The Complete Fairy Tales in Verse and Prose

L'intégrale des contes en vers et en prose

A DUAL-LANGUAGE BOOK

Charles Perrault

Edited and Translated by
STANLEY APPELBAUM

*Chère Sanson
Je te souhaite bon courage
en tout ce que tu fais.
Monsieur M
mai, 2007*

DOVER PUBLICATIONS, INC.
Mineola, New York

Bibliographical Note

This Dover edition, first published in 2002, includes the unabridged French texts of all the tales, prefaces, morals, etc., as first published in volume form in 1694 (2nd ed., 1695), for the verse tales, and 1697, for the prose tales; further bibliographical data, including earlier appearances of some of the tales, will be found in the Introduction. The French texts are accompanied by new English translations by Stanley Appelbaum, who also wrote the Introduction and the footnotes.

Library of Congress Cataloging-in-Publication Data

Perrault, Charles, 1628–1703.
    [Contes des fées. English & French]
    The complete fairy tales in verse and prose : a dual-language book = L'intégrale des contes en vers et en prose / Charles Perrault ; edited and translated by Stanley Appelbaum.
        p. cm.
    ISBN 0-486-42476-6 (pbk.)
    1. Fairy tales—France—Translations into English. I. Title: Contes en vers et en prose. II. Appelbaum, Stanley. III. Title.

PQ1877 .A26 2002

2002074158

Manufactured in the United States of America
Dover Publications, Inc., 31 East 2nd Street, Mineola, N.Y. 11501

Contents

Annexe: "Peau d'Ane" en prose /
Appendix: Prose Version of "Donkey-Skin"

Introduction

Charles Perrault: Life and Works

Born in Paris in 1628, Charles Perrault was the youngest surviving son[1] of a distinguished family. His father was an eminent lawyer. His brother Pierre (1608–1680) was a royal tax administrator from 1654 until his retirement under a cloud in 1664. His brother Nicolas (1611–1661) was a professor at the Sorbonne, losing his post because of his adherence to Jansenism, an unorthodox religious movement. His brother Claude (1613–1688) was a major architect in the king's service, but is no longer credited with the 1667 design for the Louvre colonnade, which is now attributed to the circle of the architect Louis Le Vau (1612–1670).

Charles attended the Collège de Beauvais from about 1636 to about 1644, and was already writing while a schoolboy. He completed his studies on his own; it is unclear whether this was a voluntary or a forced decision. In 1651 he received his law degree, but he is said to have handled only two cases. His father died in 1652. His first published work, a satire written in collaboration with others, appeared in 1653.

Perrault's extensive career in government began in 1654, when he became clerk to his brother Pierre. By 1658 he was in the circle of the powerful finance minister Nicolas Fouquet (1615–1680), whom the envious Louis XIV ruined in 1661. In that circle Perrault could have met the poet Jean de La Fontaine (1621–1695), whose works remained prestigious models for his own odes and narratives.

In 1663 Perrault became clerk to Bouquet's successor, Jean-Baptiste Colbert (1619–1683). In 1665 he became head of the royal building commission. Also in the 1660s, he became a member of what would become the Academy of Inscriptions and Belles-Lettres. He has been viewed as the overseer of the king's personality cult, an overall cultural minister supervising the book trade and having a hand in

---

[1] His twin brother lived only six months.

the construction and furnishing of palaces, the striking of medals, and related activities. His highest honor arrived in 1671, when he was elected to the Académie Française (which had been granted its royal charter as recently as 1635).

In 1672, Perrault, at 44, married the 19-year-old Marie Guichon, who bore him four children before she died in 1678, not long after the birth of Pierre Perrault (later called Pierre Darmancour). The folktales that the widower told his children as he raised them without a mother were to become the basis of his most famous works.

By the early 1680s, Perrault's political career was disintegrating, and he resigned his last government office in 1683. In the preceding year, he had returned to true creative writing after a lapse of 22 years (though he had been churning out—and would continue to do so—reams of adulatory odes and sycophantic addresses, speeches, letters, memoirs, descriptions of royal and noble festivities, and the like, not to mention translations of old and new Latin odes, hymns, and fables).

In 1687, with his long poem "Le siècle de Louis le Grand" (The Age of Louis the Great), he unleashed one of the great disputes in French (and European) literary history, that between the "ancients" and the "moderns." A "modern," he believed that contemporary French writing was equal, or even superior, to the devoutly venerated Greco-Roman works; among his chief opponents were Boileau and Racine (a formal reconciliation between Perrault and Boileau would not occur until 1694).

Meanwhile, the king's intolerant revocation in 1685 of the Edict of Nantes, which had insured religious freedom for Huguenots (French Protestants), induced Perrault to write pious Catholic works for the rest of his life: legends, biographies of early saints and of contemporary religious leaders, and reflections of current events.

Between 1688 and 1697 Perrault published his formal magnum opus, part of the above-mentioned dispute, the five dialogues (eventually appearing in four volumes) collectively known as *Le parallèle des anciens et des modernes*. His tales, published between 1691 and 1697, are discussed in the following sections of this Introduction. Another major pro-"modern" work, written between 1696 and 1700, was *Les hommes illustres qui ont paru en France pendant ce siècle* (etc.) (The Famous Men Who Have Appeared in France During This Century).

In 1697 Perrault's son Pierre, the possible author or co-author of the prose tales (see below), was convicted of manslaughter. Perrault got him off by paying a heavy indemnity. Pierre died in 1700 while

serving as an army lieutenant. In 1702 Perrault completed the manuscript of his memoirs; not published until 1909, they are self-serving and not altogether reliable. He kept writing and publishing until the year of his death, in Paris, 1703.

Perrault's Tales: General Remarks

Although grave French literary historians emphasize the great merit of such works as *Le parallèle* and *Les hommes illustres*, both at home and abroad Perrault will always be chiefly associated with his *contes*, which have exerted a vast influence on oral and written storytelling everywhere (it is too great an exaggeration, however, to call him "the creator of the artistic fairy tale").

Perrault had already emerged as a narrator in such brief works as the prose story "Le miroir" (The Mirror; 1661),[2] the poem "La peinture" (Painting; 1668; on the origin of the silhouette), and the prose-and-verse miscellany "Le labyrinthe (de Versailles)" (1679).

During the 17th century in France there had been sporadic writings about fairies and the supernatural; here again, La Fontaine was an influence on Perrault. Fairy tales were already an accepted genre of literary-salon recitations, and the great letter-writer Madame de Sévigné mentions Mother Goose stories (see below) in 1656. By 1690 there were already formal literary fairy tales in France;[3] but Perrault's more "democratic" tales, about and for children of all social classes, still created a sensation when they appeared. (Fairy tales, both homely and high-flown, were cultivated, chiefly by women writers, throughout the 18th century in France, giving way, in the early 19th, to radically new approaches in the Romantic movement.)

Folktales were an integral part of Perrault's household while his children were growing up; he considered them traditional property, and had no hesitation in publishing them under his name in properly embellished form.

In 1691, the verse tale "Grisélidis," already accompanied by the

---

[2]"Le miroir" contains a fascinating parallel to one motif in "La belle au bois dormant": after the hero is killed, the god of love is powerless to resuscitate him, but he *can* alter fate by making his body incorruptible (the hero's body is metallized, and he becomes the first mirror). The vanity of women, and their obsession with their appearance, so often alluded to in the famous tales, are already satirized here.
[3]In that year, one was interpolated into a novel by Madame d'Aulnoy (Marie-Catherine Le Jumel de Barneville, comtesse d'Aulnoy; 1650–1705).

epistle "A Monsieur ***," was published (as "La Marquise de Saluces[4] ou La patience de Grisélidis. Nouvelle") in an annual publication of the Académie Française, *Recueil de plusieurs pièces d'éloquence et de poésie présentées à l'Académie française pour les prix de 1691*. Later that year it was published separately in Paris by Jean-Baptiste Coignard, who had already been publishing material by Perrault since at least 1675.

In 1693, the verse tale "Les souhaits ridicules" was published in the November issue of the magazine *Le Mercure galant*.

In 1694, those two tales, with the addition of "Peau d'Ane" (which may have appeared separately somewhere in late 1693), comprised the first full publication of the verse tales: *Grisélidis, nouvelle. Avec le conte de Peau-d'Ane et celui des Souhaits ridicules*. The earliest known version of this volume, published by Coignard's widow and his son (with the same Christian name), bears the notice "second edition." The Preface did not appear until the "fourth edition" (no third is known) of 1695, which is the source of the French text that appears in this Dover volume.

In 1695, a professional copyist who had done other work for Perrault prepared a manuscript that is now in the Pierpont Morgan Library in New York. It contains early versions of the first five prose tales, as well as the epistle "A Mademoiselle" (signed "P. P."). The manuscript, illustrated by seven painted miniatures, is titled "Contes de ma mère l'Oie" (spelling modernized; Mother Goose Tales). There is great controversy over the origin of the "Mother Goose" designation: From a fable about a goose instructing her brood? From a goose-footed statue (Queen Pédauque) in old churches? From fairies who left goose tracks? Merely a phrase for "impossible events"?

In 1696, another variant of "La belle au bois dormant" appeared anonymously in the February *Mercure galant*; some scholars believe it may have been written by Perrault's kinswoman (niece? cousin?) Marie-Jeanne L'Héritier de Villandon (1664–1734), who had included four *contes* in her *Oeuvres mêlées* (Miscellany) of 1695. A private letter written on September 23, 1696, informs us that the Parisian publisher Claude Barbin was printing a volume of "Mother Goose tales." On October 28, the *privilège* (exclusive license to publish) for the prose tales was granted to Pierre Perrault Darmancour, who ceded it to Barbin; the *privilège* was registered on January 11, 1697.

In 1697 Barbin issued two editions (the French text in this Dover

---

[4]Or: "Salusses." (Actually, Saluzzo, in the Piedmont region of Italy.)

volume is that of the second) of the prose tales. Although the frontis-
piece still read "Mother Goose tales," the formal title was *Histoires ou
contes du temps passé. Avec des moralités* (Stories or Tales of Olden
Days. With Morals).[5]

Unlike many folktales (such as those by the Brothers Grimm) which
are called "fairy tales" incorrectly, Perrault's really are; in fact, he introduced fairies into plots which had dispensed with them previously.[6]
He also endowed the French literary folktale with representations of
everyday life in various milieux, domestic bliss in humble surround-
ings, the conspicuous consumption of high society, fashions and
modes (often viewed satirically). Did his prose tales reflect the incip-
ient political stirrings of the lower classes? Or, on the other hand, were
they written in defense of the higher classes, which were then under
attack from ultra-pious groups? There was probably a subtle combination of motives and external influences. At any rate, the elaborate
Greco-Roman mythology featured prominently in the (earlier) verse
tales disappears in the prose tales, which are more folksy in general.
The tales have also been seen as a nostalgic idealization of the past,
and as a pro-"modern" weapon in that literary dispute, since they were
chiefly in prose (a "modern" virtue), they concerned the supernatural,
and they were based ostensibly on home-grown rather than Greco-
Roman traditions.

The verse morals to the prose tales are worldly-wise, and often offer
unexpected, nearly cynical observations on the story lines.

Controversy has raged over the authorship of the prose tales. The
epistle introducing them was signed by Charles Perrault's son Pierre,
at least as early as 1695, when he was 17,[7] and it was to him that the
privilège was granted. Moreover, a pirated Dutch edition of 1697
unequivocally attributes the prose tales to him, and a private commu-
nication in 1700 shows an equal lack of doubt about it. Opponents of
this view have an easy time of pointing to the literary maturity of the

---

[5]In 1704, the year after Charles Perrault's death, Barbin's widow published the first
volume of a work that was to revolutionize European storytelling, Antoine Galland's
translation of the *Thousand and One Nights.*   [6]Whether fairies were ancient gods who
had come down in the world, or nature spirits, or spirits of the dead (fairies who give
gifts to people at birth do seem to be descendants of norns, fates, parcae, and fortu-
nae), they had played a strong part in French tradition via Celtic transmission through
Brittany and because of their prominent role in Arthurian and other medieval
romances. (English fairies are a mixture of Celtic and Germanic elements: dwarfs,
kobolds, etc.)   [7]It is sickening to the scholarly mind to tote up the number of refer-
ence works in various languages that repeat the misapprehension that Pierre was 10
when the tales appeared (1695? 1697?).

prose style and the sophisticated remarks on all sorts of worldly matters. A recent view offers a compromise: Pierre set down the tales as
he had heard them at home, and his father tidied them up, with many
personal additions. (Nevertheless, no edition of the tales known to this
editor bears an author's credit on either the cover or the title page
other than to Charles Perrault.)

The verse tales fell into a long-lasting neglect soon after their first
appearance, whereas the prose tales were frequently republished, and
were translated into numerous languages; the first English translation,
by Robert Samber, appeared in 1729. It was not until 1781 that the
publisher Lamy brought out his volume of all of Perrault's tales, calling it *Contes de fées* (the designation *Contes* for these tales has
remained current in France to this day). The 1781 volume was only
the second to include "Grisélidis" since 1695. It also added a newly
written anonymous prose rendering of "Peau d'Ane," which in subsequent decades was often substituted for the authentic verse version in
Perrault editions. Though the prose version is justly considered as
stylistically inferior, it delighted the fastidious Gustave Flaubert, who
thought it was authentic and liked it best of all the tales! Not actually
by Perrault, it is nevertheless included as an appendix in this Dover
volume, as lagniappe, and for the sake of ultra-completeness.

The Individual Tales

The Verse Tales

Like La Fontaine's fables and verse *contes,* Perrault's verse tales are
written in stanzas with varying numbers of lines, line lengths, and
rhyme schemes. The lines that begin at the left margin in this Dover
volume are alexandrines, 12-syllable lines (syllables containing a mute
e and appearing at the end of a line are not included in the syllable
count). Every singly indented line contains 10 syllables; doubly
indented lines have 8 syllables; and so on (with each further indent,
2 fewer syllables).

"Grisélidis." This, the only non-supernatural tale in the Perrault
collection, was based directly on story X, 10 (Tenth Story of the Tenth
Day) in Boccaccio's *Decameron* (ca. 1350). No direct source is known
for Boccaccio's telling, but there are various medieval narratives about
unjustly put-upon, "tested" wives, including the *lai* (narrative poem of
moderate length) "Le freisne" by Marie de France (ca. 1160) and the

verse romance of chivalry *Erec et Enide* by Chrétien de Troyes (ca. 1170). The most famous retelling based on Boccaccio is Chaucer's "Clerk's Tale" in *The Canterbury Tales* (ca. 1400).

In the earliest form of Perrault's version, he called his heroine "Griselde" to be closer to Boccaccio's "Griselda," but he later changed it to the form already long current in France, "Grisélidis." (Boccaccio's story had been translated into Latin by his friend Petrarch in 1374, and the first of many French translations had appeared as early as 1389.)

Perrault added more motivation for the behavior of both the prince and his wife, and made the prince's odd psychology more understandable to his own contemporaries (though it is still based on the age-old medical theory of the four "humors" or "temperaments"). He gave the prince's daughter a lover, for symmetry in the story line, just as Racine, in his play *Phèdre* (1677), had given his virginal hero Hippolyte a sweetheart not found in his source, Euripides. Perrault also added many satirical thrusts, and supplied such new picturesque tableaux as the hunt and the (very anachronistic) wedding festivities. To a small extent, he expurgated Boccaccio: the heroine is not stripped bare to symbolize her transformation from farm girl to sovereign, and when she is dismissed by her husband, she is not wearing merely a shift.

"Peau d'Ane." This belongs to the widespread group of folktales designated as Catskin or Cap o' Rushes, in which the heroine is forced to assume an ugly disguise; the second part of the story, in which she becomes a menial until her beauty is triumphantly revealed, is a variant on the Cinderella story. In France, by Perrault's time, the phrase "Peau d'Ane" connoted not merely some version of this particular tale, but also the concept of folktale in general; when La Fontaine, in his fable "Le pouvoir des fables" (The Power of Fables; VIII, 4), states that he'd take great pleasure in hearing "Peau d'Ane" narrated at that very moment, he may possibly mean any folktale; and some scholars believe that this wasn't unmitigated praise, but should be taken to mean he'd take pleasure *even* in a silly story like "Peau d'Ane" (or a folktale in general).

The incest motif in Perrault's version already appears in the 13th-century narrative poem *La Belle Hélène de Constantinople*. The animal skin and the identifying ring are to be found in the huge prose romance *Perceforest* (completed 1344). In his *Propos rustiques* (Rural Conversations) of 1548 (section V), Noël du Fail mentions a "Peau d'Ane" as forming part of a rustic storyteller's repertoire. In the very

short final story (CXXIX) in *Les nouvelles récréations et joyeux devis* (New Pastimes and Merry Chats) of 1558, by Bonaventure des Périers (though this story occurs in a portion of the book that is merely attributed to him), a girl nicknamed "Peau d'Ane" is forced to wear a donkey skin to discourage her ardent suitors.

A very close parallel to the first part of Perrault's tale occurs in the fourth story in the Italian writer Gianfrancesco Straparola's collection *Le piacevoli notti* (The Enjoyable Nights; 1550–1553; available to Perrault in a French translation). The prince of Salerno falls in love with his own daughter after promising his dying wife that he will remarry only if her ring fits the new bride [ring-test motif, like the shoe-test in the Cinderella story; but Perrault makes a different use of the ring]. The young woman receives advice from her nurse [Perrault, typically for him, calls in a fairy godmother]. From this point on, Straparola's story differs, employing a whole battery of other folktale motifs; there are no skins or beautiful gowns, though the princess does live in reclusion until she is discovered and married to a man of her choice.

The Italian writer Giambattista Basile, in his *Pentameron* (aka *Cunto de li cunti*, Tale of the Tales; 1634–1636; in Neapolitan dialect), has a girl-in-ugly-disguise story, "L'orsa" (The She-Bear; II, 6).

A major retelling of the story subsequent to Perrault is "Allerleirauh" (All-Kinds-of-Fur), No. 65 in the *Kinder- und Hausmärchen* (Children's and Domestic Tales) by the Brothers Grimm (1812 ff).

The wondrous gowns occur in a vast number of folktales, not only the "Peau d'Ane" type. The donkey that defecates gold appears in Basile's very first story, "L'uerco" (The Wild Man), and in the Grimms' "Tischchendeckdich, Goldesel und Knüppel aus dem Sack" (Table-Set-Yourself, Gold-Donkey, and Cudgel-Out-of-the-Sack; No. 36).

Perrault states the moral of the story at the end, without separating it out as a *moralité,* as in the prose tales.

The 1781 prose version of "Peau d'Ane," supplied as an appendix to this Dover volume, sets the story in pagan times (references to "the gods" and a "druid"). It follows Perrault's verse narrative closely, but adds numerous interminable rationalizations of the characters' actions, and other expatiations, especially (but not only) in the part about the prince's illness and his conversations with his parents.

"Les souhaits ridicules." This extremely familiar farce seems to have entered European literature via translations from Indo-Persian-Arabic sources, and was already at home in medieval France (Marie

de France, 12th century; the *fabliau* corpus; etc.). La Fontaine, in his fable "Les souhaits" (The Wishes; VII, 5), makes the wish-granting divinity a Hindu spirit (a reflection of the story's ultimate source?), but keeps the story on a high philosophical plane, free of such low-comedy elements as the very phallic pudding. Perrault makes the divinity Jupiter; this not only places his version in a Greco-Roman atmosphere (the Aesopic tradition), but also avoids any confrontation with Christian dogma. Here again, a moral is supplied without a distinctive heading.

The Prose Tales

"La belle au bois dormant." A very close parallel to this Little Briar Rose–type story (the designation is from the Grimms' version, "Dornröschen," No. 50) occurs in Basile's "Sole, Luna e Talia" (Sun, Moon, and Talia; *Pentameron* V, 5). The maiden Talia's father is warned by an astrologer that she will suffer from a flax splinter, and he forbids the use of flax in his house; but Talia looks out a window and sees an old woman spinning. She handles the flax and dies. Her father seats her body on a velvet chair in their château. During a royal hunt, the king, a married man, follows his stray falcon there, and has intercourse with Talia while she sleeps. Nine months later, she gives birth to twins, Sun and Moon, who are brought up in the château by fairies; the babes accidentally suck out the splinter; she awakens, and the king is delighted with his second household. But the queen gets wind of this, and plans to have the children served up to their father for dinner; the compassionate cook saves the children and serves goat. At a critical moment for Talia, the king learns how he has been deceived; he has the queen burned, and makes his new family legitimate.

The varied motifs and elements of Perrault's version have long separate histories. The cantankerous fairy who declares that the newly christened princess must die goes back to Eris, the goddess of discord who ultimately caused the Trojan War by instigating a beauty contest among the major goddesses (other Greek goddesses were equally touchy on occasion). In the *Jeu de folie* (or *feuillée*) by the *trouvère* Adam de la Halle (probably 1276), there are three fairies at a banquet, one of whom pronounces a curse when she becomes disgruntled. Gift-giving fairies are found in several medieval romances, including the above-mentioned *Perceforest,* which also has an incident about a girl suffering from a spindle prick after offending a goddess. The mitigation of a curse that cannot be totally set aside is a common folktale

motif, as are the discovery of a girl in a castle and her disenchanting by an arriving lover.

The theme of the long slumber has parallels in ancient Asian and European tales, such as that of the Seven Sleepers of Ephesus (literary ancestors of Rip Van Winkle), and in the Norse/Germanic story of Brünnhilde, put to sleep by a magic thorn. The alternation of the seasons, with hibernation in winter, has been seen as the ultimate source of this theme; whereas psychologists view the princess's slumber as an avoidance of conjugal life, the phallic spindle being her enemy.

Most of the popular retellings of the story for children follow the Grimms rather than Perrault, in that they end the story with the general reawakening and the subsequent rejoicing. Perrault, like Basile, added the (altogether distinct) story of the heroine's children, from another folktale cycle about child-eaters and offspring who are secretly spirited away from their mother, often by a "compassionate executioner."[8]

"Le Petit Chaperon Rouge." This has been called a literary (fairy) tale rather than a true folktale embellished, because no direct source for the Perrault version is known, and it itself is the general source for later versions; it is also unusual for its unhappy ending. (The Grimms' version, "Rotkäppchen," No. 26, adopts the rescuing hunter from other German sources, and saves both the heroine and her grandmother, turning the tale into a typical Big Swallow story, in which characters live after being gulped down hastily.)

One of the great mysteries about this story: what did Perrault have in mind with regard to the *chaperon* headgear? Apparently, in the Middle Ages, a *chaperon* was a sort of padded stocking cap (more specifically, a wide, soft, baggy hat in the 14th century), but by 1630 in France it seems to have referred to a velvet headdress; others say it was merely a velvet band added to a bonnet. In heraldry, *chaperon* definitely means a hood, and "hood" is used in this new translation, partly out of familiarity; the term "riding hood" (whatever it was supposed to mean; our heroine doesn't go riding) has been standard in English ever since the above-mentioned Samber translation in 1729.

---

[8]There is no need here to enumerate the many creative works based on this Perrault tale. By far the most important of these is Tchaikovsky's ballet *Sleeping Beauty* (1890), which makes amusing reuse of some of the characters' names in Perrault: Aurora, the name of the princess's little daughter in the story, becomes her own name; the young king's troublesome neighbor in the story, Cantalabutte, lends his name to the court majordomo in the ballet; and in the ballet libretto, the principal good fairy, who continues to appear throughout, is called the Lilac Fairy, possibly after the fairy by that name in the 1781 prose version of "Peau d'Ane."

There is further controversy over the connotations of our heroine's wearing the *chaperon*. Was she overstepping her village limitations (and thus courting disaster) by wearing a headdress reserved for the bourgeoisie? There is absolutely no internal evidence for this, even in Perrault's humorously sententious *moralité*. Even more dubious is the contention that the *chaperon* also alludes to the chaperon (person) who protects virginal girls, and that the *chaperon's* being *petit* meant that our heroine was insufficiently protected against the wolf!

Among the outré interpretations that the story has inspired in more recent days are: the identification of the wolf as a werewolf; the discovery that it reflects an initiation ritual for seamstresses in "sewing communities"; and any number of explanations of the *chaperon's* redness (denoting the Devil, menstruation, the red hat worn by non-conformists, etc., etc.).

"La Barbe-Bleue." This specific story, and the villain's name, were quite possibly invented by Perrault, but there are worldwide folktale analogies. It is a story about a broken taboo. It is a story about a monster-husband (compare Cupid and Psyche, and Beauty and the Beast). It represents a large group of tales in which some powerful man (king, rich merchant, sorcerer) marries three or seven sisters, whom he kills or imprisons, except for the last one, who kills him (or has him killed) after he discovers that she knows the truth (there are various plot mechanisms for this discovery); she then resuscitates or liberates her sisters (some folklorists believe that the happy ending was not part of the original tale-type).

In Basile's story "Cannetella" (*Pentameron* III, 1), there is a killer of girls and a forbidden room, and elements similar to Perrault also occur in "Le tre corune" (The Three Crowns; *Pentameron* IV, 6). Subsequent to Perrault, the Grimms have two analogous stories, "Der Räuberbräutigam" (The Robber Bridegroom; No. 40), in which an allegedly rich suitor induces the heroine to visit him at his forest home, really the lair of murderous bandits, and "Fitchers Vogel" (Fitcher's Bird; No. 46), in which a sorcerer successively kidnaps three sisters, the last of whom gains mastery over him because she avoids getting blood on his enchanted egg when she enters the forbidden room; she reassembles her sisters and brings them back to life, and their brothers burn the sorcerer in his house.

In view of the wide distribution of this tale-type, it is pointless to try to identify a historical precedent (such as Gilles de Rais) for Perrault's Bluebeard. Perrault had current French society in mind: his villain is an extremely wealthy financier who owns several fancy homes and

possesses such up-to-date treasures as full-length mirrors. His story is very well told, being remarkable for Sister Anne's incantatory lines ("All I see is the sun . . .") and the quick intercutting at the climax between the heroine, her sister, her husband, and her brothers, analogous to a D. W. Griffith "chase."

Here again, modern folklorists have let their imagination run riot. Does the color of the villain's beard represent a misuse of the royal blue? Does he continue to wear the obviously repellent beard because it is hiding a mark made by the Devil? Is he a solar hero, an alchemist, a proto-psychiatrist? Is his home a tribal house for male initiation ceremonies?

The dramatic nature of Perrault's story was soon recognized, and a number of operas and operettas were based on it in the 18th and 19th centuries. Two really important Bluebeard operas of the early 20th century were Paul Dukas's *Ariane et Barbe-bleue* (completed 1906; libretto by Maurice Maeterlinck) and Béla Bartók's *A kékszakállú herceg vára* ([Duke] Bluebeard's Castle; 1911; libretto by Béla Balázs).

"Le Maître Chat ou Le Chat Botté." This story appears to have been the invention of Straparola ("Constantino Fortunato," *Le piacevoli notti* XI, 1): of three sons in Bohemia, one inherits a (female) white cat, which curries favor with the king by bringing him a hare; the hero takes a bath, to clean his sores and rashes, *before* he bathes in the river as in Perrault; after he weds the princess, thanks to his false prestige, he has no decent home to take her to; people are induced to state that the land they are on belongs to the hero, who temporarily occupies a masterless castle the owner of which conveniently dies while away; the hero becomes king.

In Basile's story "Gagliuso" (*Pentameron* II, 4), the cat is male; the hero is greatly confused by the rich clothes he gets to wear through the cat's ruse; and, at the end, he badly fails a test of gratitude that the cat prepares for him.

The boots were apparently Perrault's contribution, and some scholars think that his Puss is a satire on the finance minister Colbert. The name Carabas that the cat bestows on its master may possibly recall that of a traditional fool in Alexandria or of a resort town in Turkey (Turks were highly newsworthy in Perrault's day; both Molière and Racine wrote a play on a Turkish subject.) The meaning of *maître* in the phrase *le Maître Chat* is in dispute, probably needlessly. One finds it stated that it is a belittling form of address, as from a nobleman to an artisan, and/or that it suggests a teacher, because the cat teaches its

master how to live. But the adjectival use of *maître*, with a feminine form *maîtresse*, is well attested in French with the meaning "capable; wonderful; outstanding (in a person's or thing's particular way). To take examples from Perrault's tales alone (surely a sensible procedure), the gold-defecating donkey in "Peau d'Ane" is called a *maître âne* (possibly, a "wonder donkey," but a very reliable French scholar plumps for the meaning "egregious"), and the rat who becomes Cendrillon's coachman has a *maîtresse barbe* ("marvelous whiskers"). Thus, in this new Dover translation *le Maître Chat* is rendered as "the Capable Cat."

The tale is one of hundreds in world folk literature involving grateful animals (not always a cat) helping their feckless masters. (A different, more naturalistic, type of aid from a cat in folktales is exemplified by the English ballad about Dick Whittington, ca. 1600; the hero sends his cat abroad as a mercantile venture, and makes his fortune when it arrives in a foreign land that is overrun by rodents because cats are unknown there.) Perrault's cat is also a traditional trickster, a folktale character who gets ahead by means of ruses, often cruel ones. Other folktale themes in Perrault's tale: the poorest legacy proves to be the best; the youngest son, for all his disadvantages, becomes the most successful.

The ogre,[9] who doesn't appear in the original Straparola version, was apparently a favorite figure for Perrault. The metamorphoses he undergoes in Perrault's tale recall the universal folktale motif of the transformation-contest between a master sorcerer and his apprentice. Wagner had no qualms about using the motif in his very serious music drama *Das Rheingold,* where Loge and Alberich substitute for Puss and the ogre. (In other ogre-versus-trickster folktales, the ogre is duped into listening to good stories all night, and he bursts when dawn suddenly arrives.) Many other folktale motifs familiar from other stories appear in variant versions of the Puss tale.

"Les fées." Somewhat oddly titled, because there is only one fairy in it, this Perrault tale is one of the thousand or so folktales since the 15th century that contrast the actions of a good and a bad girl who are rewarded according to their merits. Basile's *Pentameron* has two such stories; in "Le tre ffate" (The Three Fairies; III, 10) one girl is

---

[9]The word is probably derived ultimately from Orcus, a Latin term for the underworld (Hades) or its ruler. It appears in the form *uerco* in the above-mentioned Basile story of that title. Perrault had already introduced and glossed *ogre* in his verse dedication to "Peau d'Ane," and is said to have used it in his scholarly work *Le parallèle.* Scholars state that the word does not appear in 17th-century French dictionaries.

rewarded with pearls, the other with lice; the other Basile story, "Le doje pizzelle" (The Two Cakes; IV, 7), is even closer to Perrault: the good girl, sent for water, gives an old woman her cake and returns home spewing pearls, lilies, and other flowers; the bad girl, who refuses to share her cake, foams at the mouth and produces lice and brambles; the good girl's brother praises her to the king, who eventually marries her after all sorts of adventures, typical of several other tale-types, that do not occur in Perrault.

Closer to Perrault in time and place was the treatment of the story in the 1695 book *Les enchantements de l'éloquence* (The Charms of Eloquence; a defense of courtly speech) by his above-mentioned kinswoman Marie-Jeanne L'Héritier. In the Grimms' version of the story, "Frau Holle" (No. 24), the girls get to spend time in the otherwordly realm of the title character, a folk figure who was once a Norse/Germanic goddess.

"Cendrillon ou La petite pantoufle de verre." Cinderella is the world's best-known folktale, occurring in many versions; over five hundred have been collected in Europe alone, and there is a record of a 9th-century version from China. Certain elements of the story are of great antiquity: in his *Varia Historia,* the Italian author Claudius Aelianus (Aelian; ca. 170–ca. 235 A.D.), who wrote in Greek, tells the one-paragraph story (XIII, 33) of the beautiful Egyptian courtesan Rhodopis, whose sandal was stolen by an eagle while she was bathing outdoors; flying to Memphis, the bird dropped the sandal into the lap of the pharaoh Psammetichus, who, judging from the elegance of the footgear that its owner must be outstandingly beautiful, instituted a search for the wearer throughout Egypt, and finally married Rhodopis.[10]

The most complete literary rendering of the Cinderella story before Perrault is the one in Basile's *Pentameron,* "La gatta cenerentola" (The Ashy Cat; I, 6; there is no real cat, it's just a nickname for the heroine Zezolla). Poor Zezolla has to put up with *two* successive evil stepmothers (she murders the first on the advice of the eventual second), becoming the drudge for the second one's numerous children. As in the Grimms' version ("Aschenputtel"; No. 21), her father, leaving on a journey, asks his daughters what gifts they would like him to bring back (a motif essential to "La Belle et la Bête," by Marie Le Prince de Beaumont, 1711–1780); but in Basile, the father is off to

---

[10]The antiquity of this motif makes it hard to agree with those scholars who view the shoe-test in the Cinderella story as an old marriage custom.

Sardinia, home of a fairy who has been recommended to Zezolla as a protectress. In Sardinia, the father forgets his promise to contact the fairy, and his ship is becalmed until he does so. He brings back to Zezolla a date tree, from which issues a fairy who will dress and undress Zezolla at opportune moments so she can go around in finery without her stepsisters' knowledge (the Grimms' version also uses the tree device to make the heroine elegant, but in their version the tree cutting is obtained by the father without a fairy's intervention, and the heroine plants it on her mother's grave). When Zezolla attends a fête in her fancy dress, the king is smitten with her; on two occasions she escapes by throwing gold and jewels in front of the servant sent to follow her; the third time, she loses her slipper, the king searches for its owner, and marries her.

Though the various versions of the Cinderella story have different plot mechanisms for dressing the heroine in finery, Perrault's version, with the fairy godmother, the metamorphosed pumpkin and small animals, and the glass slippers, is by far the most widespread today, thanks especially to the musical entertainments (ballet, animated film, television show, etc.) based on it directly. Perrault was apparently the inventor of the *glass* slippers (the commentators who insisted that he meant to write *vair,* "squirrel fur," rather than *verre,* have fallen out of favor) and of the injunction to return home by midnight.

The "ash" element in the heroine's name recurs in versions recorded in Germanic, Slavic, and other language groups; it seems to have been inspired by the sight of cats keeping warm in hearth ashes, and reflects the heroine's dirty condition and drudgery. Ashes have also been an age-old symbol of affliction (as when they are coupled with "sackcloth"), and lying in ashes indicates despondency in folktale heroes, who generally shake off their torpor and go into action.

"Riquet à la Houppe." Despite a certain quaint charm, this story (the furthest in Perrault's collection from having folk roots; truly a "literary fairy tale") must unfortunately be considered as an inept plagiarism. Catherine Bernard (1622–1712) had just told it, much better, in an episode of her 1696 novel *Inès de Cordoue* (Inés of Cordova).

In *Inès,* a nobleman of Granada has a stupid daughter named Atama. One day a horridly ugly man emerges from the ground and states that he will make her intelligent if she promises to marry him in a year. She agrees, and he immediately gives her a verse charm that does the job. But she falls in love with a man named Arada, not rich but handsome. She *doesn't* forget the deadline for the marriage; on that day, the ground beneath her opens and she sees her fiancé

Riquet, who is the king of the gnomes; he gives her the choice of being his queen or returning home just as stupid as formerly. She feels compelled to wed Riquet, but she sends word to Arada to visit her. Suspicious of her new happiness, Riquet makes her stupid in the daytime, but every night she gives Riquet a sleeping potion and goes off to meet Arada. When Riquet discovers this, he turns Arada into a clone of himself, leaving Atama with two ugly men whom she cannot tell apart. Bernard ends her story with the cynical observation that Atama probably lost nothing thereby, because eventually a lover becomes like just another husband.

In addition to the incomparably feebler ending that Perrault provided (with the hackneyed moral that love for a person makes him or her good-looking to the beholder), he further spoiled Bernard's story by offering no explanation whatsoever for Riquet's subterranean activities. And if the mincing, insufferably arch, courtly dialogues that Perrault's hero and heroine take part in are a touchstone for intelligence, then maybe ignorance is really bliss.

The motif of intelligence achieved through love appears in a number of literary works, including story V, 1 of Boccaccio's *Decameron,* "Cimone amando divien savio . . ." (By falling in love, Cimone becomes wise). The marriage of a maiden to a monster recalls the Cupid and Psyche and the Beauty and the Beast stories.

The name Riquet may be short for Henriquet; it may be a word for "disfigured" in the Normandy dialect (Bernard was from Rouen); or it may be a malicious allusion to Pierre-Paul de Riquet, a political protégé of the finance minister Colbert.

"Le Petit Poucet." Not a true Tom Thumb story (Perrault's hero is merely small—very small, indeed, at birth—but has no adventures to compare with those of the Grimms' diminutive Daumesdick and Daumerling),[11] Perrault's tale is an uneasy combination of the theme of children deserted in the woods (like Hänsel and Gretel in the Grimms' No. 15) and a typical giant-killer story with a trickster hero.

The Hänsel and Gretel element had already been treated in Basile's story "Nennillo e Nennella" (*Pentameron* V, 8), in which the children's father remarries to their misfortune; at the instigation of his shrewish wife, he leads them into the forest, but *he himself* leaves a trail of ashes for them to follow. When they arrive home, their stepmother is furious, and forces their father to take them out again; this time he

---

[11]In "Daumesdick" (Big-as-a-Thumb; No. 37) and "Daumerlings Wanderschaft" (Thumbling's Travels; No. 45), respectively. The theme of unusually small people goes far back into antiquity; cf. the Pygmies mentioned in Homer's *Iliad.*

leaves a trail of bran, which is eaten by a donkey. The rest of the story, quite long and complicated, is very different from anything in Perrault or the Grimms, and may safely be omitted here. (Perrault refers to a famine, a common occurrence in 17th-century France.)

The young-hero-versus-ogre theme, with which Perrault continues, is a very popular one in Europe. Among the regularly recurring features of such stories are: spending the night in the ogre's home, switching headgear with his own child(ren),[12] and stealing his treasures, either during the one-and-only visit, or on a return visit, which is variously motivated.

Perrault's ending is really out of place; it is satirical and thoroughly literary and unfolklike. His Thumbling's service as a military courier refers to the incessant wars, entailing battles fought far from home, that were an integral part of the foreign policy of Louis XIV. Perrault's mockery of the ladies of the court parallels that in "Grisélidis" (the prince's diatribe), "Peau d'Ane" (the finger-slimming episode), and "Cendrillon" (the stepsisters).

The Nature of This Edition

Based on the above-mentioned editions of 1695 (for the verse tales), 1697 (the second edition of that year, for the prose tales), and 1781 (for the prose "Peau d'Ane"), the French text offered here (like the corresponding translation) is absolutely complete, including all prefaces, epistles, verse dedications, and morals. This is possibly the most complete English-language volume of the tales.

The translation is as literal as possible (without distorting the English), and also the most accurate one known to the translator, who has made every endeavor to reflect the semantic nuances of the 17th-century vocabulary. The verses have been translated into literal prose, but line-for-line wherever English syntax allows. Any attempt to reproduce original rhymes and meters inevitably alters the meaning.[13]

As is customary in most modern editions of Perrault, his spelling, capitalization, punctuation, and paragraphing have been modernized, but not a word has been basically altered, or omitted.

---

[12]The motif of switching headgear to avoid death was already used in the 5th-century B.C. *Ino* of Euripides (the play is lost, but the plot is preserved in an ancient summary).   [13]And the absolutely vile pseudopoetic renderings of the verse morals to Perrault's prose tales contained in a very recent folktale collection are the best possible argument in favor of the approach adopted in this Dover edition!

Contes en vers
Verse Tales

Préface

La manière dont le public a reçu les pièces de ce recueil, à mesure qu'elles lui ont été données séparément, est une espèce d'assurance qu'elles ne lui déplairont pas en paraissant toutes ensemble. Il est vrai que quelques personnes qui affectent de paraître graves, et qui ont assez d'esprit pour voir que ce sont des contes faits à plaisir, et que la matière n'en est pas fort importante, les ont regardées avec mépris; mais on a eu la satisfaction de voir que les gens de bon goût n'en ont pas jugé de la sorte.

Ils ont été bien aises de remarquer que ces bagatelles n'étaient pas de pures bagatelles, qu'elles renfermaient une morale utile, et que le récit enjoué dont elles étaient enveloppées n'avait été choisi que pour les faire entrer plus agréablement dans l'esprit et d'une manière qui instruisît et divertît tout ensemble. Cela devrait me suffire pour ne pas craindre le reproche de m'être amusé à des choses frivoles. Mais comme j'ai affaire à bien des gens qui ne se payent pas de raisons et qui ne peuvent être touchés, que par l'autorité et par l'exemple des Anciens, je vais les satisfaire là-dessus.

Les fables milésiennes si célèbres parmi les Grecs, et qui ont fait les délices d'Athènes et de Rome, n'étaient pas d'une autre espèce que les fables de ce recueil. L'histoire de la Matrone d'Éphèse est de la même nature que celle de Grisélidis: ce sont l'une et l'autre des nouvelles, c'est-à-dire des récits de choses qui peuvent être arrivées, et qui n'ont rien qui blesse absolument la vraisemblance. La fable de Psyché écrite par Lucien et par Apulée est une fiction toute pure et un conte de vieille comme celui de Peau d'Ane. Aussi voyons-nous qu'Apulée le fait raconter par une vieille femme à une jeune fille que

Preface

The manner in which the public has received the items in this collection as they were published individually is a sort of reassurance that they will not cease to please now that they appear in a single volume. It is true that certain persons who put on an air of gravity and who are bright enough to see that these are stories written for no special purpose, and that the subject matter is not very serious, have looked on them with scorn; but the author has had the satisfaction of seeing that people of good taste have not made the same judgment.

They were very glad to ascertain that these trifles were not mere trifles, that they contained a useful moral code, and that the playful style in which they were told was chosen solely to instill them in the reader's mind more pleasantly, and in a way that would instruct and entertain at the same time. That should be sufficient to keep me from fearing the reproach that I had wasted my time on frivolities. But since I am dealing with many people who refuse to listen to reason and can only be persuaded by the authority and example of classical antiquity, I shall satisfy them on that count.

The Milesian tales[1] so famous among the Greeks, the delight of both Athens and Rome, were no different from the stories in this collection. The tale of the Matron of Ephesus[2] is of the same nature as that of Griselidis: they are both *novelle*; that is, narrations of events that could really have occurred, with no element that runs absolutely counter to probability. The story of Psyche written by Lucian and by Apuleius[3] is just as thoroughly fictional—an old wives' tale—as that of Donkey-Skin. Thus we note that Apuleius has it told by an old woman to a young girl who has been abducted by

---

[1]Amusing tales, often risqué. [2]Included in the *Satyricon* of Petronius (1st century A.D.): a seemingly inconsolable widow has casual sex with a soldier while still mourning at her husband's tomb. [3]In two prose works of the 2nd century A.D., the Greek-language story "Lucius, or the Ass," attributed to Lucian of Samosata, and Apuleius's Latin novel *Metamorphoses* (aka The Golden Ass), a man is transformed into a donkey, but only Apuleius tells the story of Cupid and Psyche.

3

des voleurs avaient enlevée, de même que celui de Peau d'Ane est conté tous les jours à des enfants par leurs gouvernantes, et par leurs grands-mères. La fable du laboureur qui obtint de Jupiter le pouvoir de faire comme il lui plairait la pluie et le beau temps, et qui en usa de telle sorte, qu'il ne recueillit que de la paille sans aucuns grains, parce qu'il n'avait jamais demandé ni vent, ni froid, ni neige, ni aucun temps semblable; chose nécessaire cependant pour faire fructifier les plantes: cette fable, dis-je, est de même genre que le conte des Souhaits ridicules, si ce n'est que l'un est sérieux et l'autre comique; mais tous les deux vont à dire que les hommes ne connaissent pas ce qu'il leur convient, et sont plus heureux d'être conduits par la Providence, que si toutes choses leur succédaient selon qu'ils le désirent.

Je ne crois pas qu'ayant devant moi de si beaux modèles dans la plus sage et la plus docte Antiquité, on soit en droit de me faire aucun reproche. Je prétends même que mes fables méritent mieux d'être racontées que la plupart des contes anciens, et particulièrement celui de la Matrone d'Éphèse et celui de Psyché, si l'on les regarde du côté de la morale, chose principale dans toute sorte de fables, et pour laquelle elles doivent avoir été faites. Toute la moralité qu'on peut tirer de la Matrone d'Éphèse est que souvent les femmes qui semblent les plus vertueuses le sont le moins, et qu'ainsi il n'y en a presque point qui le soient véritablement.

Qui ne voit que cette morale est très mauvaise, et qu'elle ne va qu'à corrompre les femmes par le mauvais exemple, et à leur faire croire qu'en manquant à leur devoir elles ne font que suivre la voie commune. Il n'en est pas de même de la morale de Grisélidis, qui tend à porter les femmes à souffrir de leurs maris, et à faire voir qu'il n'y en a point de si brutal ni de si bizarre, dont la patience d'une honnête femme ne puisse venir à bout.

A l'égard de la morale cachée dans la fable de Psyché, fable en elle-même très agréable et très ingénieuse, je la comparerai avec celle de Peau d'Ane quand je la saurai, mais jusqu'ici je n'ai pu la deviner. Je sais bien que Psyché signifie l'âme; mais je ne comprends point ce qu'il faut entendre par l'Amour qui est amoureux de Psyché, c'est-à-dire de l'âme, et encore moins ce qu'on ajoute, que Psyché devait être heureuse, tant qu'elle ne connaîtrait point celui dont elle était aimée, qui était l'Amour, mais qu'elle serait très malheureuse dès le moment qu'elle viendrait à le connaître: voilà pour moi une énigme impénétrable. Tout ce qu'on peut dire, c'est que cette fable de même que la plupart de celles qui nous restent des Anciens n'ont été faites que pour plaire sans égard aux bonnes mœurs qu'ils négligeaient beaucoup.

robbers, just as the story of Donkey-Skin is narrated daily to children by their governesses and by their grandmothers. The fable of the plowman who received from Jupiter the power of controlling the weather according to his wishes, but made such use of it that he harvested only straw without grain because he had never requested wind, cold, snow or any similar climatic condition, though these are necessary for making plants bear grain: that fable, I say, is of the same type as the story of the Ludicrous Wishes, except that one is serious and the other is funny; but both of them teach us that people fail to see what is good for them and are more pleased to be guided by Providence than to have everything work out according to their desires.

Having before me such fine precedents from the wisest and most learned men of ancient times, I do not believe anyone has the right to reproach me in any way. In fact, I claim that my stories are more worthy of being told than most ancient tales, especially those of the Matron of Ephesus and of Psyche, if they are examined from the standpoint of morality, which is a principal element of all kinds of fables, and ought to be the reason why they were told in the first place. The only moral to be derived from the Matron of Ephesus is that frequently the women who seem most virtuous are really the least, and that therefore there are almost none who are truly virtuous.

Who can fail to see that this is a very bad moral, which serves only to corrupt women through its bad example, by making them think that, if they are lax in their duties, they are merely doing what most women do? The case is not the same with the moral of the Griselidis story, which helps persuade women to be patient with their husbands, showing them that there is no husband so brutal or so capricious that a respectable woman's patience cannot be a match for him.

With regard to the morality concealed in the story of Psyche, a story that is very pleasant and ingenious in itself, I will compare it to that of Donkey-Skin whenever I find out what it is, but up to now I have been unable to divine it. I know that Psyche means the soul; but I fail to understand what is meant by having Love fall in love with Psyche—that is, the soul—and I understand even less the additional fact that Psyche was supposed to be happy just as long as she was ignorant of who her lover was (he was Love), but would be very unhappy just as soon as she found out: this is a puzzle I simply cannot solve. All that can be said is that this story and most of the others extant from ancient times were invented merely for pleasure with no regard to propriety, which they dealt with quite casually.

Il n'en est pas de même des contes que nos aïeux ont inventés pour leurs enfants. Ils ne les ont pas contés avec l'élégance et les agréments dont les Grecs et les Romains ont orné leurs fables; mais ils ont toujours eu un très grand soin que leurs contes renfermassent une moralité louable et instructive. Partout la vertu y est récompensée, et partout le vice y est puni. Ils tendent tous à faire voir l'avantage qu'il y a d'être honnête, patient, avisé, laborieux, obéissant, et le mal qui arrive à ceux qui ne le sont pas. Tantôt ce sont des fées qui donnent pour don à une jeune fille qui leur aura répondu avec civilité, qu'à chaque parole qu'elle dira, il lui sortira de la bouche un diamant ou une perle; et à une autre fille qui leur aura répondu brutalement, qu'à chaque parole il lui sortira de la bouche une grenouille ou un crapaud. Tantôt ce sont des enfants qui pour avoir bien obéi a leur père ou à leur mère deviennent grands seigneurs, ou d'autres, qui ayant été vicieux et désobéissants, sont tombés dans des malheurs épouvantables.

Quelque frivoles et bizarres que soient toutes ces fables dans leurs aventures, il est certain qu'elles excitent dans les enfants le désir de ressembler à ceux qu'ils voient devenir heureux, et en même temps la crainte des malheurs où les méchants sont tombés par leur méchanceté. N'est-il pas louable à des pères et à des mères, lorsque leurs enfants ne sont pas encore capables de goûter les vérités solides et dénuées de tous agréments, de les leur faire aimer, et si cela se peut dire, les leur faire avaler, en les enveloppant dans des récits agréables et proportionnés à la faiblesse de leur âge. Il n'est pas croyable avec quelle avidité ces âmes innocentes, et dont rien n'a encore corrompu la droiture naturelle, reçoivent ces instructions cachées; on les voit dans la tristesse et dans l'abattement, tant que le héros ou l'héroïne de conte sont dans le malheur, et s'écrier de joie quand le temps de leur bonheur arrive; de même qu'après avoir souffert impatiemment la prospérité du méchant ou de la méchante, ils sont ravis de les voir enfin punis comme ils le méritent. Ce sont des semences qu'on jette qui ne produisent d'abord que des mouvements de joie et de tristesse, mais dont il ne manque guère d'éclore de bonnes inclinations.

J'aurais pu rendre mes contes plus agréables en y mêlant certaines choses un peu libres dont on a accoutumé de les égayer; mais le désir de plaire ne m'a jamais assez tenté pour violer une loi que je me suis imposée de ne rien écrire qui pût blesser ou la pudeur ou la bienséance. Voice un madrigal qu'une jeune demoiselle° de beaucoup d'esprit a composé sur ce sujet, et qu'elle a écrit au-dessous du conte de Peau d'Ane que je lui avais envoyé.

°Mademoiselle Lhéritier.

The same is not true of the tales that our own ancestors invented for their children. They did not tell them with the elegance and charm with which the Greeks and Romans adorned their stories, but they were always very careful to have their tales contain a praiseworthy, instructive moral. Virtue is always rewarded in them and vice is always punished. They all try to show the advantages of being honest, patient, prudent, diligent, and obedient, and the evil which overtakes those who are not. In one tale, fairies give a girl who answered them politely the gift that, with every word she speaks, a diamond or pearl will fall from her lips, whereas another girl, who answers rudely, has a frog or toad fall from her lips with every word. In others, children who have dutifully obeyed their father or mother thereby become great lords, whereas other children, who were vice-ridden and disobedient, fall into horrible misfortune.

However frivolous and odd the events in all these tales may be, they definitely instill in children the wish to be like the people they see becoming happy, and, at the same time, fear of the misfortune into which malicious people have fallen through their malice. Is it not praiseworthy in fathers and mothers, at a time when their children are not yet able to enjoy solid truths devoid of all pleasurable trappings, to make them love these truths and, if one may say so, to make them swallow them, by coating them with pleasant narratives suitable to their tender age? It is unbelievable, how avidly these innocent souls, whose inborn rectitude has not yet been corrupted in any way, take in these concealed teachings; they display sadness and dejection whenever the hero or heroine of the tale is in trouble, and they shout with joy when the time for their happiness arrives; likewise, after showing impatience at the prosperity of an evil man or woman, they are delighted to see them finally punished as they deserve. These are seeds being sown; at first they produce only spurts of joy or sadness, but they seldom fail to result in a propensity for good.

I could have made my tales more entertaining by adding some risqué elements, with which authors have grown accustomed to enliven them; but I have never been so tempted by a desire to please as to break a rule which I imposed upon myself; never to write anything that might offend either modesty or propriety. Here is a madrigal that a most intelligent young lady* has written on this subject, inscribing it below the story of Donkey-Skin that I had sent her:

---

*Mlle. L'Héritier. [Footnote in original. See Introduction for her identity. Some scholars believe that Perrault wrote these verses himself.]

Le conte de Peau d'Ane est ici raconté
       Avec tant de naïveté,
       Qu'il ne m'a pas moins divertie,
Que quand auprès du feu ma nourrice ou ma mie
Tenaient en le faisant mon esprit enchanté.
On y voit par endroits quelques traits de satire,
       Mais qui sans fiel et sans malignité,
A tous également font du plaisir à lire:
Ce qui me plaît encor dans sa simple douceur,
       C'est qu'il divertit et fait rire,
       Sans que mère, époux, confesseur,
       Y puissent trouver à redire.

The tale of Donkey-Skin is narrated here
    in so plain and candid a fashion
    that it amused me just as much
as when, beside the fireplace, my nurse or my governess
held my mind spellbound as they told it.
Here and there it contains some elements of satire,
    but satire which, without bile and without viciousness,
gives every reader equal pleasure.
Another thing I like about its simple sweetness
    is that it is entertaining and laugh-provoking
    even though no mother, husband, or confessor
    can find anything in it to reproach.

Grisélidis

A Mademoiselle**

En vous offrant, jeune et sage beauté,
   Ce modèle de patience,
   Je ne me suis jamais flatté
Que par vous de tout point il serait imité,
   C'en serait trop en conscience.

   Mais Paris où l'homme est poli,
   Où le beau sexe né pour plaire
   Trouve son bonheur accompli,
   De tous côtés est si rempli
   D'exemples du vice contraire,
   Qu'on ne peut en toute saison,
   Pour s'en garder ou s'en défaire,
   Avoir trop de contrepoison.

   Une dame aussi patiente
Que celle dont ici je relève le prix,
   Serait partout une chose étonnante,
   Mais ce serait un prodige à Paris.

   Les femmes y sont souveraines,
   Tout s'y règle selon leurs vœux,
   Enfin c'est un climat heureux
   Qui n'est habité que de reines.
   Ainsi je vois que de toutes façons,
   Grisélidis y sera peu prisée,
Et qu'elle y donnera matière de risée,
   Par ses trop antiques leçons.

Griselidis

To Mademoiselle***[4]

In offering to you, young and well-mannered beauty,
*   this model of patience,*
I never deluded myself into thinking
that you would imitate it in every detail:
*   that would really be too much.*

But Paris, where people are polished,
where the fair sex, born to please,
find their happiness perfected,
is so full everywhere
of examples of the opposite vice
that, at all times, one cannot,
to prevent it or get rid of it,
have too much antidote.

A lady as patient
as the one whose praises I here sing
*   would be amazing anywhere,*
*   but in Paris she'd be a miracle of nature.*

Here the women rule,
*   here everything is governed by their wishes;*
*   in short, it's a fortunate region*
*   inhabited by queens alone.*
Thus I see that, in every way,
Griselidis will be little appreciated here,
and that she will provide laughing matter
*   with her outmoded lessons.*

---

[4]Unidentified.

Ce n'est pas que la patience
Ne soit une vertu des dames de Paris,
Mais par un long usage elles ont la science
De la faire exercer par leurs propres maris.

Grisélidis: Nouvelle

Au pied des célèbres montagnes
Où le Pô s'échappant de dessous ses roseaux,
Va dans le sein des prochaines campagnes
Promener ses naissantes eaux,
Vivait un jeune et vaillant prince,
Les délices de sa province:
Le Ciel, en le formant, sur lui tout à la fois
Versa ce qu'il a de plus rare,
Ce qu'entre ses amis d'ordinaire il sépare,
Et qu'il ne donne qu'aux grands rois.

Comblé de tous les dons et du corps et de l'âme,
Il fut robuste, adroit, propre au métier de Mars,
Et par l'instinct secret d'une divine flamme,
Avec ardeur il aima les beaux-arts.
Il aima les combats, il aima la victoire,
Les grands projets, les actes valeureux,
Et tout ce qui fait vivre un beau nom dans l'histoire;
Mais son cœur tendre et généreux
Fut encor plus sensible à la solide gloire
De rendre ses peuples heureux.

Ce tempérament héroïque
Fut obscurci d'une sombre vapeur
Qui, chagrine et mélancolique,
Lui faisait voir dans le fond de son cœur
Tout le beau sexe infidèle et trompeur:
Dans la femme où brillait le plus rare mérite,
Il voyait une âme hypocrite,
Un esprit d'orgueil enivré,
Un cruel ennemi qui sans cesse n'aspire
Qu'à prendre un souverain empire
Sur l'homme malheureux qui lui sera livré.

It is not that patience
is not a virtue for Parisian ladies,
but through long experience they have learned
how to make their husbands practice it.

Griselidis: A *Novella*

At the foot of the famous mountains
where the Po, escaping from beneath its reeds,
proceeds to pour its springing waters
into the bosom of the nearby countryside,
there lived a young, valiant prince,
the delight of his province:
Heaven, in shaping him, poured all its rarest gifts
upon him at once,
gifts it usually parcels out among its friends
and gives only to great kings.

Endowed with every favor of body and soul,
he was robust, skillful, suited to the trade of Mars,
and by the hidden inspiration of a divine flame
he passionately loved the fine arts.
He loved combat, he loved victory,
grand projects, valorous deeds,
and all that makes a fair name live through history;
but his tender, noble heart
was even more open to the solid glory
of making his subjects happy.

This heroic temperament
was darkened by a gloomy vapor
which, moody and melancholy,
made him, at the bottom of his heart, view
the entire fair sex as being faithless and deceitful:
in the woman in whom the rarest merit shone
he saw a hypocritical soul,
a mind drunk with pride,
a cruel enemy with one unceasing desire:
to take complete control
over any unfortunate man who fell into her hands.

Le fréquent usage du monde,
Où l'on ne voit qu'époux subjugués ou trahis,
Joint à l'air jaloux du pays,
Accrut encor cette haine profonde.
Il jura donc plus d'une fois
Que quand même le Ciel pour lui plein de tendresse
Formerait une autre Lucrèce,
Jamais de l'hyménée il ne suivrait les lois.

Ainsi, quand le matin, qu'il donnait aux affaires,
Il avait réglé sagement
Toutes les choses nécessaires
Au bonheur du gouvernement,
Que du faible orphelin, de la veuve oppressée,
Il avait conservé les droits,
Ou banni quelque impôt qu'une guerre forcée
Avait introduit autrefois,
L'autre moitié de la journée
A la chasse était destinée,
Où les sangliers et les ours,
Malgré leur fureur et leurs armes
Lui donnaient encor moins d'alarmes
Que le sexe charmant qu'il évitait toujours.

Cependant ses sujets que leur intérêt presse
De s'assurer d'un successeur
Qui les gouverne un jour avec même douceur,
A leur donner un fils le conviaient sans cesse.

Un jour dans le palais ils vinrent tous en corps
Pour faire leurs derniers efforts;
Un orateur d'une grave apparence,
Et le meilleur qui fût alors,
Dit tout ce qu'on peut dire en pareille occurrence.
Il marqua leur désir pressant
De voir sortir du prince une heureuse lignée
Qui rendît à jamais leur État florissant;
Il lui dit même en finissant
Qu'il voyait un astre naissant

The customary way of the world,
where we see nothing but henpecked or cheated husbands,
   when combined with the jealousy prevalent in that country,
   increased that deep-seated hatred even more.
   Thus, he swore more than once
that, even if Heaven, full of tenderness for him,
   were to create a new Lucrece,[5]
he would never submit to the laws of marriage.

Thus, when in the morning, which he regularly devoted to business,
   he had made wise arrangements
   for all things necessary
   to the happiness of the realm,
after he had protected the rights of the weak orphan
   and the oppressed widow,
or revoked some tax which an unavoidable war
   had introduced in the past,
   the second half of his day
   was dedicated to the hunt,
   in which boars and bears,
   despite their rage and their natural weapons,
   were even less frightening to him
than the charming sex, which he always avoided.

Nevertheless, his subjects, goaded by their interest
   in being assured of a successor
who would rule them with the same light hand one day,
never stopped urging him to give them a son.

One day they came to the palace in a group
   to make one last attempt;
   an orator of grave appearance,
   the best there was at the time,
said all that can be said on such an occasion.
   He emphasized their urgent desire
to see the prince give rise to a fortunate lineage
that would make their state forever prosperous;
   he even told him, in conclusion,
   that he saw a star rising,

---

[5]Lucretia, the ancient Roman matron who preferred suicide to (even forced) adultery.

Issu de son chaste hyménée
Qui faisait pâlir le croissant.

D'un ton plus simple et d'une voix moins forte,
Le prince à ses sujets répondit de la sorte:

«Le zèle ardent, dont je vois qu'en ce jour
Vous me portez aux nœuds du mariage,
Me fait plaisir, et m'est de votre amour
        Un agréable témoignage;
        J'en suis sensiblement touché,
Et voudrais dès demain pouvoir vous satisfaire:
    Mais à mon sens l'hymen est une affaire
Où plus l'homme est prudent, plus il est empêché.

    Observez bien toutes les jeunes filles;
    Tant qu'elles sont au sein de leurs familles,
        Ce n'est que vertu, que bonté,
        Que pudeur, que sincérité,
        Mais sitôt que le mariage
        Au déguisement a mis fin,
        Et qu'ayant fixé leur destin
        Il n'importe plus d'être sage,
        Elles quittent leur personnage,
        Non sans avoir beaucoup pâti,
        Et chacune dans son ménage
        Selon son gré prend son parti.

L'une d'humeur chagrine, et que rien ne récrée,
        Devient une dévote outrée,
        Qui crie et gronde à tous moments;
        L'autre se façonne en coquette,
        Qui sans cesse écoute ou caquette,
        Et n'a jamais assez d'amants;
Celle-ci des beaux-arts follement curieuse,
        De tout décide avec hauteur,
        Et critiquant le plus habile auteur,
        Prend le forme de précieuse;
        Cette autre s'érige en joueuse,
perd tout, argent, bijoux, bagues, meubles de prix,
        Et même jusqu'à ses habits.

as the issue of his chaste marriage,
which would make the Crescent turn pale.[6]

In a simpler tone and a quieter voice,
the prince replied to his subjects as follows:

"The ardent zeal with which I see you today
leading me into the bonds of marriage,
gives me pleasure, and is a welcome testimony
    of your love to me;
    I am sincerely touched by it;
and I would like to be able to satisfy you as early as tomorrow:
    but, as I see it, marriage is a matter
in which, the more prudent a man is, the more awkward his situation is.

Take a good look at all young women:
while they are still in the bosom of their families,
    they are all virtue, all kindness,
    all modesty, all sincerity,
    but as soon as marriage
    has put an end to that masquerade,
    and, now that their fate has been settled,
    it is no longer necessary to be well-behaved,
    they drop their mask,
    not without having suffered greatly,
    and each woman in her household
    makes her decisions just as she wishes.

One, of a gloomy temperament, whom nothing amuses,
    becomes a religious fanatic,
    shouting and scolding all the time;
    another becomes a flirt
    who does nothing but listen or chatter,
    and never has enough male admirers;
another, madly smitten with the fine arts,
    makes haughty judgments on all matters
  and, critical of the most skillful author,
    becomes an affected patron of "culture";
    another turns out to be a gambler
and loses everything, money, jewelry, valuables, expensive furnishings,
    and even her clothes.

[6]Wars against the Turks were a constant topic in the Europe of Perrault's day.

Dans la diversité des routes qu'elles tiennent,
    Il n'est qu'une chose où je voi
    Qu'enfin toutes elles conviennent,
    C'est de vouloir donner la loi.
Or je suis convaincu que dans le mariage
    On ne peut jamais vivre heureux,
    Quand on y commande tous deux;
Si donc vous souhaitez qu'à l'hymen je m'engage,
    Cherchez une jeune beauté
    Sans orgueil et sans vanité,
    D'une obéissance achevée,
    D'une patience éprouvée,
    Et qui n'ait point de volonté,
Je la prendrai quand vous l'aurez trouvée.»

Le prince ayant mis fin à ce discours moral,
    Monte brusquement à cheval,
    Et court joindre à perte d'haleine
Sa meute qui l'attend au milieu de la plaine.

Après avoir passé des prés et des guérets,
Il trouve ses chasseurs couchés sur l'herbe verte;
    Tous se lèvent et tous alerte,
Font trembler de leurs cors les hôtes des forêts.
    Des chiens courants l'aboyante famille,
    Deçà, delà, parmi le chaume brille,
    Et les limiers à l'œil ardent
Qui du fort de la bête à leur poste reviennent,
    Entraînent en les regardant
    Les forts valets qui les retiennent.

    S'étant instruit par un des siens
    Si tout est prêt, si l'on est sur la trace,
Il ordonne aussitôt qu'on commence la chasse,
    Et fait donner le cerf aux chiens.
    Le son des cors qui retentissent,
    Le bruit des chevaux qui hennissent
Et des chiens animés les pénétrants abois,
Remplissent la forêt de tumulte et de trouble,
Et pendant que l'écho sans cesse les redouble,
S'enfoncent avec eux dans les plus creux du bois.

In the variety of paths they take
    there is only one point on which I see
    them all agreeing:
    their desire to rule the roost.
Now, I am convinced that in a marriage
    it is impossible ever to lead a happy life
    when both partners give the orders;
therefore, if you want me to enter matrimony,
    seek out a young beauty
    free of pride and vanity,
    one of total obedience
    and tested patience,
    and with no will of her own,
and I'll marry her as soon as you find her."

Having finished that moral speech, the prince
    mounted his horse without delay
    and breathlessly rode out to catch up with
his pack of hounds awaiting him in mid-plain.

After passing meadows and fields,
he found his huntsmen lying on the green grass;
    they all got up and all, bestirring themselves,
made the forest-dwellers tremble at the sound of their horns.
    The barking family of running dogs
    flashed to and fro amid the grass,
    and the eager-eyed sleuth-hounds,
returning to their post from the beast's lair,
    by their looks urged on
    the strong keepers who held them back.

    Being informed by one of his men
    that all was ready and they had picked up a scent,
he immediately ordered the hunt to begin,
    and loosed the dogs upon the stag.
    The sound of the echoing horns,
    the noise of the neighing horses,
and the ear-piercing barks of the lively hounds
filled the forest with tumult and chaos,
and while the echoes constantly repeated them,
the sounds penetrated the densest parts of the forest along with
                those who produced them.

Le prince, par hasard ou par sa destinée,
    Prit une route détournée
    Où nul des chasseurs ne le suit;
    Plus il court, plus il s'en sépare:
    Enfin à tel point il s'égare
Que des chiens et des cors il n'entend plus le bruit.

L'endroit où le mena sa bizarre aventure,
    Clair de ruisseaux et sombre de verdure,
Saisissait les esprits d'une secrète horreur;
    La simple et naïve nature
    S'y faisait voir et si belle et si pure,
    Que mille fois il bénit son erreur.

    Rempli des douces rêveries
Qu'inspirent les grands bois, les eaux et les prairies,
Il sent soudain frapper et son cœur et ses yeux
    Par l'objet le plus agréable,
    Le plus doux et le plus aimable
    Qu'il eût jamais vu sous les cieux.

    C'était une jeune bergère
    Qui filait aux bords d'un ruisseau,
    Et qui conduisant son troupeau,
    D'une main sage et ménagère
    Tournait son agile fuseau.

Elle aurait pu dompter les cœurs les plus sauvages;
    Des lys, son teint a la blancheur,
    Et sa naturelle fraîcheur
S'était toujours sauvée à l'ombre des bocages:
Sa bouche, de l'enfance avait tout l'agrément,
Et ses yeux qu'adoucit une brune paupière,
    Plus bleus que n'est le firmament,
    Avaient aussi plus de lumière.

Le prince, avec transport, dans le bois se glissant,
Contemple les beautés dont son âme est émue,
    Mais le bruit qu'il fait en passant
De la belle sur lui fit détourner la vue;
    Dès qu'elle se vit aperçue,
D'un brillant incarnat la prompte et vive ardeur
    De son beau teint redoubla la splendeur,

Whether by chance or by fate, the prince
    took a bypath
    on which none of the huntsmen followed him;
    the farther he went, the more he became separated from them;
    finally he was so lost
that he no longer heard the sound of the hounds and horns.

The place where his odd adventure had led him,
  with its clear streams and dark foliage,
assailed his spirits with a secret awe;
    simple, unspoiled nature
  displayed itself there in such beauty and purity
  that he blessed his straying a thousand times.

    Filled with the sweet daydreams
that great forests, waters, and grasslands inspire,
he suddenly felt his heart and eyes being smitten
    by the most pleasant young woman,
    the gentlest and most lovable,
    that he had ever seen beneath the skies.

    It was a young shepherdess
  who was spinning by the side of a brook
  and, while guiding her flock,
  was turning her agile spindle
  with a well-trained, housewifely hand.

She could have subdued the wildest hearts;
    her complexion had the whiteness of lilies,
    and her skin, naturally light and smooth,
had always been protected by the shade of the groves:
her mouth had all the charm of a child's,
and her eyes, set off by dark lids,
    were bluer than the sky
    and even brighter, too.

The prince, slipping into the woods in his ardor,
observed the beauties that had touched his heart,
    but the sound he made while passing
made the beauty turn her eyes in his direction;
    the moment she found herself observed,
the prompt, lively flush of a bright red
  made her lovely complexion twice as splendid,

Et sur son visage épandue,
Y fit triompher la pudeur.

Sous le voile innocent de cette honte aimable,
Le prince découvrit une simplicité,
  Une douceur, une sincérité,
  Dont il croyait le beau sexe incapable,
  Et qu'il voit là dans toute leur beauté.

Saisi d'une frayeur pour lui toute nouvelle,
Il s'approche interdit, et plus timide qu'elle,
  Lui dit d'une tremblante voix,
Que de tous ses veneurs il a perdu la trace,
  Et lui demande si la chasse
  N'a point passé quelque part dans le bois.

«Rien n'a paru, seigneur, dans cette solitude,
Dit-elle, et nul ici que vous seul n'est venu;
  Mais n'ayez point d'inquiétude,
Je remettrai vos pas sur un chemin connu.

    —De mon heureuse destinée
Je ne puis, lui dit-il, trop rendre grâce aux Dieux;
  Depuis longtemps je fréquente ces lieux,
Mais j'avais ignoré jusqu'à cette journée
  Ce qu'ils ont de plus précieux.»

Dans ce temps elle voit que le prince se baisse
    Sur le moite bord du ruisseau,
  Pour étancher dans le cours de son eau
    La soif ardente qui le presse.
    «Seigneur, attendez un moment»,
    Dit-elle, et courant promptement
  Vers sa cabane, elle y prend une tasse
    Qu'avec joie et de bonne grâce,
  Elle présente à ce nouvel amant.

Les vases précieux de cristal et d'agate
    Où l'or en mille endroits éclate,
Et qu'un art curieux avec soin façonna,
N'eurent jamais pour lui, dans leur pompe inutile,
  Tant de beauté que le vase d'argile
    Que la bergère lui donna.

and, spreading over her face,
made modesty triumph there.

Beneath the innocent veil of that lovable sense of shame
the prince discovered a simplicity,
a sweetness, a sincerity,
of which he thought the fair sex was incapable,
and which he saw there in all their beauty.

Assailed by an alarm that was quite new to him,
he approached in confusion and, more timid than she,
told her in a trembling voice
that he had lost trace of all his huntsmen,
and asked her whether the hunt
had not passed by somewhere in those woods.

"I have seen nothing in this solitude, my lord,"
she replied, "and no one has come but you;
but have no fears,
I shall guide your steps back to a familiar path."

"For such a fortunate stroke of fate,"
he said, "I cannot thank the Gods too much;
I have been in these places very often,
but up to today I was unaware
of the most precious thing they contained."

Meanwhile, she saw the prince stoop down
by the moist side of the brook
to quench in the current of its water
the strong thirst that he felt.
"My lord, wait a moment,"
she said, and, running swiftly
to her cottage, she fetched a cup there
which she joyfully and graciously
presented to her new admirer.

The precious vessels of crystal and agate,
on which gold gleams in a thousand places,
and which a skillful art painstakingly fashioned,
never possessed for him, in their useless pomp,
as much beauty as the clay cup
that the shepherdess gave him.

Cependant pour trouver une route facile
    Qui mène le prince à la ville,
Ils traversent des bois, des rochers escarpés
    Et de torrents entrecoupés;
Le prince n'entre point dans de route nouvelle
Sans en bien observer tous les lieux d'alentour,
    Et son ingénieux amour
    Qui songeait au retour,
    En fit une carte fidèle.

    Dans un bocage sombre et frais
    Enfin la bergère le mène,
Où de dessous ses branchages épais
Il voit au loin dans le sein de la plaine
Les toits dorés de son riche palais.

    S'étant séparé de la belle,
    Touché d'une vive douleur,
    A pas lents il s'éloigne d'elle,
Chargé du trait qui lui perce le cœur;
Le souvenir de sa tendre aventure
Avec plaisir le conduisit chez lui.
Mais dès le lendemain il sentit sa blessure,
Et se vit accablé de tristesse et d'ennui.
Dès qu'il le peut il retourne à la chasse,
    Où de sa suite adroitement
    Il s'échappe et se débarrasse
    Pour s'égarer heureusement.
Des arbres et des monts les cimes élevées,
    Qu'avec grand soin il avait observées,
Et les avis secrets de son fidèle amour,
Le guidèrent si bien que malgré les traverses
      De cent routes diverses,
De sa jeune bergère il trouva le séjour.

Il sut qu'elle n'a plus que son père avec elle,
    Que Grisélidis on l'appelle,
Qu'ils vivent doucement du lait de leurs brebis,
Et que de leur toison qu'elle seule elle file,
    Sans avoir recours à la ville,
    Ils font eux-mêmes leurs habits.

Meanwhile, in order to find an easy path
  for the prince to follow to his city,
they crossed forests, rugged boulders,
  and torrents interrupted by the terrain;
the prince did not enter any new path
without carefully noting all the places around it,
  and his ingenious love,
  with his return in mind,
  drew a reliable map of them.

  The shepherdess finally led him
  into a dark, cool grove
where, beneath its dense branches,
he saw in the distance, in the heart of the plain,
the gilded roofs of his rich palace.

  After taking leave of the beauty,
  feeling a keen pain,
  he walked away from her with slow steps,
burdened with the dart that had pierced his heart;
the recollection of his amorous adventure
brought him home pleasurably.
But the very next day he felt his wound
and found himself overwhelmed by sadness and unease.
  As soon as he could, he went hunting again;
  in the course of it he cleverly slipped away
  from his followers, to be rid of them,
  and to lose his way happily.
The lofty tops of the trees and hills,
  which he had observed with great diligence,
and the secret promptings of his faithful love,
were such good guides that, despite the crisscrossings
   of a hundred different paths,
he found the dwelling place of his young shepherdess.

He learned that she had only her father with her,
  that she was called Griselidis,
that they lived quietly from the milk of their sheep,
and that from their wool, which she spun by herself,
  without having recourse to the city
  they made their own clothes.

Plus il la voit, plus il s'enflamme
Des vives beautés de son âme;
Il connaît en voyant tant de dons précieux,
     Que si la bergère est si belle,
     C'est qu'une légère étincelle
De l'esprit qui l'anime a passé dans ses yeux.

     Il ressent une joie extrême
D'avoir si bien placé ses premières amours;
Ainsi sans plus tarder, il fit dès le jour même
Assembler son conseil et lui tint ce discours:

     «Enfin aux lois de l'hyménée
     Suivant vos vœux je me vais engager;
Je ne prends point ma femme en pays étranger,
Je la prends parmi vous, belle, sage, bien née,
Ainsi que mes aïeux ont fait plus d'une fois,
     Mais j'attendrai cette grande journée
     A vous informer de mon choix.»
     Dès que la nouvelle fut sue,
     Partout elle fut répandue.
On ne peut dire avec combien d'ardeur
     L'allégresse publique
     De tous côtés s'explique;
     Le plus content fut l'orateur,
     Qui par son discours pathétique
Croyait d'un si grand bien être l'unique auteur.
     Qu'il se trouvait homme de conséquence!
«Rien ne peut résister à la grande éloquence»,
     Disait-il sans cesse en son cœur.

Le plaisir fut de voir le travail inutile
     Des belles de toute la ville
     Pour s'attirer et mériter le choix
Du prince leur seigneur, qu'un air chaste et modeste
Charmait uniquement et plus que tout le reste,
     Ainsi qu'il l'avait dit cent fois.

D'habit et de maintien toutes elles changèrent,
     D'un ton dévot elles toussèrent,
     Elles radoucirent leurs voix,
     De demi-pied les coiffures baissèrent,

The more he saw her, the more he was ignited
  by the bright beauties of her soul;
seeing so many precious talents, he knew
    that, if the shepherdess was so beautiful,
    it was because a light spark
of the spirit that animated her had taken refuge in her eyes.

  He felt an extreme joy
at having bestowed his first love on such a worthy person;
and so, with no further delay, that very day
he convoked his council and made this speech to them:

  "Finally, in deference to your wishes,
  I shall submit to the laws of matrimony;
I have not chosen my wife in a foreign land,
I have chosen her from among you, beautiful, discreet, well born,
just as my ancestors did more than once;
    but I shall await that great day
    before informing you of my choice."
    As soon as the news was learned,
    it was spread abroad in all quarters.
It cannot be told how eagerly
      the public's joy
      was expressed on all sides;
    the most contented man was the orator,
    who was sure that his heartfelt speech
had been the sole cause of such great good fortune.
  How important he considered himself!
"Nothing can resist lofty eloquence."
    he repeated ceaselessly to himself.

It was entertaining to watch the useless labor
      of all the beauties in town
    to attract and deserve selection
by their lord the prince, whom a chaste and modest air
alone could delight, more than anything else,
    as he had said a hundred times.

They all changed their clothes and behavior,
    they coughed in a pious tone,
    they softened their voices,
    their headgear grew six inches shorter,

La gorge se couvrit, les manches s'allongèrent,
A peine on leur voyait le petit bout des doigts.

Dans la ville avec diligence,
Pour l'hymen dont le jour s'avance,
On voit travailler tous les arts:
Ici se font de magnifiques chars
D'une forme toute nouvelle,
Si beaux et si bien inventés,
Que l'or qui partout étincelle
En fait la moindre des beautés.

Là, pour voir aisément et sans aucun obstacle
Toute la pompe du spectacle,
On dresse de longs échafauds,
Ici de grands arcs triomphaux
Où du prince guerrier se célèbre la gloire,
Et de l'amour sur lui l'éclatante victoire.

Là, sont forgés d'un art industrieux,
Ces feux qui par les coups d'un innocent tonnerre,
En effrayant la terre,
De mille astres nouveaux embellissent les cieux.
Là d'un ballet ingénieux
Se concerte avec soin l'agréable folie,
Et là d'un opéra peuplé de mille dieux,
Le plus beau que jamais ait produit l'Italie,
On entend répéter les airs mélodieux.

Enfin, du fameux hyménée,
Arriva la grande journée.

Sur le fond d'un ciel vif et pur,
A peine l'aurore vermeille
Confondait l'or avec l'azur,
Que partout en sursaut le beau sexe s'éveille;
Le peuple curieux s'épand de tous côtés,
En différents endroits des gardes sont postés
Pour contenir la populace,
Et la contraindre à faire place.
Tout le palais retentit de clairons,
De flûtes, de hautbois, de rustiques musettes,

their bosoms were covered, their sleeves were lengthened,
their fingertips could scarcely be seen.

    In town every artisan
    could be seen working diligently
    for the wedding, which was approaching:
  here, magnificent coaches were made,
    of a model so new,
    so lovely and so well contrived
    that the gold sparkling all over them
    was the least of their attractions.

Here, in order to see clearly, without any impediment,
    the full splendor of the spectacle,
    long bleachers were erected,
    and here, tall triumphal arches
in which were celebrated the warlike prince's glory
and love's glowing victory over him.

    Here, there were forged by industrious craft
those fires which, frightening the earth with the claps
      of a harmless thunder,
adorn the skies with a thousand new stars.
    Here, the pleasant folly
of an ingenious ballet was carefully arranged,
and here, there could be heard the rehearsal of the melodious airs
of an opera peopled by a thousand gods,
the most beautiful one that Italy ever produced.

    Finally the great day
    of the much talked-of wedding arrived.

    Against the background of a bright, clear sky,
    scarcely was vermilion dawn
    mingling gold with the blue,
when everywhere the fair sex awoke with a start;
in its curiosity the populace crowded on all sides,
in various places guards were posted
    to contain the rabble
    and force them to make way.
  The whole palace echoed with bugles,
flutes, oboes, and rustic bagpipes,

Et l'on n'entend aux environs
Que des tambours et des trompettes.

Enfin le prince sort entouré de sa cour,
    Il s'élève un long cri de joie,
Mais on est bien surpris quand au premier détour,
De la forêt prochaine on voit qu'il prend la voie,
        Ainsi qu'il faisait chaque jour.
    «Voilà, dit-on, son penchant qui l'emporte,
Et de ses passions, en dépit de l'amour,
        La chasse est toujours la plus forte.»

        Il traverse rapidement
Les guérets de la plaine et gagnant la montagne,
Il entre dans le bois au grand étonnement
        De la troupe qui l'accompagne.

Après avoir passé par différents détours,
Que son cœur amoureux se plaît à reconnaître,
        Il trouve enfin la cabane champêtre,
        Où logent ses tendres amours.

    Grisélidis de l'hymen informée,
        Par la voix de la renommée,
    En avait pris son bel habillement;
Et pour en aller voir la pompe magnifique,
        De dessous sa case rustique
        Sortait en ce même moment.

    «Où courez-vous si prompte et si légère?
        Lui dit le prince en l'abordant
        Et tendrement la regardant;
Cessez de vous hâter, trop aimable bergère:
La noce où vous allez, et dont je suis l'époux,
        Ne saurait se faire sans vous.

    Oui, je vous aime, et je vous ai choisie
        Entre mille jeunes beautés,
Pour passer avec vous le reste de ma vie,
Si toutefois mes vœux ne sont pas rejetés.

—Ah! dit-elle, seigneur, je n'ai garde de croire
Que je sois destinée à ce comble de gloire,
        Vous cherchez à vous divertir.

and all around nothing was heard
but drums and trumpets.

Finally the prince emerged in the midst of his court;
a long shout of joy was raised,
but people were quite surprised when, at the first turning,
he was seen to follow the path to the nearby forest,
as he did every day.
"See!" they said; "his hobby is carrying him away,
and, in spite of love, the strongest
of his passions is still the hunt."

He swiftly crossed
the fields in the plain and, reaching the mountain,
he entered the woods to the great astonishment
of the troop accompanying him.

After making various turns,
which his loving heart was pleased to recognize,
he finally found the rural cottage
in which his tender love dwelt.

Griselidis, informed of the marriage
by the voice of Fame,
had put on her best clothes for the occasion;
and in order to go and see the splendid ceremony,
at that very moment
she was leaving her rustic hut.

"Where are you running to so nimbly and lightly?"
the prince said to her as he approached her
and looked at her tenderly;
"do not be in a hurry, most lovable shepherdess:
the wedding you are going to, in which I am groom,
cannot take place without you.

Yes, I love you, and I have chosen you
from among a thousand young beauties,
in order to spend the rest of my life with you,
assuming that my wishes are not refused."

"Oh," she said, "my lord, I do not dare to believe
that I am destined for that pinnacle of glory;
you are trying to amuse yourself."

—Non, non, dit-il, je suis sincère,
   J'ai déjà pour moi votre père,
(Le prince avait eu soin de l'en faire avertir).
   Daignez, bergère, y consentir,
   C'est là tout ce qui reste à faire.
Mais afin qu'entre nous une solide paix
      Éternellement se maintienne,
Il faudrait me jurer que vous n'aurez jamais
      D'autre volonté que la mienne.

—Je le jure, dit-elle, et je vous le promets;
Si j'avais épousé le moindre du village,
   J'obéirais, son joug me serait doux;
      Hélas! combien donc davantage,
      Si je viens à trouver en vous
      Et mon seigneur et mon époux.»

      Ainsi le prince se déclare,
Et pendant que la cour applaudit à son choix,
Il porte la bergère à souffrir qu'on la pare
Des ornements qu'on donne aux épouses des rois.
Celles qu'à cet emploi leur devoir intéresse
Entrent dans la cabane, et là diligemment
Mettent tout leur savoir et toute leur adresse
A donner de la grâce à chaque ajustement.

      Dans cette hutte où l'on se presse
      Les dames admirent sans cesse
      Avec quel art la pauvreté
      S'y cache sous la propreté;
      Et cette rustique cabane,
Que couvre et rafraîchit un spacieux platane,
      Leur semble un séjour enchanté.

Enfin, de ce réduit sort pompeuse et brillante
      La bergère charmante;
      Ce ne sont qu'applaudissements
   Sur sa beauté, sur ses habillements;
      Mais sous cette pompe étrangère
Déjà plus d'une fois le prince a regretté
      Des ornements de la bergère
      L'innocente simplicité.

"No, no," he said, "I am sincere;
    I already have your father on my side"
(the prince had taken care to have him notified);
    "shepherdess, deign to consent,
    that is the only thing lacking now.
But, in order that a firm peace may last
    eternally between us,
you must swear to me that you will never have
    a will other than mine."

"I swear," she said, "and I promise you that;
if I had wed the lowliest man in the village,
    I would obey, his yoke would be sweet to me;
        alas! how much more so, then,
        since I have come to find in you
        both my lord and my husband."

And so the prince makes the announcement,
and while his court was applauding his choice,
he induced the shepherdess to let herself be adorned
with the ornaments given to the brides of kings.
The ladies whose duty that task was
entered the cottage, and there diligently
applied all their knowledge and all their skill
to lend grace to every adornment.

    In that hut into which they crowded
    the ladies ceaselessly wondered
    at the art with which poverty
    was concealed there beneath cleanliness;
    and that rustic cabin,
shaded and kept cool by a wide plane tree,
    seemed like an enchanted dwelling to them.

Finally the charming shepherdess left that retreat
        pompously and brilliantly clad;
    applause was universally bestowed
    on her beauty, on her attire;
    but, seeing that unfamiliar pomp,
more than once already the prince had missed
    the innocent simplicity
    of the shepherdess's adornments.

Sur un grand char d'or et d'ivoire,
La bergère s'assied pleine de majesté;
    Le prince y monte avec fierté,
    Et ne trouve pas moins de gloire
A se voir comme amant assis à son côté
Qu'à marcher en triomphe après une victoire;
    La cour les suit et tous gardent le rang
Que leur donne leur charge ou l'éclat de leur sang.

La ville dans les champs presque toute sortie
    Couvrait les plaines d'alentour,
    Et du choix du prince avertie,
Avec impatience attendait son retour.
Il paraît, on le joint. Parmi l'épaisse foule
Du peuple qui se fend le char à peine roule;
Par les longs cris de joie à tout coup redoublés
    Les chevaux émus et troublés
    Se cabrent, trépignent, s'élancent,
    Et reculent plus qu'ils n'avancent.

    Dans le temple on arrive enfin,
    Et là par la chaîne éternelle
    D'une promesse solennelle,
Les deux époux unissent leur destin;
    Ensuite au palais ils se rendent,
    Où mille plaisirs les attendent,
Où la danse, les jeux, les courses, les tournois,
Répandent l'allégresse en différents endroits;
    Sur le soir le blond Hyménée
De ses chastes douceurs couronna la journée.

Le lendemain, les différents États
    De toute la Province
Accourent haranguer la princesse et le prince
    Par la voix de leurs magistrats.

    De ses dames environnée,
   Grisélidis, sans paraître étonnée,
    En princesse les entendit,
    En princesse leur répondit.
Elle fit toute chose avec tant de prudence,
Qu'il sembla que le Ciel eût versé ses trésors
    Avec encor plus d'abondance

On a grand gold-and-ivory carriage
the shepherdess took her seat, full of majesty;
    the prince ascended with boldness,
    and discovered no less glory
in finding himself seated beside her as a lover
than in marching in triumph after a victory;
    the court followed them, each one keeping the place
assigned to him by position or nobility of blood.

The townsfolk, nearly all of whom had come out to the fields,
    was covering the plain all around,
    and, informed of the prince's choice,
was awaiting his return impatiently.
He appeared; they joined him. Amid the dense crowd
of the people making way, the carriage could hardly move;
the horses, frightened and made shy by the long shouts of joy
        that were redoubled at every moment,
        reared, stamped, darted forward,
        and retreated more than they advanced.

    They finally reached the church,
    and there, by the eternal chain
    of a solemn vow,
  the two newlyweds joined their destinies together;
    then they proceeded to the palace,
    where a thousand pleasures awaited them,
where dancing, games, tilting at the ring, and tournaments
spread joy in various places;
    in the evening the blonde god of marriage
crowned the day with his chaste delights.

    The next day, the various Estates of the nation
        came from the whole territory
to address the princess and prince
        through the voice of their magistrates.

    Surrounded by her ladies,
  Griselidis, showing no sign of surprise,
    listened to them like a princess
    and replied to them like a princess.
She did everything so prudently
that Heaven seemed to have poured its treasures
        even more plentifully

Sur son âme que sur son corps.
Par son esprit, par ses vives lumières,
Du grand monde aussitôt elle prit les manières,
Et même dès le premier jour
Des talents, de l'humeur des dames de sa cour,
Elle se fit si bien instruire,
Que son bon sens jamais embarrassé
Eut moins de peine à les conduire
Que ses brebis du temps passé.

Avant la fin de l'an, des fruits de l'hyménée
Le Ciel bénit leur couche fortunée;
Ce ne fut pas un prince, on l'eût bien souhaité;
Mais la jeune princesse avait tant de beauté
Que l'on ne songea plus qu'à conserver sa vie;
Le père qui lui trouve un air doux et charmant
La venait voir de moment en moment,
Et la mère encor plus ravie
La regardait incessamment.

Elle voulut la nourrir elle-même:
«Ah! dit-elle, comment m'exempter de l'emploi
Que ses cris demandent de moi
Sans une ingratitude extrême?
Par un motif de nature ennemi
Pourrais-je bien vouloir de mon enfant que j'aime
N'être la mère qu'à demi?»

Soit que le prince eût l'âme un peu moins enflammée
Qu'aux premiers jours de son ardeur,
Soit que de sa maligne humeur
La masse se fût rallumée,
Et de son épaisse fumée
Eût obscurci ses sens et corrompu son cœur,
Dans tout ce que fait la princesse,
Il s'imagine voir peu de sincérité.
Sa trop grande vertu le blesse,
C'est un piège qu'on tend à sa crédulité;
Son esprit inquiet et de trouble agité
Croit tous les soupçons qu'il écoute,
Et prend plaisir à révoquer en doute
L'excès de sa félicité.

on her soul than on her body.
Through her intelligence, through her great inborn brightness,
she immediately adopted the manners of high society,
    and, from the very first day,
she gained such insight into the talents and moods
        of the ladies of her court
    that her good sense, never at a loss,
        had less trouble guiding them
        than guiding her sheep in the past.

Before a year had passed, Heaven blessed
    their happy bed with the fruits of matrimony;
it was not a prince, though that was wished for;
but the young princess was so beautiful
that their sole care was to preserve her life;
her father, who found her sweet and charming,
    came to see her all the time,
        and her mother, even more delighted,
        kept looking at her constantly.

She decided to nurse her herself:
"Oh," she said, "how can I beg off from the duty
        that her cries demand of me
        without being extremely ungrateful?
    For a reason contrary to nature
could I really wish to be only half a mother
        to the child that I love?"

Whether the prince's heart was now a little less ardent
        than in the first days of his passion,
        or whether the residue of his melancholy
        caught fire again
        and with its thick smoke
was clouding his senses and tainting his heart,
        in everything that the princess did
he imagined that he found little sincerity.
        Her too-great virtue offended him,
as if it were a snare laid for his gullibility;
his restless mind, stirred by confusion,
        lent credence to every suspicion he heard,
    and took pleasure in calling into doubt
        the excess of his happiness.

Pour guérir les chagrins dont son âme est atteinte,
Il la suit, il l'observe, il aime à la troubler
    Par les ennuis de la contrainte,
    Par les alarmes de la crainte,
    Par tout ce qui peut démêler
    La vérité d'avec la feinte.
  «C'est trop, dit-il, me laisser endormir;
    Si ses vertus sont véritables,
  Les traitements les plus insupportables
    Ne feront que les affermir.»

  Dans son palais il la tient resserrée,
Loin de tous les plaisirs qui naissent à la cour,
Et dans sa chambre, où seule elle vit retirée,
    A peine il laisse entrer le jour.
    Persuadé que la parure
    Et le superbe ajustement
Du sexe que pour plaire a formé la nature
    Est le plus doux enchantement
    Il lui demande avec rudesse
Les perles, les rubis, les bagues, les bijoux
  Qu'il lui donna pour marque de tendresse,
Lorsque de son amant il devint son époux.

    Elle dont la vie est sans tache,
    Et qui n'a jamais eu d'attache
    Qu'à s'acquitter de son devoir,
    Les lui donne sans s'émouvoir,
Et même, le voyant se plaire à les reprendre,
    N'a pas moins de joie à les rendre
    Qu'elle en eut à les recevoir.

  «Pour m'éprouver mon époux me tourmente,
Dit-elle, et je vois bien qu'il ne me fait souffrir
Qu'afin de réveiller ma vertu languissante,
Qu'un doux et long repos pourrait faire périr.
S'il n'a pas ce dessein, du moins suis-je assurée
Que telle est du Seigneur la conduite sur moi
Et que de tant de maux l'ennuyeuse durée
N'est que pour exercer ma constance et ma foi.

    Pendant que tant de malheureuses
    Errent au gré de leurs désirs

To cure the cares with which his soul was stricken,
he followed her, observed her, delighted in upsetting her
    with the nuisance of constraint,
    with the alarms of fear,
    with every means that could distinguish
    truth from pretense.
   "I have let myself be caught napping long enough," he said;
    if her virtues are real,
the most unbearable treatment
    will only strengthen them."

He kept her penned up in his palace,
far from all the pleasures that the court provides,
and in her room, where she lived in solitary retirement,
    he scarcely allowed daylight to enter.
    Convinced that jewelry
    and splendid ornaments
are the dearest delight of that sex
    which nature created to please,
    he harshly asked her for
the pearls, rubies, rings, and gems
   that he had given her as a token of his affection
when, from being her suitor, he became her husband.

    She, whose life was spotless,
    and who had never felt any attachment
    except to the performance of her duties,
    gave them to him without a qualm.
In fact, seeing him glad to have them back,
    she felt no less joy in returning them
    than she had felt in receiving them.

   "My husband is tormenting me to test me,"
she said, "and I realize that he is making me suffer merely
in order to rekindle my flagging virtue,
which a lengthy, sweet repose might destroy.
If that is not his purpose, at least I am certain
that the Lord is guiding me in this manner
and that the troublesome duration of so many woes
is merely to make me exert my constancy and my faith.

    While so many wretched women
    stray, as their desires lead them,

Par mille routes dangereuses,
    Après de faux et vains plaisirs;
Pendant que le Seigneur dans sa lente justice
    Les laisse aller aux bords du précipice
        Sans prendre part à leur danger,
Par un pur mouvement de sa bonté suprême,
    Il me choisit comme un enfant qu'il aime,
        Et s'applique à me corriger.

Aimons donc sa rigueur utilement cruelle,
    On n'est heureux qu'autant qu'on a souffert,
        Aimons sa bonté paternelle
        Et la main dont elle se sert.»

Le prince a beau la voir obéir sans contrainte
    A tous ses ordres absolus:
«Je vois le fondement de cette vertu feinte,
Dit-il, et ce qui rend tous mes coups superflus,
        C'est qu'ils n'ont porté leur atteinte
        Qu'à des endroits où son amour n'est plus.

Dans son enfant, dans la jeune princesse,
    Elle a mis toute sa tendresse;
    A l'éprouver si je veux réussir,
        C'est là qu'il faut que je m'adresse,
        C'est là que je puis m'éclaircir.»

Elle venait de donner la mamelle
    Au tendre objet de son amour ardent,
Qui couché sur son sein se jouait avec elle,
        Et riait en la regardant:
«Je vois que vous l'aimez, lui dit-il, cependant
Il faut que je vous l'ôte en cet âge encor tendre,
Pour lui former les mœurs et pour la préserver
De certains mauvais airs qu'avec vous l'on peut prendre;
        Mon heureux sort m'a fait trouver
    Une dame d'esprit qui saura l'élever
Dans toutes les vertus et dans la politesse
        Que doit avoir une princesse.

along a thousand perilous paths
in pursuit of false, vain pleasures;
while the Lord in His slow-moving justice
allows them to approach the brink of the abyss
without being concerned for their danger,
by a pure action of His supreme goodness
He had chosen me as a beloved child
and is taking the trouble to chasten me.

Thus, let me love His usefully cruel harshness;
one is only happy to the extent that one has suffered;
let me love His paternal kindness
and the hand it is making use of."

In vain the prince saw her obey without constraint
all his absolute orders:
"I see the basis for this feigned virtue,"
he said, "and the thing that makes all my efforts useless
is that they have only been aimed
at places where her love no longer exists.

It is in her child, in the young princess,
that she has placed all her affection;
if I wish to test her successfully,
it is there that I must turn,
it is there that I can learn the truth."

She had just given her breast
to the tender object of her ardent love,
who, lying on her bosom, was playing with her
and was laughing while looking at her:
"I see that you love her," he said to her, "and yet
I must take her away from you at her still tender age,
in order to bring her up properly and to protect her
against certain evil ways she might adopt from you;[7]
My luck has allowed me to find
an intelligent lady who can raise her
with all the virtues and polish
that a princess should have.

---

[7]Or: "against certain diseases she might catch from you." Both connotations were
probably intended by Perrault.

Disposez-vous à la quitter,
On va venir pour l'emporter.»

Il la laisse à ces mots, n'ayant pas le courage,
    Ni les yeux assez inhumains,
    Pour voir arracher de ses mains
    De leur amour l'unique gage;
Elle de mille pleurs se baigne le visage,
    Et dans un morne accablement
Attend de son malheur le funeste moment.

Dès que d'une action si triste et si cruelle
Le ministre odieux à ses yeux se montra,
    «Il faut obéir», lui dit-elle;
Puis prenant son enfant qu'elle considéra,
    Qu'elle baisa d'une ardeur maternelle,
Qui de ses petits bras tendrement la serra,
    Toute en pleurs elle le livra.
    Ah! que sa douleur fut amère!
    Arracher l'enfant ou le cœur
    Du sein d'une si tendre mère,
    C'est la même douleur.

    Près de la ville était un monastère,
    Fameux par son antiquité,
Où des vierges vivaient dans une règle austère,
Sous les yeux d'une abbesse illustre en piété.
    Ce fut là que dans le silence,
    Et sans déclarer sa naissance,
On déposa l'enfant, et des bagues de prix,
    Sous l'espoir d'une récompense
Digne des soins que l'on en aurait pris.

Le prince qui tâchait d'éloigner par la chasse
    Le vif remords qui l'embarrasse
    Sur l'excès de sa cruauté,
    Craignait de revoir la princesse,
Comme on craint de revoir une fière tigresse
    A qui son faon vient d'être ôté;
    Cependant il en fut traité
    Avec douceur, avec caresse,
    Et même avec cette tendresse
Qu'elle eut aux plus beaux jours de sa prospérité.

Make ready to let her go,
people are coming to take her away."

Saying this, he left her, not having the heart,
or the inhuman eyes,
to watch the sole pledge of their love
being torn from her hands;
her face was bathed in a thousand tears,
and in gloomy dejection
she awaited the dire moment of her misfortune.

As soon as the hateful executor of such a sad
and cruel act appeared before her,
"I must obey," she said to him;
then, picking up her child, taking a long look at her,
and kissing her with a mother's passion
as the infant tenderly hugged her with her little arms,
she handed her over, bathed in tears.
Ah! How bitter her sorrow was!
To snatch a child or the very heart
from the breast of such a loving mother:
the pain is the same.

Near the city was a convent,
famous for its great age,
in which virgins lived following an austere rule,
under the guidance of an abbess well known for her piety.
It was there that, in silence,
and without declaring her high birth,
they deposited the child, along with costly valuables,
with the promise of a reward
worthy of the care the nuns would take of her.

The prince, who was trying, by means of the hunt, to repress
the keen remorse that troubled him
on account of his excessive cruelty,
feared to see the princess again,
as a man fears to see again a tigress
from whom her cub has just been taken;
nevertheless, she received him
with gentleness, with kind attentions,
and even with the tenderness
she had felt in the loveliest days of her prosperity.

Par cette complaisance et si grande et si prompte,
    Il fut touché de regret et de honte;
    Mais son chagrin demeura le plus fort:
Ainsi, deux jours après, avec des larmes feintes,
Pour lui porter encor de plus vives atteintes,
    Il lui vint dire que la mort
De leur aimable enfant avait fini le sort.

Ce coup inopiné mortellement la blesse,
    Cependant malgré sa tristesse,
Ayant vu son époux qui changeait de couleur,
    Elle parut oublier son malheur,
    Et n'avoir même de tendresse
Que pour le consoler de sa fausse douleur.

    Cette bonté, cette ardeur sans égale
      D'amitié conjugale,
Du prince tout à coup désarmant la rigueur,
Le touche, le pénètre et lui change le cœur,
    Jusque-là qu'il lui prend envie
    De déclarer que leur enfant
    Jouit encore de la vie;
Mais sa bile s'élève et fière lui défend
    De rien découvrir du mystère
    Qu'il peut être utile de taire.

Dès ce bienheureux jour telle des deux époux
    Fut la mutuelle tendresse,
Qu'elle n'est point plus vive aux moments les plus doux
    Entre l'amant et la maîtresse.

Quinze fois le soleil, pour former les saisons,
Habita tour à tour dans ses douze maisons,
    Sans rien voir qui les désunisse;
    Que si quelquefois par caprice
    Il prend plaisir à la fâcher,
    C'est seulement pour empêcher
    Que l'amour ne se ralentisse,
Tel que le forgeron qui pressant son labeur,
    Répand un peu d'eau sur la braise
    De sa languissante fournaise
    Pour en redoubler la chaleur.

At that great and prompt obligingness
    he was smitten with regret and shame;
    but his melancholia still prevailed;
and so, two days later, with feigned tears,
in order to strike her even deadlier blows,
    he came to tell her that death
had ended the days of their dear child.

That unexpected blow wounded her fatally,
    and yet, despite her sadness,
having seen her husband turn pale,
    she seemed to forget her own grief
    and it even seemed that all her tenderness
was aimed at consoling him for his false sorrow.

    That goodness, that unequaled warmth
        of marital friendship,
suddenly disarming the prince's severity,
touched him, sank into him, and changed his heart
    to such an extent that he felt the urge
    to announce that their child
    still enjoyed life;
but his melancholia surged up and fiercely forbade him
    to reveal anything of the mystery
    that it might be useful to maintain.

From that sad day on, the mutual affection
    of the two spouses was such
that it is not livelier at the sweetest moments
    shared by a lover and his mistress.

Fifteen times the sun, to create the seasons,
had resided in turn in his twelve mansions
    without seeing anything that could separate the pair;
    if at times by caprice
    he took pleasure in grieving her,
    it was merely to prevent
    her love from growing cold,
just as a blacksmith at his labors
    will sprinkle a little water on the embers
    of his dying blaze
    to redouble its heat.

Cependant la jeune princesse
Croissait en esprit, en sagesse;
A la douceur, à la naïveté
Qu'elle tenait de son aimable mère,
Elle joignit de son illustre père
    L'agrèable et noble fierté;
L'amas de ce qui plaît dans chaque caractère
    Fit une parfaite beauté.

Partout comme un astre elle brille;
Et par hasard un seigneur de la cour,
Jeune, bien fait et plus beau que le jour,
    L'ayant vu paraître à la grille,
Conçut pour elle un violent amour.
Par l'instinct qu'au beau sexe a donné la nature
    Et que toutes les beautés ont
    De voir l'invisible blessure
Que font leurs yeux, au moment qu'ils la font,
    La princesse fut informée
    Qu'elle était tendrement aimée.

Après avoir quelque temps résisté
Comme on le doit avant que de se rendre,
    D'un amour également tendre
    Elle l'aima de son côté.

Dans cet amant, rien n'était à reprendre,
Il était beau, vaillant, né d'illustres aïeux
    Et dès longtemps pour en faire son gendre
    Sur lui le prince avait jeté les yeux.
Ainsi donc avec joie il apprit la nouvelle
    De l'ardeur tendre et mutuelle
    Dont brûlaient ces jeunes amants;
Mais il lui prit une bizarre envie
De leur faire acheter par de cruels tourments
    Le plus grand bonheur de leur vie.

«Je me plairai, dit-il, à les rendre contents;
    Mais il faut que l'inquiétude,
    Par tout ce qu'elle a de plus rude,
    Rende encor leurs feux plus constants;
    De mon épouse en même temps

Meanwhile, the young princess
was growing in intelligence and wisdom;
with the sweetness and simplicity
she had inherited from her lovable mother
she combined the noble, pleasing pride
of her illustrious father;
the sum of pleasant traits from both their natures
added up to a perfect beauty.

Everywhere she shone like a star;
and by chance a nobleman of the court,
young, well built, and handsomer than the daylight,
having seen her appear at the convent grille,
fell madly in love with her.
By the instinct that nature has given the fair sex,
and which all beauties possess,
that gift of observing the invisible wound
that their eyes inflict, at the moment it happens,
the princess was informed
that she was tenderly loved.

After resisting for awhile
as a woman does before yielding herself,
she loved him in return
with a love just as warm.

No fault could be found in this suitor;
he was handsome, brave, born of illustrious stock,
and for some time the prince had had
his eyes on him, to make him his son-in-law.
And so he was overjoyed to hear the report
of the mutual warm love
with which these young lovers were aglow;
but he conceived an odd desire
to make them pay with cruel torments
for the greatest happiness in their lives.

"I will be pleased," he said, "to make them contented;
but, first, anxiety
in its most intense form
must make their love more constant;
at the same time, I will be testing

J'exercerai la patience,
    Non point, comme jusqu'à ce jour,
Pour assurer ma folle défiance,
Je ne dois plus douter de son amour;
Mais pour faire éclater aux yeux de tout le monde
Sa bonté, sa douceur, sa sagesse profonde,
Afin que de ces dons si grands, si précieux,
        La terre se voyant parée,
        En soit de respect pénétrée,
Et par reconnaissance en rende grâce aux cieux.»

Il déclare en public que manquant de lignée,
En qui l'État un jour retrouve son seigneur,
Que la fille qu'il eut de son fol hyménée
        Étant morte aussitôt que née,
    Il doit ailleurs chercher plus de bonheur;
Que l'épouse qu'il prend est d'illustre naissance,
    Qu'en un convent on l'a jusqu'à ce jour
        Fait élever dans l'innocence,
Et qu'il va par l'hymen couronner son amour.

    On peut juger à quel point fut cruelle
Aux deux jeunes amants cette affreuse nouvelle;
Ensuite, sans marquer ni chagrin, ni douleur,
        Il avertit son épouse fidèle
        Qu'il faut qu'il se sépare d'elle
        Pour éviter un extrême malheur;
Que le peuple indigné de sa basse naissance
Le force à prendre ailleurs une digne alliance.

        Il faut, dit-il, vous retirer
    Sous votre toit de chaume et de fougère
Après avoir repris vos habits de bergère
        Que je vous ai fait préparer.»

Avec une tranquille et muette constance,
la princesse entendit prononcer sa sentence;
        Sous les dehors d'un visage serein
        Elle dévorait son chagrin,
Et sans que la douleur diminuât ses charmes,
    De ses beaux yeux tombaient de grosses larmes,
Ainsi que quelquefois au retour du printemps,
    Il fait soleil et pleut en même temps.

my wife's patience,
     not, as I have done up to now,
   in order to reassure my mad mistrust,
     since I can no longer doubt her love,
but to make evident to all the world
her goodness, her gentleness, her profound wisdom,
so that, seeing her adorned with such great
          and precious gifts, the earth
          will be imbued with respect for her,
and in its gratitude will give thanks to Heaven."

He declared in public that, having no heir
in whom the state could one day recognize its lord,
since the daughter he had obtained from his madcap marriage
          had died as soon as she was born,
     he was compelled to seek more happiness elsewhere;
the wife he was taking was of noble ancestry
     and had been brought up innocent
          in a convent until that very day,
and he was going to crown his love for her by marrying her.

   You can imagine how cruel
that terrible news was to the two young lovers;
next, displaying no vexation or sorrow,
     he informed his faithful wife
          that he had to divorce her
     in order to avoid a great misfortune;
that his people, angry over the lowness of her birth,
were forcing him to make a worthier alliance with someone else.

     "You must," he said, "withdraw
   to your roof of thatch and fern
after donning once more your shepherdess's garb,
          which I have had prepared for you."

With a tranquil, silent constancy
the princess heard her sentence pronounced;
     beneath the outward appearance of a calm face
          she digested her sorrow,
and, her grief not lessening her charms,
     big tears fell from her lovely eyes,
just as sometimes, when spring returns,
     there is sunshine and rain at the same time.

«Vous êtes mon époux, mon seigneur, et mon maître,
(Dit-elle en soupirant, prête à s'évanouir),
Et quelque affreux que soit ce que je viens d'ouïr,
    Je saurai vous faire connaître
Que rien ne m'est si cher que de vous obéir.»

Dans sa chambre aussitôt seule elle se retire,
Et là se dépouillant de ses riches habits,
    Elle reprend paisible et sans rien dire,
      Pendant que son cœur en soupire,
    Ceux qu'elle avait en gardant ses brebis.

    En cet humble et simple équipage,
Elle aborde le prince et lui tient ce langage:

    «Je ne puis m'éloigner de vous
    Sans le pardon d'avoir su vous déplaire;
    Je puis souffrir le poids de ma misère,
Mais je ne puis, seigneur, souffrir votre courroux;
Accordez cette grâce à mon regret sincère,
Et je vivrai contente en mon triste séjour,
    Sans que jamais le temps altère
Ni mon humble respect, ni mon fidèle amour.»

Tant de soumission et tant de grandeur d'âme
    Sous un si vil habillement,
Qui dans le cœur du prince en ce même moment
Réveilla tous les traits de sa première flamme,
Allaient casser l'arrêt de son bannissement.
    Ému par de si puissants charmes,
    Et prêt à répandre des larmes,
    Il commençait à s'avancer
      Pour l'embrasser,
    Quand tout à coup l'impérieuse gloire
    D'être ferme en son sentiment
    Sur son amour remporta la victoire,
Et le fit en ces mots répondre durement:

«De tout le temps passé j'ai perdu la mémoire,
    Je suis content de votre repentir,
    Allez, il est temps de partir.»

Elle part aussitôt, et regardant son père
Qu'on avait revêtu de son rustique habit,

"You are my husband, my lord, and my master,"
she said with a sigh, on the point of fainting,
"and as horrible as what I have just heard is,
    I will be able to show you
that nothing is as dear to me as obedience to you."

She immediately withdrew to her room,
and, there, taking off her rich garments,
   peacefully and wordlessly,
     while her heart was greatly troubled,
she put back on those she had worn while tending her sheep.

    In that humble and simple guise
she approached the prince and spoke to him as follows:

   "I cannot leave your side
   without receiving your pardon for having displeased you;
   I am able to bear the burden of my poverty,
but, my lord, I cannot bear your anger;
grant this favor to my sincere regret,
and I shall live happily in my sad dwelling,
    nor shall time ever impair
either my humble respect or my faithful love."

So much submissiveness and such greatness of soul
    beneath such lowly garb,
which at that very moment reawakened in the prince's heart
every pang of his earlier love,
were on the verge of revoking his decree of banishment.
    Touched by such potent charms,
    and on the point of shedding tears,
    he was beginning to step forward
       in order to kiss her,
   when suddenly the imperious glory
    of remaining steadfast in his feelings
   won the victory over his love,
and caused him to reply harshly in these words:

"I've lost the memory of all past time;
   I'm pleased by your repentance;
    go, it is time to leave."

She left at once; seeing her father,
who had been dressed again in his rural clothes,

Et qui, le cœur percé d'une douleur amère,
Pleurait un changement si prompt et si subit:
«Retournons, lui dit-elle, en nos sombres bocages,
Retournons habiter nos demeures sauvages,
Et quittons sans regret la pompe des palais;
Nos cabanes n'ont pas tant de magnificence,
    Mais on y trouve avec plus d'innocence,
Un plus ferme repos, une plus douce paix.»

    Dans son désert à grand peine arrivée,
    Elle reprend et quenouille et fuseaux,
    Et va filer au bord des mêmes eaux
        Où le prince l'avait trouvée.
        Là son cœur tranquille et sans fiel
        Cent fois le jour demande au Ciel
Qu'il comble son époux de gloire, de richesses,
Et qu'à tous ses désirs il ne refuse rien;
        Un amour nourri de caresses
        N'est pas plus ardent que le sien.

    Ce cher époux qu'elle regrette
    Voulant encore l'éprouver,
    Lui fait dire dans sa retraite
    Qu'elle ait à le venir trouver.

«Grisélidis, dit-il, dès qu'elle se présente,
Il faut que la princesse à que je dois demain
    Dans le temple donner la main,
    De vous et de moi soit contente.
Je vous demande ici tous vos soins, et je veux
Que vous m'aidiez à plaire à l'objet de mes vœux;
Vous savez de quel air il faut que l'on me serve,
    Point d'épargne, point de réserve;
Que tout sente le prince, et le prince amoureux.

    Employez toute votre adresse
    A parer son appartement,
    Que l'abondance, la richesse,
    La propreté, la politesse
    S'y fasse voir également;
    Enfin songez incessamment
    Que c'est une jeune princesse
        Que j'aime tendrement.

and who was weeping, his heart pierced with bitter grief,
over such a quick and sudden change of fortune,
"Let us return," she said, "to our shady groves,
let us return to live in our wild dwelling place,
and let us leave behind without regret the pomp of palaces;
our cottages are not so magnificent,
    but, in addition to greater innocence, we will find there
a more secure repose, a sweeter peace."

    Returning to her wilderness with great difficulty,
    she took up her distaff and spindles again
    and went to spin by the side of the same brook
        where the prince had discovered her.
        There her tranquil heart, devoid of ill feelings,
        asked Heaven a hundred times a day
to shower glory and wealth upon her husband
and not to refuse to grant any of his desires;
        a love nurtured on caresses
        could not be more ardent than hers was.

    That dear husband whom she missed,
    wishing to test her further,
    sent word to her in her retreat
    to come to see him.

"Griselidis," he said, the moment she appeared,
"the princess to whom I am to give my hand
    in church tomorrow
    must be satisfied with you and with me.
I now request of you all your care, and I want
you to help me please the woman of my desires;
you know in what way I need to be served,
    sparing no expense, holding nothing back;
let everything bespeak a prince, and a prince in love.

    Use all your skill
    to adorn her quarters;
    let abundance, wealth,
    cleanliness, and polish
    be seen there all combined;
    in short, keep in mind constantly
    that it is for a young princess
        whom I love dearly.

Pour vous faire entrer davantage
Dans les soins de votre devoir,
Je veux ici vous faire voir
Celle qu'à bien servir mon ordre vous engage.»

Telle qu'aux portes du Levant
Se montre la naissante Aurore,
Telle parut en arrivant
La princesse plus belle encore.
Grisélidis à son abord
Dans le fond de son cœur sentit un doux transport
De la tendresse maternelle;
Du temps passé, de ses jours bienheureux,
Le souvenir en son cœur se rappelle:
«Hélas! ma fille, en soi-même dit-elle,
Si le Ciel favorable eût écouté mes vœux,
Serait presque aussi grande, et peut-être aussi belle.»

Pour la jeune princesse en ce même moment
Elle prit un amour si vif, si véhément,
Qu'aussitôt qu'elle fut absente,
En cette sorte au prince elle parla,
Suivant, sans le savoir, l'instinct qui s'en mêla:

«Souffrez, seigneur, que je vous représente
Que cette princesse charmante,
Dont vous allez être l'époux,
Dans l'aise, dans l'éclat, dans la pourpre nourrie,
Ne pourra supporter, sans en perdre la vie,
Les mêmes traitements que j'ai reçus de vous.

Le besoin, ma naissance obscure,
M'avaient endurcie aux travaux,
Et je pouvais souffrir toutes sortes de maux
Sans peine et même sans murmure;
Mais elle qui jamais n'a connu la douleur,
Elle mourra dès la moindre rigueur,
Dès la moindre parole un peu sèche, un peu dure.
Hélas! seigneur, je vous conjure
De la traiter avec douceur.

—Songez, lui dit le prince avec un ton sévère,
A me servir selon votre pouvoir,

In order to make you more eager
to perform your duties with care,
I wish to show you here
the woman whom I am ordering you to serve faithfully."

Just as rising Dawn appears
when she appears at the gates of the East,
thus did the even lovelier princess
look when she arrived.
On meeting her, Griselidis
felt a sweet surge of motherly love
at the bottom of her heart;
the memory of the bygone time,
of her happy days, reawakened in her heart:
"Alas! My daughter," she said to herself,
"if kind Heaven had granted my wishes,
would be nearly this old, and perhaps just as beautiful."

At that very moment she conceived a love
for the young princess that was so keen and strong
that, as soon as the girl had left the room,
she spoke to the prince as follows,
unknowingly following the intuition that mingled with her feelings:

"My lord, permit me to remind you
that this charming princess,
whose husband you will be,
has been raised in comfort, in brilliance, in the purple,
and will not be able to bear, without dying of it,
the same treatment that I received from you.

Need and the lowliness of my birth
had inured me to labor,
and I was able to bear all sorts of woes
painlessly and even without grumbling at them;
but she, who has never known grief,
she will die at the least harshness,
at the least word that is somewhat cold or hard.
Alas, my lord, I implore you
to treat her gently."

"Keep your mind," the prince said to her severely,
"on serving me as best you can;

Il ne faut pas qu'une simple bergère
Fasse des leçons, et s'ingère
De m'avertir de mon devoir.»
Grisélidis, à ces mots, sans rien dire,
Baisse les yeux et se retire.

Cependant pour l'hymen les seigneurs invités,
Arrivèrent de tous côtés;
Dans une magnifique salle
Où le prince les assembla
Avant que d'allumer la torche nuptiale,
En cette sorte il leur parla:

«Rien au monde, après l'espérance,
N'est plus trompeur que l'apparence;
Ici l'on en peut voir un exemple éclatant.
Qui ne croirait que ma jeune maîtresse,
Que l'hymen va rendre princesse,
Ne soit heureuse et n'ait le cœur content?
Il n'en est rien pourtant.

Qui pourrait s'empêcher de croire
Que ce jeune guerrier amoureux de la gloire
N'aime à voir cet hymen, lui qui dans les tournois
Va sur tous ses rivaux remporter la victoire?
Cela n'est pas vrai toutefois.

Qui ne croirait encor qu'en sa juste colère,
Grisélidis ne pleure et ne se désespère?
Elle ne se plaint point, elle consent à tout,
Et rien n'a pu pousser sa patience à bout.

Qui ne croirait enfin que de ma destinée,
Rien ne peut égaler la course fortunée,
En voyant les appas de l'objet de mes vœux?
Cependant si l'hymen me liait de ses nœuds,
J'en concevrais une douleur profonde,
Et de tous les princes du monde
Je serais le plus malheureux.

L'énigme vous paraît difficile à comprendre;
Deux mots vont vous la faire entendre,
Et ces deux mots feront évanouir
Tous les malheurs que vous venez d'ouïr.

a simple shepherdess must not
    give me lessons, or presume
    to instruct me in my duties."
Hearing this, Griselidis, saying not a word,
    cast her eyes down and withdrew.

Meanwhile, the noblemen invited to the wedding
    arrived from every direction;
    in a magnificent hall,
    where the prince assembled them,
before the nuptial torch was lighted,
    he spoke to them as follows:

    "After hope, there is nothing in the world
        as deceptive as appearances;
here you may see a vivid example of this.
    Who would not believe that my young bride,
        whom marriage will make a princess,
        is happy and contented at heart?
            And yet, she is not at all.

    Who could keep from believing
that this young warrior, enamored with glory,
is pleased to view this wedding, he who in the tournaments
will win the victory over all his rivals?
        Nevertheless, such is not the case.

Furthermore, who would not believe that, in her righteous anger,
Griselidis is weeping and in despair?
She is *not* lamenting, she consents to everything,
and nothing has been able to overcome her patience.

Finally, who would not believe that nothing can equal
the fortunate course of my destiny,
upon viewing the charms of the woman I love?
And yet, if matrimony tied me with its bonds,
    I would become deeply unhappy,
        and of all the princes in the world
        I would be the most unfortunate.

This riddle seems hard to understand to you;
    two words will make you comprehend it,
    and those two words will cause to disappear
    all the misfortunes you have just heard recited.

Sachez, poursuivit-il, que l'aimable personne
   Que vous croyez m'avoir blessé le cœur,
      Est ma fille, et que je la donne
      Pour femme à ce jeune seigneur
      Qui l'aime d'un amour extrême,
      Et dont il est aimé de même.

   Sachez encor, que touché vivement
      De la patience et du zèle
      De l'épouse sage et fidèle
      Que j'ai chassée indignement,
   Je la reprends, afin que je répare,
Par tout ce que l'amour peut avoir de plus doux,
      Le traitement dur et barbare
      Qu'elle a reçu de mon esprit jaloux.

      Plus grande sera mon étude
      A prévenir tous ses désirs,
   Qu'elle ne fut dans mon inquiétude
      A l'accabler de déplaisirs;
Et si dans tous les temps doit vivre la mémoire
Des ennuis dont son cœur ne fut point abattu,
Je veux que plus encore on parle de la gloire
Dont j'aurai couronné sa supréme vertu.»

      Comme quand un épais nuage
        A le jour obscurci,
   Et que le ciel de toutes parts noirci,
      Menace d'un affreux orage;
Si de ce voile obscur par les vents écarté
      Un brillant rayon de clarté
      Se répand sur le paysage,
      Tout rit et reprend sa beauté;
Telle, dans tous les yeux où régnait la tristesse,
Éclate tout à coup une vive allégresse.

      Par ce prompt éclaircissement,
      La jeune princesse ravie
D'apprendre que du prince elle a reçu la vie
Se jette à ses genoux qu'elle embrasse ardemment.
Son père qu'attendrit une fille si chère,
La relève, la baise, et la mène à sa mère,
A qui trop de plaisir en un même moment

You must know," he continued, "that the lovable woman
  who you think has wounded my heart
    is my daughter, and that I am giving her
    to wife to this young lord,
    who loves her with a mighty love,
    and is loved by her in return.

  Know, as well, that, deeply moved
    by the patience and zeal
    of the wise and faithful wife
    whom I have unjustly cast off,
  I am taking her back, in order to make amends,
by all the sweetness that love contains,
    for the harsh and barbarous treatment
  she received from my jealous mind.

    My efforts to anticipate
    her every desire will be greater
  then those were, in my hours of melancholy,
    to overwhelm her with vexation;
and if the memory is to live through the ages
of the griefs that failed to vanquish her heart,
I want people to speak even more about the glory
with which I shall crown her supreme virtue."

    As when a dense cloud
      has darkened the day,
    and the sky, blackened everywhere,
      threatens us with a terrible storm;
if, out of this dark veil, which the wind lifts,
      a bright ray of sunshine
      spreads over the countryside,
      everything smiles, its beauty restored:
so, in all the eyes where sadness was reigning,
a keen joy suddenly burst forth.

    After this rapid explanation,
      the young princess, delighted
to learn that she had received her life from the prince,
fell at his feet and embraced his knees ardently.
Her father, his heart softened by so dear a daughter,
raised her up, kissed her, and led her to her mother,
who felt such an excess of joy in a single moment

Ôtait presque tout sentiment.
Son cœur, qui tant de fois en proie
Aux plus cuisants traits du malheur,
Supporta si bien la douleur,
Succombe au doux poids de la joie;
A peine de ses bras pouvait-elle serrer
    L'aimable enfant que le Ciel lui renvoie,
        Elle ne pouvait que pleurer.

«Assez dans d'autres temps vous pourrez satisfaire,
    Lui dit le prince, aux tendresses du sang;
Reprenez les habits qu'exige votre rang,
    Nous avons des noces à faire.»

Au temple on conduisit les deux jeunes amants,
        Où la mutuelle promesse
        De se chérir avec tendresse
Affermit pour jamais leurs doux engagements.
Ce ne sont que plaisirs, que tournois magnifiques,
        Que jeux, que danses, que musiques,
        Et que festins délicieux,
Où sur Grisélidis se tournent tous les yeux,
        Où sa patience éprouvée
        Jusques au Ciel est élévée
        Par mille éloges glorieux:
Des peuples réjouis la complaisance est telle
        Pour leur prince capriceux,
Qu'ils vont jusqu'à louer son épreuve cruelle,
        A qui d'une vertu si belle,
Si séante au beau sexe, et si rare en tous lieux,
        On doit un si parfait modèle.

A Monsieur°°° en lui envoyant Grisélidis

Si je m'etais rendu à tous les différents avis qui m'ont été donnés
sur l'ouvrage que je vous envoie, il n'y serait rien demeuré que le
conte tout sec et tout uni, et en ce cas j'aurais mieux fait de n'y pas
toucher et de le laisser dans son papier bleu où il est depuis tant d'années. Je le lus d'abord à deux de mes amis.

that she nearly lost consciousness.
Her heart, which had so often been prey
to the most painful darts of misfortune,
and had withstood sorrow so firmly,
succumbed to the gentle weight of joy;
she was barely able to clasp in her arms
   the lovable child that Heaven was restoring to her;
   all she could do was cry.

"On other occasions," the prince said to her,
  you will have enough time to satisfy your maternal feelings;
put on again the clothing that your rank demands,
   we have a wedding to celebrate."

The two young lovers were led to the church,
   where the mutual vow
   to cherish each other tenderly
put a final seal on their loving attachment.
There followed nothing but amusements, magnificent tournaments,
   games, dances, concerts,
   and delicious banquets,
at which all eyes were turned toward Griselidis,
   and at which her proven patience
   was lauded to the skies
   in a thousand glorious encomiums:
the overjoyed people were so indulgent
   toward their capricious prince
that they went so far as to praise his cruel trial,
   to which they owed such a perfect model
of a virtue so lovely, so becoming to the fair sex,
   and so unusual anywhere.

To Monsieur***,[8] with a Copy of "Griselidis"

If I had agreed with all the different opinions I have been given on the work I am sending you, nothing would have been left of it but the dry, uniform narrative, and in that case I would have done better not to have handled it and to have left it in its blue wrappers,[9] where it had remained for so many years. First I read it to two friends of mine.

[8]Not identified; probably an invention of Perrault's   [9]Referring to the customary wrappers of 17th-century chapbooks.

«Pourquoi, dit l'un, s'étendre si fort sur le caractère de votre héros? Qu'a-t-on à faire de savoir ce qu'il faisait le matin dans son conseil, et moins encore à quoi il se divertissait l'après-dînée? Tout cela est bon à retrancher.

—Ôtez-moi, je vous prie, dit l'autre, la réponse enjouée qu'il fait aux députés de son peuple qui le pressent de se marier; elle ne convient point à un prince grave et sérieux. Vous voulez bien encore, poursuivit-il, que je vous conseille de supprimer la longue description de votre chasse? Qu'importe tout cela au fond de votre histoire? Croyez-moi, ce sont de vains et ambitieux ornements, qui appauvrissent votre poème au lieu de l'enrichir. Il en est de même, ajouta-t-il, des préparatifs qu'on fait pour le mariage du prince, tout cela est oiseux et inutile. Pour vos dames qui rabaissent leurs coiffures, qui couvrent leurs gorges, et qui allongent leurs manches, froide plaisanterie aussi bien que celle de l'orateur qui s'applaudit de son éloquence.

—Je demande encore, reprit celui qui avait parlé le premier, que vous ôtiez les réflexions chrétiennes de Grisélidis, qui dit que c'est Dieu qui veut l'éprouver; c'est un sermon hors de sa place. Je ne saurais encore souffrir les inhumanités de votre prince, elles me mettent en colère, je les supprimerais. Il est vrai qu'elles sont de l'histoire, mais il n'importe. J'ôterais encore l'épisode du jeune seigneur qui n'est là que pour épouser la jeune princesse, cela allonge trop votre conte.

—Mais, lui dis-je, le conte finirait mal sans cela.

—Je ne saurais que vous dire, répondit-il, je ne laisserais pas que de l'ôter.»

A quelques jours de là, je fis la même lecture à deux autres de mes amis, qui ne me dirent pas un seul mot sur les endroits dont je viens de parler, mais qui en reprirent quantité d'autres.

«Bien loin de me plaindre de la rigueur de votre critique, leur dis-je, je me plains de ce qu'elle n'est pas assez sévère: vous m'avez passé une infinité d'endroits que l'on trouve très dignes de censure.

—Comme quoi? dirent-ils.

—On trouve, leur dis-je, que le caractère du prince est trop étendu, et qu'on n'a que faire de savoir ce qu'il faisait le matin et encore moins l'après-dînée.

—On se moque de vous, dirent-ils tous deux ensemble, quand on vous fait de semblables critiques.

—On blâme, poursuivis-je, la réponse que fait le prince à ceux qui

"Why," asked one of them, "expatiate so broadly on the character of your hero? Who needs to know what he used to do every morning in his council, much less how he entertained himself in the afternoon? All of that deserves to be cut."

"Please," said the other, "delete the playful reply he makes to the delegates from his people who urge him to marry; it isn't befitting a grave and serious prince." He continued: "Do you mind my also advising you to omit your long description of the hunt? What does all that have to do with your basic story? Trust me, those are vain and pretentious ornaments that impoverish your poem instead of enriching it. The same holds," he added, "for the preparations made for the prince's wedding; all of that is superfluous and unnecessary. As for your ladies lowering their headdresses, covering their bosoms, and lengthening their sleeves: a poor joke, just like the one about the orator congratulating himself on his eloquence."

"I also request," continued the one who had spoken first, "that you delete the Christian reflections made by Griselidis when she says that it's God who wishes to test her; that's a sermon which is out of place. Nor can I abide your prince's inhuman actions; they put me in a rage, and I'd do away with them. It's true that they're part of the story, but that doesn't matter. I'd also delete the episode with the young nobleman, who exists only to marry the young princess; it makes your story too long."

"But," I countered, "the story would end badly without it."

"I don't know what to say about that," he replied, "but, all the same, I'd delete it."

A few days later, I read the same text to two other friends of mine, who said not a single word about the passages I have just mentioned, but criticized a number of others.

"Far from complaining of the severity of your criticism," I told them, "I complain that it isn't harsh enough: you let me get away with any number of passages that have been found eminently worthy of censure."

"Such as?" they asked.

"People have found," I replied, "that I spent too much time on the prince's character, and that nobody needs to know what he did every morning, much less in the afternoon."

"They're pulling your leg," they said simultaneously, "when they make criticisms like that."

I continued: "They find fault with the prince's reply to those who

le pressent de se marier, comme trop enjouée et indigne d'un prince grave et sérieux.

—Bon, reprit l'un d'eux; et où est l'inconvénient qu'un jeune prince d'Italie, pays où l'on est accoutumé à voir les hommes les plus graves et les plus élevés en dignité dire des plaisanteries, et qui d'ailleurs fait profession de mal parler et des femmes et du mariage, matières si sujettes à la raillerie, se soit un peu réjoui sur cet article? Quoi qu'il en soit, je vous demande grâce pour cet endroit comme pour celui de l'orateur qui croyait avoir converti le prince, et pour le rabaissement des coiffures; car ceux qui n'ont pas aimé la réponse enjouée du prince, ont bien la mine d'avoir fait main basse sur ces deux endroits-là.

—Vous l'avez deviné, lui dis-je. Mais d'un autre côté, ceux qui n'aiment que les choses plaisantes n'ont pu souffrir les réflexions chrétiennes de la princesse, qui dit que c'est Dieu qui la veut éprouver. Ils prétendent que c'est un sermon hors de propos.

—Hors de propos? reprit l'autre; non seulement ces réflexions conviennent au sujet, mais elles y sont absolument nécessaires. Vous aviez besoin de rendre croyable la patience de votre héroïne; et quel autre moyen aviez-vous que de lui faire regarder les mauvais traitements de son époux comme venant de la main de Dieu? Sans cela, on la prendrait pour la plus stupide de toutes les femmes, ce qui ne ferait pas assurément un bon effet.

—On blâme encore, leur dis-je, l'épisode du jeune seigneur qui épouse la jeune princesse.

—On a tort, reprit-il; comme votre ouvrage est un véritable poème, quoique vous lui donniez le titre de nouvelle, il faut qu'il n'y ait rien à désirer quand il finit. Cependant si la jeune princesse s'en retournait dans son convent sans être mariée après s'y être attendue, elle ne serait point contente ni ceux qui liraient la nouvelle.»

Ensuite de cette conférence, j'ai pris le parti de laisser mon ouvrage tel à peu près qu'il a été lu dans l'Académie. En un mot, j'ai eu soin de corriger les choses qu'on m'a fait voir être mauvaises en elles-mêmes; mais à l'égard de celles que j'ai trouvées n'avoir point d'autre défaut que de n'être pas au goût de quelques personnes peut-être un peu trop délicates, j'ai cru n'y devoir pas toucher.

Est-ce une raison décisive
D'ôter un bon mets d'un repas,
Parce qu'il s'y trouve un convive
Qui par malheur ne l'aime pas?

are urging him to marry, calling it too playful and unworthy of a grave and serious prince."

"Well, well!" one of them countered. "Please tell me what's wrong with having a young prince from Italy—a country where people are used to see the most serious and highly placed men tell jokes—and, moreover, a prince who habitually speaks ill of both women and marriage (topics so often the subject of mockery) speak somewhat laughingly on that subject? However that may be, I implore you to spare that passage and the one about the orator who thought he had converted the prince, and the one about lowering the headgear; because the people who didn't like the prince's playful reply are just the sort who would pounce on those two passages as well."

"You guessed it," I said. "But on the other hand, those who like only witty things couldn't stand the Christian reflections of the princess when she says that it's God who wishes to test her. They claim it's a sermon that doesn't belong there."

"Doesn't belong there?" my other friend said. "Not only do those reflections befit the subject, they're absolutely necessary to it. You needed to make your heroine's patience believable, and what other means were at your disposal than to have her view her husband's ill treatment of her as coming from the hand of God? Otherwise readers would take her for the stupidest of all women, which certainly wouldn't have a good effect."

I said: "They also find fault with the episode about the young nobleman who marries the young princess."

"Well, they're wrong," he replied; "since your piece is a true narrative poem, though you've called it a *novella,* it's important to have no loose ends when it concludes. So, if the young princess returned to her convent unmarried after expecting to be, she wouldn't be satisfied, and neither would the readers of the story."

After that discussion I decided to leave my work more or less as it was when it was read in the Académie. In a word, I carefully corrected the things that people convinced me were intrinsically bad; but with regard to the things I found to have no other fault than not being to the taste of a few people who may be a bit too fastidious, I thought it best to leave them alone.

Is it a cogent reason
to omit a good dish from a meal
if a single guest present
unfortunately doesn't like it?

Il faut que tout le monde vive,
Et que les mets, pour plaire à tous,
Soient différents comme les goûts.

Quoi qu'il en soit, j'ai cru devoir m'en remettre au public qui juge toujours bien. J'apprendrai de lui ce que j'en dois croire, et je suivrai exactement tous ses avis, s'il m'arrive jamais de faire une seconde édition de cet ouvrage.

Everyone must be allowed to live,
and dishes, if everyone is to be pleased,
must be as varied as tastes.

However that may be, I felt it my duty to appeal to the public, always the best judge. I will learn from my readers what opinion I ought to have of my poem, and I shall follow all their comments religiously if I ever need to prepare a second edition of this work.

Peau d'Ane

A Madame la marquise de L***

Il est des gens de qui l'esprit guindé,
Sous un front jamais déridé,
Ne souffre, n'approuve et n'estime
Que le pompeux et le sublime;
Pour moi, j'ose poser en fait
Qu'en de certains moments l'esprit le plus parfait
Peut aimer sans rougir jusqu'aux marionnettes;
Et qu'il est des temps et des lieux
Où le grave et le sérieux
Ne valent pas d'agréables sornettes.
Pourquoi faut-il s'émerveiller
Que la raison la mieux sensée,
Lasse souvent de trop veiller,
Par des contes d'ogre* et de fée
Ingénieusement bercée,
Prenne plaisir à sommeiller?

Sans craindre donc qu'on me condamne
De mal employer mon loisir,
Je vais, pour contenter votre juste désir,
Vous conter tout au long l'histoire de Peau d'Ane.

Peau d'Ane

Il était une fois un roi,
Le plus grand qui fût sur la terre,

---

*Homme sauvage qui mangeait les petits enfants.

Donkey-Skin

To the Marquise de L***[10]

There are people whose prim minds,
 beneath brows never unwrinkled,
 cannot abide, approve, or esteem
 anything but the pompous and the sublime;
 as for me, I dare to assert
that, at certain moments, the most perfect mind
can enjoy even marionettes without blushing;
 and that there are times and places
 in which gravity and seriousness
are worth less than pleasant trifles.
 Why should anyone be surprised
 if the most sensible rational mind,
 often wearied with excessive watchfulness,
 is skillfully rocked to sleep
 by tales of ogre* and fairy,
 and takes pleasure in drowsing?

Thus, without fear of being censured
for making bad use of my leisure hours,
in order to satisfy your legitimate wishes I shall
tell you the complete story of Donkey-Skin.

Donkey-Skin

There was once a king,
the greatest on earth,

---

[10]Lambert; she conducted a literary salon at her home.   *"A wild man who ate little children." [Footnote in the original text.]

Aimable en paix, terrible en guerre,
Seul enfin comparable à soi:
Ses voisins le craignaient, ses États étaient calmes,
Et l'on voyait de toutes parts
Fleurir, à l'ombre de ses palmes,
Et les vertus et les beaux-arts.
Son aimable moitié, sa compagne fidèle,
Était si charmante et si belle,
Avait l'esprit si commode et si doux
Qu'il était encor avec elle
Moins heureux roi qu'heureux époux.
De leur tendre et chaste hyménée
Plein de douceur et d'agrément,
Avec tant de vertus une fille était née
Qu'ils se consolaient aisément
De n'avoir pas de plus ample lignée.

Dans son vaste et riche palais
Ce n'était que magnificence;
Partout y fourmillait une vive abondance
De courtisans et de valets;
Il avait dans son écurie
Grands et petits chevaux de toutes les façons;
Couverts de beaux caparaçons,
Roides d'or et de broderie;
Mais ce qui surprenait tout le monde en entrant,
C'est qu'au lieu le plus apparent,
Un maître âne étalait ses deux grandes oreilles.
Cette injustice vous surprend,
Mais lorsque vous saurez ses vertus nonpareilles,
Vous ne trouverez pas que l'honneur fût trop grand.
Tel et si net le forma la nature
Qu'il ne faisait jamais d'ordure
Mais bien beaux écus au soleil
Et louis de toute manière,
Qu'on allait recueillir sur la blonde litière
Tous les matins à son réveil.

Or le Ciel qui parfois se lasse
De rendre les hommes contents,

lovable in peace, fear-inspiring in war,
in short, one who could only be compared to himself:
his neighbors feared him, his Estates[11] were calm,
      and on all sides one could see
      both the virtues and the fine arts
      flourishing in the shade of his victory-palms.
His lovable wife, a faithful helpmate,
      was so charming and beautiful,
   and had such an obliging, sweet nature,
      that, at her side, he was even
      more fortunate as a husband than as a king.
      From their loving and chaste marriage,
      full of sweetness and pleasure,
a daughter had been born, so virtuous
      that they readily consoled themselves
   for not having further children.

      In his huge, sumptuous palace
      everything was magnificent;
everywhere a brisk multitude
      of courtiers and servants swarmed;
      in his stable he had
horses large and small of every breed,
      covered with beautiful caparisons
      that were stiff with gold and embroidery;
but what surprised everyone who entered
      was that in the most prominent place
stood an egregious donkey with its two big ears.
      That injustice may surprise you,
but when you hear about its matchless powers,
you won't find the honor excessive.
   Nature had created it so cleanly
      that it never deposited feces
      but, instead, beautiful three-franc pieces with the sign of the sun
      and twenty-franc pieces of all sorts,
which the grooms collected on its yellow litter
      every morning when it awoke.

      Now, Heaven, which is sometimes tired
      of making people happy

---

[11]That is: the clergy, the nobility, and the merchant class (commons).

Qui toujours à ses biens mêle quelque disgrâce,
    Ainsi que la pluie au beau temps,
    Permit qu'une âpre maladie
Tout à coup de la reine attaquât les beaux jours.
    Partout on cherche du secours;
Mais ni la Faculté qui le grec étudie,
    Ni les charlatans ayant cours,
Ne purent tous ensemble arrêter l'incendie
Que la fièvre allumait en s'augmentant toujours.

    Arrivée à sa dernière heure
    Elle dit au roi son époux:
    «Trouvez bon qu'avant que je meure
    J'exige une chose de vous;
    C'est que s'il vous prenait envie
De vous remarier quand je n'y serai plus . . .
    —Ah! dit le roi, ces soins sont superflus,
    Je n'y songerai de ma vie,
    Soyez en repos là-dessus.
    —Je le crois bien, reprit la reine,
Si j'en prends à témoin votre amour véhément;
    Mais pour m'en rendre plus certaine,
    Je veux avoir votre serment,
Adouci toutefois par ce tempérament
Que si vous rencontrez une femme plus belle,
    Mieux faite et plus sage que moi,
Vous pourrez franchement lui donner votre foi
    Et vous marier avec elle.»
    Sa confiance en ses attraits
Lui faisait regarder une telle promesse
  Comme un serment, surpris avec adresse,
    De ne se marier jamais.
Le prince jura donc, les yeux baignés de larmes,
    Tout ce que la reine voulut;
    La reine entre ses bras mourut,
Et jamais un mari ne fit tant de vacarmes.
A l'ouïr sangloter et les nuits et les jours,
On jugea que son deuil ne lui durerait guère,
    Et qu'il pleurait ses défuntes amours
Comme un homme pressé qui veut sortir d'affaire.

On ne se trompa point. Au bout de quelques mois

and always mingles some misfortune with its blessings,
    just as rain alternates with fair weather,
    allowed a severe illness
to attack the queen's happy days all of a sudden.
    Aid was sought everywhere,
but neither the Faculty that studies Greek,
    nor the charlatans currently in vogue,
were able, all combined, to put out the fire
that her fever kindled, growing steadily greater.

    When her last hour had come,
    she said to her husband the king:
    "Please permit me, before I die,
    to ask one favor of you:
    if you should feel the desire
to marry again after I am gone . . ."
    "Oh," said the king, "that is a needless worry;
    I would never think of it as long as I lived,
    rest easy on that account."
    "I believe you," the queen replied,
"judging by your strong love for me;
    but to reassure myself even more,
    I wish to have your oath on it,
nevertheless softened by the following palliative:
if you meet a woman more beautiful,
    more shapely, and of better conduct than myself,
you may readily plight your faith to her
    and marry her."
    Her confidence in her own attractions
caused her to view such a promise
    as an oath, adroitly extorted,
        never to remarry.
Thus the monarch swore, his eyes wet with tears,
    to do just as the queen desired;
        the queen died in his arms,
and never did a husband make such a commotion.
Hearing him sob night and day,
people thought that his mourning would not last long,
    and that he was lamenting his lost love
like a busy man who wants to get the business over with.

They were not mistaken. After a few months

Il voulut procéder à faire un nouveau choix;
  Mais ce n'était pas chose aisée,
  Il fallait garder son serment
  Et que la nouvelle épousée
  Eût plus d'attraits et d'agrément
Que celle qu'on venait de mettre au monument.

  Ni la cour en beautés fertile,
  Ni la campagne, ni la ville,
  Ni les royaumes d'alentour
  Dont on alla faire le tour,
  N'en purent fournir une telle;
  L'infante seule était plus belle
  Et possédait certains tendres appas
  Que la défunte n'avait pas.
  Le roi le remarqua lui-même
  Et brûlant d'un amour extrême,
  Alla follement s'aviser
Que par cette raison il devait l'épouser.
  Il trouva même un casuiste
Qui jugea que le cas se pouvait proposer.
  Mais la jeune princesse triste
  D'ouïr parler d'un tel amour,
  Se lamentait et pleurait nuit et jour.

  De mille chagrins l'âme pleine,
  Elle alla trouver sa marraine,
  Loin, dans une grotte à l'écart
De nacre et de corail richement étoffée.
  C'était une admirable fée
  Qui n'eut jamais de pareille en son art.
  Il n'est pas besoin qu'on vous die
Ce qu'était une fée en ces bienheureux temps;
  Car je suis sûr que votre mie
Vous l'aura dit dès vos plus jeunes ans.

  «Je sais, dit-elle, en voyant la princesse,
  Ce qui vous fait venir ici,
Je sais de votre cœur la profonde tristesse;
  Mais avec moi n'ayez plus de souci.
  Il n'est rien qui vous puisse nuire
Pourvu qu'à mes conseils vous vous laissiez conduire.

he decided to go ahead and choose a new bride;
    but it was not an easy matter:
    he felt bound by his oath,
    and his new wife
    had to be more attractive and charming
than the one who had just been consigned to her tomb.

    Neither the royal court, rich in beauties,
    nor the countryside, nor the town,
    nor the kingdoms round about,
    which were all inspected,
    were able to provide such a woman;
    only the crown princess was more beautiful
and possessed certain amorous attractions
    that her late mother lacked.
    The king himself became aware of this
    and, on fire with a powerful love,
    came to the mad conclusion
that, for that very reason, he ought to marry her.
    He even found a casuist
who deemed that the case could be logically argued.
    But the young princess, saddened
    to hear talk of such a love,
    lamented and wept night and day.

    Her soul filled with a thousand griefs,
    she went to visit her godmother,
    far away, in a remote grotto
richly adorned with mother-of-pearl and coral.
    She was a wonderful fairy
    who was never equaled in her skill.
    I have no need to tell you
what a fairy was in those fortunate days,
    because I am sure that your governess
    told you when you were still very young.

    On seeing the princess, she said, "I know
    what brings you here,
I know the profound sadness of your heart;
    but, with me on your side, have no more cares.
    Nothing can harm you
as long as you let yourself be guided by my advice.

Votre père, il est vrai, voudrait vous épouser;
    Écouter sa folle demande
    Serait une faute bien grande,
Mais sans le contredire on le peut refuser.

    Dites-lui qu'il faut qu'il vous donne
    Pour rendre vos désirs contents,
Avant qu'à son amour votre cœur s'abandonne,
Une robe qui soit de la couleur du temps.
Malgré tout son pouvoir et toute sa richesse,
Quoique le Ciel en tout favorise ses vœux,
Il ne pourra jamais accomplir sa promesse.»

    Aussitôt la jeune princesse
L'alla dire en tremblant à son père amoureux
    Qui dans le moment fit entendre
    Aux tailleurs les plus importants
Que s'ils ne lui faisaient, sans trop le faire attendre,
Une robe qui fût de la couleur du temps,
Ils pouvaient s'assurer qu'il les ferait tous pendre.

    Le second jour ne luisait pas encor
    Qu'on apporta la robe désirée;
    Le plus beau bleu de l'empyrée
N'est pas, lorsqu'il est ceint de gros nuages d'or,
    D'une couleur plus azurée.
De joie et de douleur l'infante pénétrée
    Ne sait que dire ni comment
    Se dérober à son engagement.
    «Princesse, demandez-en une,
    Lui dit sa marraine tout bas,
    Qui plus brillante et moins commune,
    Soit de la couleur de la lune.
    Il ne vous la donnera pas.»
A peine la princesse en eut fait la demande
    Que le roi dit à son brodeur:
«Que l'astre de la nuit n'ait pas plus de splendeur
Et que dans quatre jours sans faute on me la rende.»

Le riche habillement fut fait au jour marqué,
    Tel que le roi s'en était expliqué.
Dans les cieux où la nuit a déployé ses voiles,
La lune est moins pompeuse en sa robe d'argent

It is true, your father would like to marry you;
to heed his mad request
would be a very big mistake,
but you can dissuade him without refusing him outright.

Tell him that he must give you,
to gratify your wishes
before you abandon your heart to his love,
a gown that is the color of the sky.
Despite all his power and all his wealth,
even though Heaven grants all his wishes,
he will never be able to keep his promise."

Immediately the young princess
went tremblingly to make this request of her enamored father,
who made known at once
to the most prominent tailors
that if they did not make for him, without letting him wait too long,
a gown that was the color of the sky,
they could be assured he would hang them all.

The following day no sooner dawned
than the requested gown was delivered;
the most beautiful blue of the empyrean,
when ringed by great golden clouds, is not
of a more azure color.
The princess, stricken with joy and sorrow,
did not know what to say nor how
to get out of her promise.
"Princess, ask for one,"
her godmother said to her quietly,
"that is more brilliant and less common:
one that is the color of the moon.
He will be unable to give it to you."
Scarcely had the princess requested it
when the king said to his embroiderer:
"The luminary of the night must not shine more brightly,
and it must be delivered to me in four days without fail."

The sumptuous garment was ready on the day specified,
and was exactly as the king had described.
In the skies over which night has spread her veils,
the moon is less splendid in her silver gown,

Lors même qu'au milieu de son cours diligent
Sa plus vive clarté fait pâlir les étoiles.

La princesse admirant ce merveilleux habit,
Était à consentir presque délibérée;
     Mais par sa marraine inspirée,
     Au prince amoureux elle dit:
     «Je ne saurais être contente
Que je n'aie une robe encore plus brillante
     Et de la couleur du soleil.»
Le prince qui l'aimait d'un amour sans pareil,
Fit venir aussitôt un riche lapidaire
     Et lui commanda de la faire
D'un superbe tissu d'or et de diamants,
Disant que s'il manquait à le bien satisfaire,
Il le ferait mourir au milieu des tourments.

Le prince fut exempt de s'en donner la peine,
     Car l'ouvrier industrieux,
     Avant la fin de la semaine,
    Fit apporter l'ouvrage précieux,
     Si beau, si vif, si radieux,
     Que le blond amant de Clymène,
     Lorsque sur la voûte des cieux
     Dans son char d'or il se promène,
D'un plus brillant éclat n'éblouit pas les yeux.

L'infante que ces dons achèvent de confondre,
A son père, à son roi ne sait plus que répondre.
Sa marraine aussitôt la prenant par la main:
    «Il ne faut pas, lui dit-elle à l'oreille,
     Demeurer en si beau chemin;
     Est-ce une si grande merveille
    Que tous ces dons que vous en recevez,
    Tant qu'il aura l'âne que vous savez,
    Qui d'écus d'or sans cesse emplit sa bourse?
Demandez-lui la peau de ce rare animal.
     Comme il est toute sa ressource,
Vous ne l'obtiendrez pas, ou je raisonne mal.»

     Cette fée était bien savante,

even when, in the midst of her assiduous court,
her brightest glow makes the stars look pale.

The princess, marveling at that wonderful garment,
was almost of a mind to consent,
        but, on her godmother's advice,
        she said to the lovesick monarch:
        "I will not be satisfied
until I have a gown more brilliant still,
        one the color of the sun."
The monarch, who loved her with a matchless love,
immediately sent for a wealthy jeweler
        and ordered him to make it
from a superb fabric of gold and diamonds,
saying that if he did not satisfy him perfectly,
he would put him to death after torturing him.

The monarch need not have worried,
        for the diligent artisan,
        before the end of the week,
    delivered the priceless piece of work,
        so beautiful, so bright, so radiant,
        that the blonde lover of Clymene,[12]
        when he drives his golden chariot
        over the vault of the skies,
does not dazzle men's eyes with a brighter glow.

The princess, finally disconcerted by these gifts,
had no more reply to make to her father and her king.
Immediately her godmother took her by the hand
    and whispered in her ear, "You must not
        falter on such a noble path;
        are all these gifts you receive from him
    such a big surprise,
        seeing that he possesses the donkey you know of,
    which constantly fills his purse with golden three-franc pieces?
Ask him for the skin of that rare animal.
        Since it is his sole resource,
you will not obtain it, if my reasoning is correct.

        That fairy was very intelligent,

---

[12]The sun god, Apollo. Clymene bore him his son Phaethon.

Et cependant elle ignorait encor
Que l'amour violent pourvu qu'on le contente,
    Compte pour rien l'argent et l'or;
La peau fut galamment aussitôt accordée
    Que l'infante l'eut demandée.

    Cette peau quand on l'apporta
    Terriblement l'épouvanta
Et la fit de son sort amèrement se plaindre.
Sa marraine survint et lui représenta
Que quand on fait le bien on ne doit jamais craindre;
    Qu'il faut laisser penser au roi
    Qu'elle est tout à fait disposée
A subir avec lui la conjugale loi,
Mais qu'au même moment, seule et bien déguisée,
Il faut qu'elle s'en aille en quelque État lointain
Pour éviter un mal si proche et si certain.

«Voici, poursuivit-elle, une grande cassette
    Où nous mettrons tous vos habits,
    Votre miroir, votre toilette,
    Vos diamants et vos rubis.
    Je vous donne encor ma baguette;
    En la tenant en votre main,
La cassette suivra votre même chemin
    Toujours sous la terre cachée;
    Et lorsque vous voudrez l'ouvrir,
A peine mon bâton la terre aura touchée
Qu'aussitôt à vos yeux elle viendra s'offrir.

    Pour vous rendre méconnaissable,
La dépouille de l'âne est un masque admirable.
    Cachez-vous bien dans cette peau,
On ne croira jamais, tant elle est effroyable,
    Qu'elle renferme rien de beau.»

    La princesse ainsi travestie
De chez la sage fée à peine fut sortie,
    Pendant la fraîcheur du matin,
    Que le prince qui pour la fête
    De son heureux hymen s'apprête,
Apprend tout effrayé son funeste destin.
Il n'est point de maison, de chemin, d'avenue,

and yet she was still unaware
that a violent love, if it sees it may be gratified,
    counts money and gold as nothing;
gallantly, the skin was granted as soon
    as the princess had requested it.

    When it was brought to her, that skin
    gave her a terrible fright
and made her lament her fate bitterly.
Her godmother arrived and explained to her
that a person who does the right thing need never be afraid;
    she told her she must allow the king to think
    she was completely agreeable
to enter matrimony with him;
but, at the same time, alone and well disguised,
she must depart for some distant country
to avoid an evil so imminent and so certain.

"Here," she continued, "is a large casket,
    in which we shall put all your gowns,
    your mirror, your makeup cloth,
    your diamonds, and your rubies.
    In addition, I am giving you my wand;
    when you hold it in your hand,
the casket will follow your exact path,
    though it is always concealed underground;
    and whenever you want to open it,
scarcely will my wand have touched the ground
when it will immediately appear before you.

    In order to make yourself unrecognizable,
the donkey's skin is an admirable disguise.
    Conceal yourself thoroughly in this skin;
it is so frightful that no one will ever think
    it contains anything beautiful."

    Disguised in that manner, the princess
had scarcely left the wise fairy's home,
    while the morning was still cool,
    when the monarch, making ready
    to celebrate his happy wedding,
learned in great alarm of his gloomy fate.
There was no house, road, or avenue

Qu'on ne parcoure promptement;
    Mais on s'agite vainement,
On ne peut deviner ce qu'elle est devenue.

Partout se répandit un triste et noir chagrin;
    Plus de noces, plus de festin,
    Plus de tarte, plus de dragées;
Les dames de la cour, toutes découragées,
    N'en dînèrent point la plupart;
Mais du curé surtout la tristesse fut grande,
    Car il en déjeuna fort tard,
    Et qui pis est n'eut point d'offrande.

L'infante cependant poursuivait son chemin,
Le visage couvert d'une vilaine crasse;
    A tous passants elle tendait la main,
Et tâchait pour servir de trouver une place.
Mais les moins délicats et les plus malheureux
La voyant si maussade et si pleine d'ordure,
Ne voulaient écouter ni retirer chez eux
    Une si sale créature.

Elle alla donc bien loin, bien loin, encor plus loin;
Enfin elle arriva dans une métairie
    Où la fermière avait besoin
    D'une souillon, dont l'industrie
Allât jusqu'à savoir bien laver des torchons
    Et nettoyer l'auge aux cochons.

On la mit dans un coin au fond de la cuisine
    Où les valets, insolente vermine,
    Ne faisaient que la tirailler,
    La contredire et la railler;
    Ils ne savaient quelle pièce lui faire,
    La harcelant à tout propos;
    Elle était la butte ordinaire
De tous leurs quolibets et de tous leurs bons mots.

Elle avait le dimanche un peu plus de repos;
Car, ayant du matin fait sa petite affaire,
Elle entrait dans sa chambre et tenant son huis clos,
Elle se décrassait, puis ouvrait sa cassette,
    Mettait proprement sa toilette,

that was not promptly investigated,
   but their bustling was in vain;
they had no idea what had become of her.

A sad, dark sorrow spread everywhere;
   no more wedding, no more banquet,
   no more cake, no more sugar plums;
the ladies of the court, completely disheartened,
   had no midday meal, for the most part;
but the priest's sadness was especially great,
   because this made him take breakfast very late,
   and, even worse, he received no offering.

Meanwhile, the princess was following her path,
her face hidden under ugly grime;
   she held out her hand to every passerby,
and tried to find a position as a servant.
But even the least fastidious and most wretched people,
seeing her so dirty and full of filth,
refused to hear her out or to take into their house
        such a foul creature.

And so she traveled very far, very far, and even farther;
finally she arrived at a tenant farm
      where the farmer's wife needed
      a scullion with just enough skill
to wash out the dishcloths thoroughly
      and clean the pigs' trough.

She was placed in a corner at the back of the kitchen,
   where the farmhands, those insolent vermin,
      did nothing but pester her,
      contradict her, and make fun of her;
   they did not know what prank to play on her next,
      bothering her at every moment;
      she was the regular butt
of all their jibes and all their jokes.

On Sundays she had a little more rest,
because, having finished her chores in the morning,
she would go into her room, shut the door,
and wash off the grime; then, opening her casket,
      she would lay out her cosmetics cloth neatly

Rangeait dessus ses petits pots.
Devant son grand miroir, contente et satisfaite,
De la lune tantôt la robe elle mettait,
Tantôt celle où le feu du soleil éclatait,
  Tantôt la belle robe bleue
Que tout l'azur des cieux ne saurait égaler,
Avec ce chagrin seul que leur traînante queue
Sur le plancher trop court ne pouvait s'étaler.
Elle aimait à se voir jeune, vermeille et blanche
Et plus brave cent fois que nulle autre n'était;
  Ce doux plaisir la sustentait
  Et la menait jusqu'à l'autre dimanche.

  J'oubliais à dire en passant
  Qu'en cette grande métairie
  D'un roi magnifique et puissant
  Se faisait la ménagerie,
  Que là, poules de Barbarie,
  Râles, pintades, cormorans,
  Oisons musqués, canes petières,
Et mille autres oiseaux de bizarres manières,
  Entre eux presque tous différents,
Remplissaient à l'envi dix cours toutes entières.

  Le fils du roi dans ce charmant séjour
  Venait souvent au retour de la chasse
    Se reposer, boire à la glace
    Avec les seigneurs de sa cour.
    Tel ne fut point le beau Céphale:
Son air était royal, sa mine martiale,
Propre à faire trembler les plus fiers bataillons.
Peau d'Ane de fort loin le vit avec tendresse,
  Et reconnut par cette hardiesse
  Que sous sa crasse et ses haillons
Elle gardait encor le cœur d'une princesse.

 «Qu'il a l'air grand, quoiqu'il l'ait négligé,
  Qu'il est aimable, disait-elle,
  Et que bienheureuse est la belle
  A qui son cœur est engagé!
D'une robe de rien s'il m'avait honorée,

and arrange the containers on it.
In front of her big mirror, happy and contented,
she would put on her gowns: now the moon gown,
now the one in which the sun's fire shone,
    now the beautiful blue gown
which all the azure in the skies could not equal,
her only regret being that their long trains
could not be unfurled to their full length on that bit of floor.
She enjoyed seeing herself young, pink-and-white,
and a hundred times better dressed than any other woman;
    that sweet pleasure kept up her spirits
    and got her through until the next Sunday.

I almost forgot to mention by the way
    that in that large farm
    a magnificent and powerful king's
    collection of rare birds was kept;
    there, Barbary fowl,
    rails, guinea hens, cormorants,
    musk-fattened goslings, bustards,
and a thousand other birds of odd appearance,
    nearly all different from one another,
vied in filling ten entire farmyards.

The son of the king frequently visited
    that charming spot when returning from the hunt,
    to rest and to drink ices
    with the gentlemen of his court.
    Handsome Cephalus[13] was no match for him:
his appearance was regal, his bearing martial,
one that would make the fiercest battalions tremble.
Donkey-Skin watched him lovingly from afar,
    and that boldness of hers made her realize
    that beneath the grime and rags
she still had the heart of a princess.

"How grand he appears, even in casual clothing!
    How charming he is," she would say,
    "and how fortunate the beauty is
    to whom his heart is promised!
If he had honored me with the gift of some worthless dress,

---

[13]In Greek mythology, a young hunter with whom the goddess of dawn fell in love.

Je m'en trouverais plus parée
Que de toutes celles que j'ai.»

Un jour le jeune prince errant à l'aventure
De basse-cour en basse-cour,
Passa dans une allée obscure
Où de Peau d'Anne était l'humble séjour.
Par hasard il mit l'œil au trou de la serrure.
Comme il était fête ce jour,
Elle avait pris une riche parure
Et ses superbes vêtements
Qui, tissus de fin or et de gros diamants,
Égalaient du soleil la clarté la plus pure.
Le prince au gré de son désir
La contemple et ne peut qu'à peine,
En la voyant, reprendre haleine,
Tant il est comblé de plaisir.
Quels que soient les habits, la beauté du visage,
Son beau tour, sa vive blancheur,
Ses traits fins, sa jeune fraîcheur
Le touchent cent fois davantage;
Mais un certain air de grandeur,
Plus encore une sage et modeste pudeur,
Des beautés de son âme assuré témoignage,
S'emparèrent de tout son cœur.

Trois fois, dans la chaleur du feu qui le transporte,
Il voulut enfoncer la porte;
Mais croyant voir une divinité,
Trois fois par le respect son bras fut arrêté.

Dans le palais, pensif il se retire,
Et là, nuit et jour il soupire;
Il ne veut plus aller au bal
Quoiqu'on soit dans le Carnaval.
Il hait la chasse, il hait la comédie,
Il n'a plus d'appétit, tout lui fait mal au cœur,
Et le fond de sa maladie
Est une triste et mortelle langueur.

Il s'enquit quelle était cette nymphe admirable
Qui demeurait dans une basse-cour,
Au fond d'une allée effroyable,

I would find myself better adorned with it
than with all the ones I own."

One day, as the prince was wandering at random
from one farmyard to another,
he entered a dark lane
in which Donkey-Skin's humble dwelling was situated.
By some chance he put his eye to the keyhole.
As that day was a holiday,
she had put on costly jewelry
and those splendid clothes of hers
which, woven of wire-drawn gold and large diamonds,
equaled the utmost brightness of the sun.
The prince watched her
as long as he liked, and, seeing her,
could hardly catch his breath,
he was so overcome with delight.
However fine her clothes were, the beauty of her face,
its lovely shape, her fair complexion,
her delicate features, and her youthful freshness
affected him a hundred times more;
but a certain air of greatness
and, even more, her well-mannered, unassuming modesty,
sure evidence of her soul's beauty,
seized his heart completely.

Three times, in the heat of the blaze that transported him,
he wanted to break down the door;
but, since he thought he was viewing a goddess,
three times his arm was restrained by respect.

Full of thought, he withdrew to the palace,
and there he sighed night and day;
he no longer wished to attend the ball
even though it was Carnival time.
He shunned the chase, he shunned the theater;
he had no more appetite, everything sickened his heart,
and the tenor of his illness
was a sad, fatal languor.

He made inquiries into the identity of that wonderful nymph
who resided in a farmyard
at the end of a horrible passage

Où l'on ne voit goutte en plein jour.
«C'est, lui dit-on, Peau d'Ane, en rien nymphe ni belle
Et que Peau d'Ane l'on appelle,
A cause de la peau qu'elle met sur son cou;
De l'amour c'est le vrai remède,
La bête en un mot la plus laide,
Qu'on puisse voir après le loup.»
On a beau dire, il ne saurait le croire;
Les traits que l'amour a tracés
Toujours présents à sa mémoire
N'en seront jamais effacés.

Cependant la reine sa mère
Qui n'a que lui d'enfant pleure et se désespère;
De déclarer son mal elle le presse en vain,
Il gémit, il pleure, il soupire,
Il ne dit rien, si ce n'est qu'il désire
Que Peau d'Ane lui fasse un gâteau de sa main;
Et la mère ne sait ce que son fils veut dire.
«O Ciel! madame, lui dit-on,
Cette Peau d'Ane est une noire taupe
Plus vilaine encore et plus gaupe
Que le plus sale marmiton.
—N'importe, dit la reine, il le faut satisfaire
Et c'est à cela seul que nous devons songer.»
Il aurait eu de l'or, tant l'aimait cette mère,
S'il en avait voulu manger.

Peau d'Ane donc prend sa farine
Qu'elle avait fait bluter exprès
Pour rendre sa pâte plus fine,
Son sel, son beurre et ses œufs frais;
Et pour bien faire sa galette,
S'enferme seule en sa chambrette.

D'abord elle se décrassa
Les mains, les bras et le visage,
Et prit un corps d'argent que vite elle laça
Pour dignement faire l'ouvrage
Qu'aussitôt elle commença.

On dit qu'en travaillant un peu trop à la hâte,
De son doigt par hasard il tomba dans la pâte

where it was completely dark in the middle of the day.
He was told, "She's Donkey-Skin, no nymph and no beauty,
    and she's called Donkey-Skin
because of the skin she puts on her neck;
    she's a real antidote to love,
    in a word: the ugliest animal
    you can see, except a wolf."
  Despite all they said, he refused to believe them;
    the marks left by love
    were always present in his memory
    and could never be erased.

    Meanwhile, his mother the queen,
who had no other child, was weeping and in despair;
she urged him in vain to identify his ailment;
    he moaned, he wept, he sighed,
  but said nothing, except that he desired
Donkey-Skin to make him a cake with her own hands;
and his mother did not know what her son had in mind.
    "Oh, heavens, madam," people told her,
  "this Donkey-Skin is a black mole,
    even uglier and more slovenly
    than the dirtiest kitchen boy."
"No matter," said the queen, "he must be satisfied,
and that is the only thing we should think about."
He would have received gold, so much did his mother love him,
    if he had wanted to eat it.

    And so, Donkey-Skin took her flour,
    which she had had bolted expressly
    to make her dough more delicate;
    she took her salt, butter, and fresh eggs;
    and to make her biscuit properly,
    she shut herself into her little room alone.

    First, she washed the grime
    off her hands, arms, and face,
and put on a silver bodice, lacing it up quickly,
    in order to do the job in a worthy manner;
    then she began the task at once.

It is told that, while she was working a little too hastily,
one of her very costly rings

Un de ses anneaux de grand prix;
Mais ceux qu'on tient savoir le fin de cette histoire
Assurent que par elle exprès il y fut mis;
Et pour moi franchement je l'oserais bien croire,
Fort sûr que, quand le prince à sa porte aborda
    Et par le trou la regarda,
    Elle s'en était aperçue:
    Sur ce point la femme est si drue
    Et son œil va si promptement
    Qu'on ne peut la voir un moment
    Qu'elle ne sache qu'on l'a vue.
Je suis bien sûr encor, et j'en ferais serment,
Qu'elle ne douta point que de son jeune amant
    La bague ne fût bien reçue.

On ne pétrit jamais un si friand morceau,
Et le prince trouva la galette si bonne
Qu'il ne s'en fallut rien que d'une faim gloutonne
    Il n'avalât aussi l'anneau.
    Quand il en vit l'émeraude admirable,
    Et du jonc d'or le cercle étroit,
    Qui marquait la forme du doigt,
Son cœur en fut touché d'une joie incroyable;
    Sous son chevet il le mit à l'instant,
    Et son mal toujours augmentant,
    Les médecins sages d'expérience,
    En le voyant maigrir de jour en jour,
    Jugèrent tous, par leur grande science,
    Qu'il était malade d'amour.

    Comme l'hymen, quelque mal qu'on en die,
Est un remède exquis pour cette maladie,
    On conclut à le marier;
    Il s'en fit quelque temps prier,
Puis dit: «Je le veux bien, pourvu que l'on me donne
    En mariage la personne
    Pour qui cet anneau sera bon.»
    A cette bizarre demande,
De la reine et du roi la surprise fut grande;
Mais il était si mal qu'on n'osa dire non.

    Voilà donc qu'on se met en quête

accidentally slipped off her finger and fell into the dough;
but those who are considered to know the secret of this story
assure us that she put it there on purpose;
as for me, frankly, I am ready to believe it,
being quite sure that, when the prince stopped at her door
    and watched her through the keyhole,
    she had noticed it:
    in such matters women are so alert,
    and their eyes move so rapidly,
      that they cannot be observed for a moment
      without their knowing they have been observed.
I am also quite sure, and I would take an oath on it,
that she had no doubt that the ring
    would be gladly received by her young admirer.

A morsel that delicious was never kneaded,
and the prince found the biscuit so good
that, but for a miracle, in his avid hunger
    he would have swallowed the ring, too.
  When he saw its remarkable emerald,
    and the narrowness of its golden band,
    which indicated the size of the finger,
his heart was stirred with unbelievable joy;
  he instantly put it under his bolster,
    and, as his malady constantly worsened,
  the doctors made wise by experience,
  seeing him grow thinner daily,
  all deemed, through their great knowledge,
    that he was lovesick.

  Since matrimony, however bad it is said to be,
is an excellent remedy for that ailment,
    they decided he should be married;
    he needed to be coaxed for awhile,
then he said: "I am willing, as long as the woman
    given to me in matrimony
    is the one that this ring fits."
    At that unusual request,
the queen and king were greatly surprised;
but he was so ill that they did not dare to refuse.

    And so, a search was instituted

De celle que l'anneau, sans nul égard du sang,
  Doit placer dans un si haut rang;
  Il n'en est point qui ne s'apprête
  A venir présenter son doigt
  Ni qui veuille céder son droit.

Le bruit ayant couru que pour prétendre au prince,
  Il faut avoir le doigt bien mince,
  Tout charlatan, pour être bienvenu,
Dit qu'il a le secret de le rendre menu;
  L'une, en suivant son bizarre caprice,
    Comme une rave le ratisse;
    L'autre en coupe un petit morceau;
Une autre en le pressant croit qu'elle l'apetisse;
    Et l'autre, avec de certaine eau,
Pour le rendre moins gros en fait tomber la peau;
    Il n'est enfin point de manœuvre
    Qu'une dame ne mette en œuvre,
Pour faire que son doigt cadre bien à l'anneau.

L'essai fut commencé par les jeunes princesses,
    Les marquises et les duchesses;
    Mais leurs doigts quoique délicats,
    Étaient trop gros et n'entraient pas.
    Les comtesses, et les baronnes,
    Et toutes les nobles personnes,
Comme elles tour à tour présentèrent leur main
    Et la présentèrent en vain.

    Ensuite vinrent les grisettes
    Dont les jolis et menus doigts,
    Car il en est de très bien faites,
Semblèrent à l'anneau s'ajuster quelquefois.
Mais la bague toujours trop petite ou trop ronde
D'un dédain presque égal rebutait tout le monde.

    Il fallut en venir enfin
    Aux servantes, aux cuisinières,
    Aux tortillons, aux dindonnières,
    En un mot à tout le fretin,
    Dont les rouges et noires pattes,
    Non moins que les mains délicates,
    Espéraient un heureux destin.

for the woman whom, with no regard to her birth, the ring
    was to raise to so high a rank;
    there was not one who did not prepare
    to come and show her finger
    or who wished to surrender her rights.

Rumor having spread that, to claim the prince,
    a woman needed to have a very slender ring finger,
  every charlatan, to receive a warm welcome,
said that he possessed the secret of slenderizing it;
  one woman, obeying his odd whim,
    grated hers like a turnip;
    another one cut a small piece off hers;
another one thought she could make hers smaller by pressing it down;
    still another, with a certain lotion,
trying to make hers less thick, made the skin fall off;
    in short, there was no device
    that some lady did not employ
to make her finger fit the ring perfectly.

The trial began with the young princesses,
    the marchionesses, and the duchesses;
    but their fingers, though delicate,
    were too thick and would not go in.
    The countesses, the baronesses,
    and all the ladies of the nobility,
showed their hands in turn, like them,
    but showed them in vain.

    Next came the girls of the commons,
    whose pretty, small fingers
    (for there are some very shapely lasses among them)
sometimes seemed to match the ring.
But the ring, always too small or too round,
rejected everyone with nearly equal disdain.

    At last it was necessary to descend
    to the maids, to the cooks,
    to the slavies, to the turkey tenders,
    in short: to all the small fry,
    whose red or black paws,
    no less than those delicate hands,
    hoped for a lucky fate.

Il s'y présenta mainte fille
Dont le doigt, gros et ramassé,
Dans la bague du prince eût aussi peu passé
Qu'un câble au travers d'une aiguille.

On crut enfin que c'était fait,
Car il ne restait en effet,
Que la pauvre Peau d'Ane au fond de la cuisine.
Mais comment croire, disait-on,
Qu'à régner le Ciel la destine!
Le prince dit: «Et pourquoi non?
Qu'on la fasse venir.» Chacun se prit à rire,
Criant tout haut: «Que veut-on dire,
De faire entrer ici cette sale guenon?»
Mais lorsqu'elle tira de dessous sa peau noire
Une petite main qui semblait de l'ivoire
Qu'un peu de pourpre a coloré,
Et que de la bague fatale,
D'une justesse sans égale
Son petit doigt fut entouré,
La cour fut dans une surprise
Qui ne peut pas être comprise.

On la menait au roi dans ce transport subit;
Mais elle demanda qu'avant que de paraître
Devant son seigneur et son maître,
On lui donnât le temps de prendre un autre habit.
De cet habit, pour la vérité dire,
De tous côtés on s'apprêtait à rire;
Mais lorsqu'elle arriva dans les appartements,
Et qu'elle eut traversé les salles
Avec ses pompeux vêtements
Dont les riches beautés n'eurent jamais d'égales;
Que ses aimables cheveux blonds
Mêlés de diamants dont la vive lumière
En faisait autant de rayons,
Que ses yeux bleus, grands, doux et longs,
Qui pleins d'une majesté fière
Ne regardent jamais sans plaire et sans blesser,
Et que sa taille enfin si menue et si fine
Qu'avecque ses deux mains on eût pu l'embrasser,
Montrèrent leurs appas et leur grâce divine,

Many a girl showed up
whose finger, fat and stumpy,
would have passed through the prince's ring with just as great difficulty
    as a cable would pass through a needle's eye.

Finally it was thought that the trial was over,
because, in fact, no one was left
but poor Donkey-Skin at the back of the kitchen.
But, people said, how could it be believed
that Heaven destined *her* to reign?
The prince said: "And why not?
Have her brought here." Everyone started laughing,
    shouting out loud: "What's the meaning of this,
having that dirty ape coming in here?"
But when she extended from beneath her black donkey-skin
a small hand that resembled ivory
    tinged with a little purple,
    and when her small finger was encircled
    by the fateful ring
    in a perfect match,
    the court was in an amazement
    that cannot be described.

She was led to the king during that sudden rapture;
but she requested that, before appearing
    in front of her lord and master,
she be given the time to put on different clothes.
To tell the truth, the thought of those clothes
    was beginning to cause universal laughter;
but when she arrived in the royal apartments,
    and had crossed the halls
    with her magnificent garments,
whose sumptuous beauty was never equaled;
    when her lovely blonde hair,
adorned with diamonds whose flashing light
    threw as many beams as there were stones,
    when her big blue eyes, soft and wide,
    which, filled with proud majesty,
never darted a glance without causing pleasure and pain,
and, finally, when her waist, so small and slender
that it could be encircled with two hands,
all displayed their charms and their divine grace,

Des dames de la cour, et de leurs ornements
    Tombèrent tous les agréments.

Dans la joie et le bruit de toute l'assemblée,
    Le bon roi ne se sentait pas
  De voir sa bru posséder tant d'appas;
    La reine en était affolée,
    Et le prince son cher amant,
    De cent plaisirs l'âme comblée,
Succombait sous le poids de son ravissement.

Pour l'hymen aussitôt chacun prit ses mesures;
Le monarque en pria tous les rois d'alentour,
  Qui, tous brillants de diverses parures,
Quittèrent leurs États pour être à ce grand jour.
On en vit arriver des climats de l'aurore,
    Montés sur le grands éléphants;
    Il en vint du rivage more,
    Qui, plus noirs et plus laids encore,
    Faisaient peur aux petits enfants;
    Enfin de tous les coins du monde,
  Il en débarque et la cour en abonde.

    Mais nul prince, nul potentat,
    N'y parut avec tant d'éclat
    Que le père de l'épousée,
    Qui d'elle autrefois amoureux
Avait avec le temps purifié les feux
    Dont son âme était embrasée.
Il en avait banni tout désir criminel
    Et de cette odieuse flamme
    Le peu qui restait dans son âme
N'en rendait que plus vif son amour paternel.
  Dès qu'il la vit: «Que béni soit le Ciel
    Qui veut bien que je te revoie,
Ma chère enfant», dit-il, et tout pleurant de joie,
    Courut tendrement l'embrasser;
Chacun à son bonheur voulut s'intéresser,
Et le futur époux était ravi d'apprendre
Que d'un roi si puissant il devenait le gendre.

    Dans ce moment la marraine arriva
    Qui raconta toute l'histoire,

all the appeal of the ladies of the court
 and of their finery was vanquished.

Amid the joy and tumult of the whole assembly,
 the good king was beside himself
 at finding his daughter-in-law possessed of so many charms;
 the queen was crazy over her,
 and the prince, her dear suitor,
 his soul filled with a hundred delights,
staggered under the weight of his rapture.

Instantly everyone began to prepare for the wedding;
the monarch invited all the kings round about,
 who, all of them splendid with various adornments,
left their realms to attend that great event.
Some were seen to arrive from Eastern climes,
 riding on large elephants;
 some, who came from Moorish shores,
 were blacker and even uglier,
 and frightened the little children;
 in short, from every corner of the world
they disembarked, and the court was full of them.

 But no ruler, no potentate
 appeared there in such glory
 as the father of the bride,
 who, formerly in love with her,
had, with time, purified the ardor
 that had blazed in his soul.
He had expelled all criminal desires from it,
 and the small residue of that odious flame
 which remained in his soul
merely made his paternal love stronger.
 As soon as he saw her, he said: "Blessed be Heaven,
 which allows me to see you again,
my dear child," and, weeping with joy,
 he ran over to embrace her tenderly;
everyone wanted to partake in his happiness,
and the future husband was delighted to learn
that he was becoming the son-in-law of so mighty a king.

 At that moment the godmother arrived
 and told the whole story;

Et par son récit acheva
De combler Peau d'Ane de gloire.

Il n'est pas malaisé de voir
Que le but de ce conte est qu'un enfant apprenne
Qu'il vaut mieux s'exposer à la plus rude peine
Que de manquer à son devoir;

Que la vertu peut être infortunée
Mais qu'elle est toujours couronnée;

Que contre un fol amour et ses fougueux transports
La raison la plus forte est une faible digue,
Et qu'il n'est point de si riches trésors
Dont un amant ne soit prodigue;

Que de l'eau claire et du pain bis
Suffisent pour la nourriture
De toute jeune créature,
Pourvu qu'elle ait de beaux habits;
Que sous le ciel il n'est point de femelle
Qui ne s'imagine être belle,
Et qui souvent ne s'imagine encor
Que si des trois beautés la fameuse querelle
S'était démêlée avec elle,
Elle aurait eu la pomme d'or.

Le conte de Peau d'Ane est difficile à croire,
Mais tant que dans le monde on aura des enfants,
Des mères et des mères-grands,
On en gardera la mémoire.

by her narrative she heaped
the last bit of glory on Donkey-Skin.

It is not difficult to see
that this tale has the aim of teaching a child
that it is better to expose oneself to the harshest suffering
    than to fail in one's duty;

    that the virtuous may be unlucky
    but are always rewarded;

that, in the face of a mad love and its violent surges,
even the firmest rational approach is a weak barrier,
  and that there are no treasures so costly
    that a man in love will hesitate to squander thim;

    that plain water and black bread
    suffice to nourish
    any young girl,
    as long as she has beautiful clothes;
  that under the sky there is no female
    who fails to imagine she is beautiful,
  and who frequently even imagines
that if that notorious dispute among the three beauties[14]
    had had her for a participant,
    she would have won the golden apple.

The tale of Donkey-Skin is hard to believe literally,
but as long as the world contains children,
    mothers, and grandmothers,
    the memory of it will be preserved.

---

[14]The beauty contest between Hera, Aphrodite, and Athena for the golden apple of the goddess of discord, which ultimately caused the Trojan War.

Les souhaits ridicules

A Mademoiselle de la C***

Si vous étiez moins raisonnable,
Je me garderais bien de venir vous conter
    La folle et peu galante fable
    Que je m'en vais vous débiter.
Une aune de boudin en fournit la matière.
    «Une aune de boudin, ma chère!
    Quelle pitié! c'est une horreur»,
    S'écriait une précieuse,
    Qui toujours tendre et sérieuse
Ne veut ouïr parler que d'affaires de cœur.
    Mais vous qui mieux qu'âme qui vive
    Savez charmer en racontant,
Et dont l'expression est toujours si naïve,
    Que l'on croit voir ce qu'on entend;
    Qui savez que c'est la manière
    Dont' quelque chose est inventé,
    Qui beaucoup plus que la matière
    De tout récit fait la beauté,
Vous aimerez ma fable et sa moralité;
J'en ai, j'ose le dire, une assurance entière.

Les souhaits ridicules

Il était une fois un pauvre bûcheron
        Qui las de sa pénible vie,
        Avait, disait-il, grande envie

The Ludicrous Wishes

To Mademoiselle de la C°°°[15]

If you were less well endowed with reason,
I would carefully avoid narrating to you
    the madcap, ungallant story
    that I am about to tell you.
The subject matter is an ell's length of black-pudding.
    "An ell's length of black-pudding, my dear!
    What an awful thing! It's terrible!"
    exclaimed a literary lady,
    who, always amorous and serious,
never wants to hear anything but love stories.
    But you, who more than any other living soul
    know how to tell stories charmingly,
always expressing yourself with such simplicity
    that your listeners think they can see what they hear;
    you who know that it is the style
    in which a story is composed
    that, much more than the subject matter,
    creates the beauty of any narrative,
you will like my story and its moral;
I venture to say that I am fully certain you will.

The Ludicrous Wishes

There was once a poor woodcutter
        who, weary of his difficult life,
        said he had a great desire

---

[15]Possibly Philis de la Charce, a military heroine in the public eye at the time.

De s'aller reposer aux bords de l'Achéron:
   Représentant, dans sa douleur profonde,
      Que depuis qu'il était au monde,
      Le Ciel cruel n'avait jamais
   Voulu remplir un seul de ses souhaits.

Un jour que, dans le bois, il se mit à se plaindre,
A lui, la foudre en main, Jupiter s'apparut.
      On aurait peine à bien dépeindre
      La peur que le bonhomme en eut.
«Je ne veux rien, dit-il, en se jetant par terre,
      Point de souhaits, point de tonnerre,
      Seigneur, demeurons but à but.
      —Cesse d'avoir aucune crainte;
Je viens, dit Jupiter, touché de ta complainte,
   Te faire voir le tort que tu me fais.
      Écoute donc. Je te promets,
Moi qui du monde entier suis le souverain maître,
D'exaucer pleinement les trois premiers souhaits
Que tu voudras former sur quoi que ce puisse être.
      Vois ce qui peut te rendre heureux,
      Vois ce qui peut te satisfaire;
Et comme ton bonheur dépend tout de tes vœux,
   Songes-y bien avant que de les faire.»

A ces mots Jupiter dans les Cieux remonta,
Et le gai bûcheron, embrassant sa falourde,
Pour retourner chez lui sur son dos la jeta.
Cette charge jamais ne lui parut moins lourde.
   «Il ne faut pas, disait-il en trottant,
   Dans tout ceci, rien faire à la légère;
      Il faut, le cas est important,
      En prendre avis de notre ménagère.
Çà, dit-il, en entrant sous son toit de fougère,
      Faisons, Fanchon, grand feu, grand chère,
      Nous sommes riches à jamais,
   Et nous n'avons qu'à faire des souhaits.»
Là-dessus tout au long le fait il lui raconte.
   A ce récit, l'épouse vive et prompte
Forma dans son esprit mille vastes projets;

to go and rest on the banks of the Acheron,[16]
   claiming, in his profound sorrow,
      that ever since he had arrived in the world,
      cruel Heaven had never
   consented to grant even one of his wishes.

One day when he started complaining in the woods,
Jupiter appeared before him, thunderbolt in hand.
      It would be hard to depict accurately
      the fright which that gave the peasant.
"I want nothing," he said, falling to the ground;
     "no wishes, no thunder,
      lord; let us say the score is even."
      "Cease to feel any fear,"
Jupiter said; "I have come, since your lament moved me,
   to show you how badly you are misjudging me.
      Listen. I promise you,
I who am the sovereign master of the whole world,
to grant in full the first three wishes
you desire to make in any category whatsoever.
      Think of what can make you happy,
      think of what can content you;
and, since your happiness depends entirely on your wishes,
   consider them carefully before uttering them."

Having said this, Jupiter reascended to the heavens,
and the happy woodcutter, placing his arms around his load of wood,
threw it onto his back to take it home.
That burden had never seemed less heavy to him.
  As he trotted along, he said, "In all this,
  I must not do anything frivolously;
     the matter is important, and I must
     hear my wife's opinion on it.
"There," he said, entering beneath his fern roof;
     "Fanny, let's make a big fire and a big meal;
     we are rich for all time,
   and all we need to do is make wishes."
Then he recounted the event to her in full detail.
   Hearing his story, his lively, quick-witted wife
planned a thousand huge projects in her mind;

---

[16]A river in the underworld (afterlife).

Mais considérant l'importance
De s'y conduire avec prudence:
«Blaise, mon cher ami, dit-elle à son époux,
    Ne gâtons rien par notre impatience;
        Examinons bien entre nous
    Ce qu'il faut faire en pareille occurrence;
Remettons à demain notre premier souhait
        Et consultons notre chevet.
—Je l'entends bien ainsi, dit le bonhomme Blaise;
Mais va tirer du vin derrière ces fagots.»
A son retour il but, et goûtant à son aise
    Près d'un grand feu la douceur du repos,
Il dit, en s'appuyant sur le dos de sa chaise:
«Pendant que nous avons une si bonne braise,
Qu'une aune de boudin viendrait bien à propos!»
A peine acheva-t-il de prononcer ces mots,
Que sa femme aperçut, grandement étonnée,
        Un boudin fort long, qui partant
        D'un des coins de la cheminée,
        S'approchait d'elle en serpentant.
        Elle fit un cri dans l'instant;
        Mais jugeant que cette aventure
        Avait pour cause le souhait
        Que par bêtise toute pure
        Son homme imprudent avait fait,
        Il n'est point de pouille et d'injure
        Que de dépit et de courroux
        Elle ne dît au pauvre époux.
«Quand on peut, disait-elle, obtenir un empire,
        De l'or, des perles, des rubis,
        Des diamants, de beaux habits,
Est-ce alors du boudin qu'il faut que l'on désire?
—Eh bien, j'ai tort, dit-il, j'ai mal placé mon choix,
        J'ai commis une faute énorme,
        Je ferai mieux une autre fois.
    —Bon, bon, dit-elle, attendez-moi sous l'orme,
Pour faire un tel souhait, il faut être bien bœuf!»
L'époux plus d'une fois, emporté de colère,
Pensa faire tout bas le souhait d'être veuf,
Et peut-être, entre nous, ne pouvait-il mieux faire:
«Les hommes, disait-il, pour souffrir sont bien nés!

but, considering the importance
of going about it prudently,
she said to her husband, "Blaise, my dear friend,
let us not spoil things by being impatient;
let us discuss fully between us
what we ought to do on such an occasion;
let us postpone our first wish until tomorrow,
and let us sleep on it."
"That is what I think, too," said peasant Blaise;
"but go and draw some wine behind that firewood."
When she returned, he drank and, comfortably enjoying
the sweetness of repose beside a roaring fire,
he said, leaning back in his chair:
"While we have such a good flame going,
an ell's length of black-pudding would come in handy!"
Scarcely had he finished uttering those words
when, to her great astonishment, his wife caught sight
of a very long black-pudding, which, starting
from one corner of the fireplace,
approached her, wriggling like a snake.
She instantly cried out;
but deeming that that adventure
was the result of the wish
which, out of sheer stupidity,
her unwise husband had made,
there was no insult or invective
that, in her vexation and anger,
she did not heap upon her poor husband.
She said, "When we are able to obtain an empire,
gold, pearls, rubies,
diamonds, fine clothes,
was it really necessary to ask for black-pudding?"
"All right, I was wrong," he said; "I made a bad choice,
I made an enormous mistake;
I will do better next time."
"Fine, fine," she said, "seeing will be believing!
To make a wish like that, a man has to be really dumb!"
More than once, her husband, wild with anger,
considered making the silent wish to be a widower,
and, between you and me, maybe that would have been the best thing:
"Men," he said, "are really born to suffer!

Peste soit du boudin et du boudin encore;
  Plût à Dieu, maudite pécore,
  Qu'il te pendît au bout du nez!»

La prière aussitôt du Ciel fut écoutée,
Et dès que le mari la parole lâcha,
  Au nez de l'épouse irritée
  L'aune de boudin s'attacha.
Ce prodige imprévu grandement le fâcha.
Fanchon était jolie, elle avait bonne grâce,
Et pour dire sans fard la vérité du fait,
  Cet ornement en cette place
  Ne faisait pas un bon effet;
Si ce n'est qu'en pendant sur le bas du visage,
  Il l'empêchait de parler aisément,
  Pour un époux merveilleux avantage,
Et si grand qu'il pensa dans cet heureux moment
  Ne souhaiter rien davantage.

  «Je pourrais bien, disait-il à part soi,
   Après un malheur si funeste,
   Avec le souhait qui me reste,
   Tout d'un plein saut me faire roi.
Rien n'égale, il est vrai, la grandeur souveraine;
   Mais encore faut-il songer
   Comment serait faite la reine,
Et dans quelle douleur ce serait la plonger
   De l'aller placer sur un trône
   Avec un nez plus long qu'une aune.
   Il faut l'écouter sur cela,
  Et qu'elle-même elle soit la maîtresse
  De devenir une grande princesse
  En conservant l'horrible nez qu'elle a,
   Ou de demeurer bûcheronne
  Avec un nez comme une autre personne,
Et tel qu'elle l'avait avant ce malheur-là.»

   La chose bien examinée,
Quoiqu'elle sût d'un sceptre et la force et l'effet,
   Et que, quand on est couronnée,
   On a toujours le nez bien fait;
Comme au désir de plaire il n'est rien qui ne cède,

The devil take the pudding, over and over;
> I wish to God, you damned ninny,
> that it was hanging from the end of your nose!"

His request was immediately granted by Heaven,
and the moment that the husband let those words slip out,
> the ell's length of pudding attached itself
> to the nose of his irritated wife.
That unforeseen marvel vexed him deeply.
Fanny was pretty, she was graceful,
and to tell the whole unvarnished truth,
> that ornament in that place
> was not particularly attractive,
except that, hanging as it did over the lower part of her face,
> it prevented her from speaking with ease;
> this is such a wonderful benefit to a husband,
such a great one, that at that happy moment he considered
> not making any more wishes at all.

He said to himself, "I could,
> after so grave a misfortune,
> use my remaining wish
> to become a king in the twinkling of an eye.
It is true that nothing equals the greatness of a sovereign,
> but I must also consider
> what my queen would look like,
and what sorrow it would plunge her into
> to place her on a throne
> with a nose longer than an ell.
> I must hear her opinion about this,
> and let her have the choice herself
> either to become a great sovereign
> while keeping the horrible nose she has,
> or to remain a woodcutter's wife
> with a nose like everyone else's,
just as she had before this catastrophe."

Having weighed the matter carefully,
even though she knew the power and effect of a scepter,
> and that, when you wear a crown,
> your nose is always shapely;
since there is nothing superior to the desire to be attractive,

Elle aima mieux garder son bavolet
    Que d'être reine et d'être laide.

Ainsi le bûcheron ne changea point d'état,
    Ne devint point grand potentat,
    D'écus ne remplit point sa bourse,
Trop heureux d'employer le souhait qui restait,
    Faible bonheur, pauvre ressource,
A remettre sa femme en l'état qu'elle était.

    Bien est donc vrai qu'aux hommes misérables,
Aveugles, imprudents, inquiets, variables,
    Pas n'appartient de faire des souhaits,
    Et que peu d'entre eux sont capables
De bien user des dons que le Ciel leur a faits.

she preferred to keep her peasant's headdress
    rather than be queen and be ugly.

And so, the woodcutter did not advance in life,
    he did not become a great potentate,
    he did not fill his purse with coin;
he was all too happy to use his remaining wish—
    a feeble happiness, a poor resource—
to restore his wife to her former condition.

    It is thus very true that for wretched mankind,
blind, unwise, restless, changeable,
    it is not fitting to make wishes,
    and that few people are capable
of making good use of the gifts Heaven has given them.

Histoires ou Contes du temps passé.
Avec des Moralités

Stories or Tales of Olden Days. With Morals

[Prose Tales]

A Mademoiselle

Mademoiselle,

On ne trouvera pas étrange qu'un enfant ait pris plaisir à composer les contes de ce recueil, mais on s'étonnera qu'il ait eu la hardiesse de vous les présenter.

Cependant, Mademoiselle, quelque disproportion qu'il y ait entre la simplicité de ces récits, et les lumières de votre esprit, si on examine bien ces contes, on verra que je ne suis pas aussi blâmable que je le parais d'abord. Ils renferment tous une morale très sensée, et qui se découvre plus ou moins, selon le degré de pénétration de ceux qui les lisent; d'ailleurs comme rien ne marque tant la vaste étendue d'un esprit, que de pouvoir s'élever en même temps aux plus grandes choses, et s'abaisser aux plus petites, on ne sera point surpris que la même princesse, à qui la nature et l'éducation ont rendu familier ce qu'il y a de plus élevé, ne dédaigne pas de prendre plaisir à de semblables bagatelles. Il est vrai que ces contes donnent une image de ce qui se passe dans les moindres familles, où la louable impatience d'instruire les enfants fait imaginer des histoires dépourvues de raison, pour s'accommoder à ces mêmes enfants qui n'en ont pas encore; mais à qui convient-il mieux de connaître comment vivent les peuples, qu'aux personnes que le Ciel destine à les conduire? Le désir de cette connaissance a poussé des héros, et même des héros de votre race, jusque dans des huttes et des cabanes, pour y voir de près et par eux-mêmes ce qui s'y passait de plus particulier: cette connaissance leur ayant paru nécessaire pour leur parfaite instruction. Quoi qu'il en soit, Mademoiselle,

To Mademoiselle[17]

Mademoiselle,

People will not think it odd that a child took pleasure in writing the tales in this collection, but they will be surprised at his boldness in dedicating them to you.

Nevertheless, Mademoiselle—however great the distance between the simplicity of these narratives and the intelligence of your mind—if these tales are closely examined, it will be seen that I am not as blameworthy as I might at first appear. They all contain a very sensible code of morality, which is discovered to a greater or lesser extent in accordance with the degree of penetration of their readers; besides, since there is nothing more indicative of a mind's vast scope than the ability to rise to the loftiest subjects and stoop to the humblest at the same time, it will not be surprising that the same princess to whom nature and upbringing have made the loftiest things familiar will not look down on the pleasure to be derived from similar trifles. It is true that these tales offer a picture of what occurs in the humblest families, in which the praiseworthy impatient desire to instruct the children causes their elders to invent stories devoid of rationality to suit the capacities of those children who have not yet reached the age of reason; but whom does it befit more to know how the common folk live than those whom Heaven has chosen to guide them? The longing for such knowledge has driven heroes, and even heroes among your ancestors, even into huts and cottages, to see personally and at first-hand the details of daily existence there, that knowledge having seemed necessary to them to complete their education. However that may be, Mademoiselle,

---

[17]The title of Élisabeth-Charlotte d'Orléans (born 1676), daughter of Philippe d'Orléans, the brother of Louis XIV.

Pouvais-je mieux choisir pour rendre vraisemblable
  Ce que la fable a d'incroyable?
  Et jamais fée au temps jadis
  Fit-elle à jeune créature,
  Plus de dons, et de dons exquis,
  Que vous en a fait la nature?

Je suis avec un très profound respect,
  Mademoiselle,

De votre altesse Royale,

Le très humble et
très obéissant serviteur,
P. DARMANCOUR.

Could I make a better choice, in order to make probable
  that which is unbelievable in the stories?
  And did a fairy in olden days
  give a young girl
  more gifts, exquisite gifts,
  than nature has given to you?

With the deepest respect, I remain,
  Mademoiselle,

Your Royal Highness's

Most humble and
most obedient servant,

P. DARMANCOUR.

La belle au bois dormant

Il était une fois un roi et une reine, qui étaient si fâchés de n'avoir point d'enfants, si fâchés qu'on ne saurait dire. Ils allèrent à toutes les eaux du monde; vœux, pèlerinages, menues dévotions, tout fut mis en œuvre, et rien n'y faisait. Enfin pourtant la reine devint grosse, et accoucha d'une fille: on fit un beau baptême; on donna pour marraines à la petite princesse toutes les fées qu'on pût trouver dans le pays (il s'en trouva sept), afin que chacune d'elles lui faisant un don, comme c'était la coutume des fées en ce temps-là, la princesse eût par ce moyen toutes les perfections imaginables.

Après les cérémonies du baptême toute la compagnie revint au palais du roi, où il y avait un grand festin pour les fées. On mit devant chacune d'elles un couvert magnifique, avec un étui d'or massif, où il y avait une cuiller, une fourchette, et un couteau de fin or, garni de diamants et de rubis. Mais comme chacun prenait sa place à table, on vit entrer une vieille fée qu'on n'avait point priée parce qu'il y avait plus de cinquante ans qu'elle n'était sortie d'une tour et qu'on la croyait morte, ou enchantée. Le roi lui fit donner un couvert, mais il n'y eut pas moyen de lui donner un étui d'or massif, comme aux autres, parce que l'on n'en avait fait faire que sept pour les sept fées. La vieille crut qu'on la méprisait, et grommela quelques menaces entre ses dents. Une des jeunes fées qui se trouva auprès d'elle l'entendit, et jugeant qu'elle pourrait donner quelque fâcheux don à la petite princesse, alla dès qu'on fut sorti de table se cacher derrière la tapisserie, afin de parler la dernière, et de pouvoir réparer autant qu'il lui serait possible le mal que la vieille aurait fait.

Cependant les fées commencèrent à faire leurs dons à la princesse. La plus jeune lui donna pour don qu'elle serait la plus belle personne du monde, celle d'après qu'elle aurait de l'esprit comme un ange, la troisième qu'elle aurait une grâce admirable à tout ce qu'elle ferait, la quatrième qu'elle danserait parfaitement bien, la cinquième qu'elle

The Beauty in the Sleeping Forest [Sleeping Beauty]

There were once a king and queen who were so grieved at having no children, so grieved that words can't say. They visited all the spas in the world; vows, pilgrimages, acts of devotion, they tried everything, and nothing was effective. Finally, however, the queen became pregnant and gave birth to a girl: they arranged a lovely christening party; they chose as godmothers for the little princess all the fairies they could locate in the country (they found seven), so that each of them could give her a gift, as was the custom of fairies in those days, and the princess might thus be endowed with all possible perfections.

After the baptismal ceremonies the entire company returned to the king's palace, where there was a great banquet for the fairies. In front of each of them was placed a magnificent setting, with a solid gold case containing a spoon, fork, and knife of purest gold, adorned with diamonds and rubies. But as everyone was sitting down at the table, they saw an old fairy come in; she hadn't been invited because for more than fifty years she hadn't left her tower and everyone thought she was dead or under a spell. The king had a setting placed for her, but there was no way of giving her a solid-gold case such as the others had received, because only seven had been made for the seven fairies. The old fairy thought she was being held in contempt, and muttered a few threats under her breath. One of the young fairies, who was sitting next to her, heard her and, thinking that she might give some grievous gift to the little princess, went and hid behind the tapestry as soon as the meal was over, so that she could be the last to speak and could thus make amends, as far as possible, for the harm done by the old fairy.

Meanwhile, the fairies began to bestow their gifts on the princess. The youngest one gave her the gift of being the most beautiful woman in the world; the next one, that of being as intelligent as an angel; the third, that of lending marvelous grace to everything she did; the fourth, that of dancing expertly; the fifth, that of singing like a nightin-

117

chanterait comme un rossignol, et la sixième qu'elle jouerait de toutes sortes d'instruments dans la dernière perfection. Le rang de la vieille fée étant venu, elle dit, en branlant la tête encore plus de dépit que de vieillesse, que la princesse se percerait la main d'un fuseau, et qu'elle en mourrait.

Ce terrible don fit frémir toute la compagnie, et il n'y eut personne qui ne pleurât. Dans ce moment la jeune fée sortit de derrière la tapisserie, et dit tout haut ces paroles:

«Rassurez-vous, roi et reine, votre fille n'en mourra pas; il est vrai que je n'ai pas assez de puissance pour défaire entièrement ce que mon ancienne a fait. La princesse se percera la main d'un fuseau; mais au lieu d'en mourir, elle tombera seulement dans un profond sommeil qui durera cent ans, au bout desquels le fils d'un roi viendra la réveiller.»

Le roi, pour tâcher d'éviter le malheur annoncé par la vieille, fit publier aussitôt un édit, par lequel il défendait à toutes personnes de filer au fuseau, ni d'avoir des fuseaux chez soi sur peine de la vie.

Au bout de quinze ou seize ans, le roi et la reine étant allés à une de leurs maisons de plaisance, il arriva que la jeune princesse courant un jour dans le château, et montant de chambre en chambre, alla jusqu'au haut d'un donjon dans un petit galetas, où une bonne vieille était seule à filer sa quenouille. Cette bonne femme n'avait point ouï parler des défenses que le roi avait faites de filer au fuseau.

«Que faites-vous là, ma bonne femme? dit la princesse.

—Je file, ma belle enfant, lui répondit la vieille qui ne la connaissait pas.

—Ah! que cela est joli, reprit la princesse, comment faites-vous? donnez-moi que je voie si j'en ferais bien autant.»

Elle n'eut pas plus tôt pris le fuseau, que comme elle était fort vive, un peu étourdie, et que d'ailleurs l'arrêt des fées l'ordonnait ainsi, elle s'en perça la main, et tomba évanouie.

La bonne vieille, bien embarrassée, crie au secours: on vient de tous côtés, on jette de l'eau au visage de la princesse, on la délace, on lui frappe dans les mains, on lui frotte les temples avec de l'eau de la reine de Hongrie; mais rien ne la faisait revenir.

Alors le roi, qui était monté au bruit, se souvint de la prédiction des fées, et jugeant bien qu'il fallait que cela arrivât, puisque les fées l'avaient dit, fit mettre la princesse dans le plus bel appartement du palais, sur un lit en broderie d'or et d'argent. On eût dit d'un ange,

gale; and the sixth, that of playing any kind of instrument with the greatest virtuosity. The turn of the old fairy having come, she said, her head shaking more in anger than through age, that the princess's hand would be jabbed by a spindle, and she would die of it.

That terrible gift made everyone assembled there shudder, and there was no one who didn't weep. At that moment the young fairy came out from behind the tapestry, and spoke these words aloud:

"Be reassured, king and queen, your daughter shall not die of it; it's true that I don't have enough power to cancel entirely what my elder has done. The princess's hand *will* be jabbed by a spindle; but, instead of dying, she will merely fall into a deep sleep lasting a hundred years, after which a king's son will come to awaken her."

The king, in an attempt to avoid the misfortune predicted by the old fairy, immediately had an edict proclaimed, in which he forbade anyone to spin with a spindle, or to keep spindles at home, on pain of death.

Fifteen or sixteen years later, when the king and queen had gone to one of their country seats, it came about that the princess, wandering through the castle one day, and climbing the stairs from one room to another, reached the very top of a tower, where there was a small garret in which a nice old lady was sitting all alone spinning with her distaff. That good lady had never heard a word about the king's prohibition of spinning with a spindle.

"What are you doing there, old grandmother?" asked the princess.

"I'm spinning, you lovely child," replied the old lady, who didn't know her.

"Oh, how pretty that is," the princess continued; "how do you do it? Let me see whether I can do the same."

No sooner had she taken the spindle, when—she being very impetuous and a little careless, and, moreover, the fairies' decree ordering matters so—she jabbed her hand with it and fell down in a faint.

The good old lady, quite flustered, called for help: people came from all sides, dashed water in the princess's face, unlaced her bodice, struck her hands, and rubbed her temples with the Queen of Hungary's lotion;[18] but nothing made her regain consciousness.

Then the king, whom the hubbub had caused to come upstairs, remembered what the fairies had foretold and, realizing that this had to happen because the fairies had said so, ordered the princess to be placed in the most beautiful apartment in the palace, on a bed of gold

---

[18]Rosemary flowers in alcohol; it was said to have cured a Hungarian queen.

tant elle était belle; car son évanouissement n'avait pas ôté les couleurs vives de son teint: ses joues étaient incarnates, et ses lèvres comme du corail; elle avait seulement les yeux fermés, mais on l'entendait respirer doucement, ce qui faisait voir qu'elle n'était pas morte.

Le roi ordonna qu'on la laissât dormir en repos, jusqu'à ce que son heure de se réveiller fût venue. La bonne fée qui lui avait sauvé la vie, en la condamnant à dormir cent ans, était dans le royaume de Mataquin, à douze mille lieues de là, lorsque l'accident arriva à la princesse; mais elle en fut avertie en un instant par un petit nain, qui avait des bottes de sept lieues (c'était des bottes avec lesquelles on faisait sept lieues d'une seule enjambée). La fée partit aussitôt, et on la vit au bout d'une heure arriver dans un chariot tout de feu, traîné par des dragons. Le roi lui alla présenter la main à la descente du chariot. Elle approuva tout ce qu'il avait fait; mais comme elle était grandement prévoyante, elle pensa que quand la princesse viendrait à se réveiller, elle serait bien embarrassée toute seule dans ce vieux château: voici ce qu'elle fit.

Elle toucha de sa baguette tout ce qui était dans ce château (hors le roi et la reine), gouvernantes, filles d'honneur, femmes de chambre, gentilshommes, officiers, maîtres d'hôtel, cuisiniers, marmitons, galopins, gardes, suisses, pages, valets de pied; elle toucha aussi tous les chevaux qui étaient dans les écuries, avec les palefreniers, les gros mâtins de basse-cour, et la petite Pouffe, petite chienne de la princesse, qui était auprès d'elle sur son lit. Dès qu'elle les eut touchés, ils s'endormirent tous, pour ne se réveiller qu'en même temps que leur maîtresse, afin d'être tout prêts à la servir quand elle en aurait besoin; les broches mêmes qui étaient au feu toutes pleines de perdrix et de faisans s'endormirent, et le feu aussi. Tout cela se fit en un moment; les fées n'étaient pas longues à leur besogne.

Alors le roi et la reine, après avoir baisé leur chère enfant sans qu'elle s'éveillât, sortirent du château, et firent publier des défenses à qui que ce soit d'en approcher. Ces défenses n'étaient pas nécessaires, car il crût dans un quart d'heure tout autour du parc une si grande quantité de grands arbres et de petits, de ronces et d'épines entrelacées les unes dans les autres, que bête ni homme n'y aurait pu passer: en sorte qu'on ne voyait plus que le haut des tours du château, encore n'était-ce que de bien loin. On ne douta point que la fée n'eût

and silver embroidery. She was so beautiful, she looked like an angel, for her swoon hadn't caused the fresh color of her complexion to fade: her cheeks were pink, and her lips like coral; she merely had her eyes closed, but her light breathing could be heard, showing that she wasn't dead.

The king commanded that she should be left to sleep peacefully until the hour of her awakening had come. The good fairy who had saved her life by sentencing her to sleep for a hundred years was in the kingdom of Mataquin, twelve thousand leagues from there, when the princess had her accident; but she was informed of it in an instant by a little dwarf who had seven-league boots (those were boots in which you could cover seven leagues[19] in a single stride). The fairy departed at once, and an hour later she could be seen arriving in a fiery chariot drawn by dragons. The king came to give her his hand as she stepped out of the chariot. She approved of everything he had done; but, since she had enormous foresight, she realized that when the princess awoke, she would be very confused to find herself all alone in that old castle; this is what she did:

With her wand she touched everyone in that castle (except the king and queen), governesses, maids of honor, ladies-in-waiting, noblemen, men who had purchased positions in the palace, majordomos, cooks, kitchen boys, spit-turners, guards, porters, pages, footmen; she also touched all the horses that were in the stables, along with the grooms, the big mastiffs in the yard, and little Pouffe, the princess's lapdog, who was next to her on her bed. As soon as she touched them, they all fell asleep, not to reawaken until their mistress did, so they could be all ready to wait on her whenever she needed them to; even the spits on the hearth, full of partridges and pheasants, went to sleep, as did the fire. All this happened in a moment; the fairies weren't slow workers.

Then the king and queen, after kissing their dear child (which didn't awaken her), left the castle and issued proclamations forbidding anyone whatsoever to approach it. These prohibitions were unnecessary, because in a quarter-hour there grew all around the park so many big and small trees, and brambles and thorns intermeshed with one another, that neither man nor beast could get through: so that only the tops of the castle towers were still visible, and even that only from a considerable distance. No one had any doubt that this, too, came out

---

[19]Twenty-one miles.

encore fait là un tour de son métier, afin que la princesse, pendant qu'elle dormirait, n'eût rien à craindre des curieux.

Au bout de cent ans, le fils du roi qui régnait alors, et qui était d'une autre famille que la princesse endormie, étant allé à la chasse de ce côté-là, demanda ce que c'était que des tours qu'il voyait au-dessus d'un grand bois fort épais; chacun lui répondit selon qu'il en avait ouï parler. Les uns disaient que c'était un vieux château où il revenait des esprits; les autres que tous les sorciers de la contrée y faisaient leur sabbat. La plus commune opinion était qu'un ogre y demeurait, et que là il emportait tous les enfants qu'il pouvait attraper, pour les pouvoir manger à son aise, et sans qu'on le pût suivre, ayant seul le pouvoir de se faire un passage au travers du bois.

Le prince ne savait qu'en croire, lorsqu'un vieux paysan prit la parole, et lui dit:

«Mon prince, il y a plus de cinquante ans que j'ai ouï dire à mon père qu'il y avait dans ce château une princesse, la plus belle du monde; qu'elle y devait dormir cent ans, et qu'elle serait réveillée par le fils d'un roi, à qui elle était réservée.»

Le jeune prince, à ce discours, se sentit tout de feu; il crut sans balancer qu'il mettrait fin à une si belle aventure; et poussé par l'amour et par la gloire, il résolut de voir sur-le-champ ce qui en était. A peine s'avança-t-il vers le bois, que tous ces grands arbres, ces ronces et ces épines s'écartèrent d'elles-mêmes pour le laisser passer: il marche vers le château qu'il voyait au bout d'une grande avenue où il entra, et ce qui le surprit un peu, il vit que personne de ses gens ne l'avait pu suivre, parce que les arbres s'étaient rapprochés dès qu'il avait été passé. Il ne laissa pas de continuer son chemin: un prince jeune et amoureux est toujours vaillant. Il entra dans une grande avant-cour où tout ce qu'il vit d'abord était capable de le glacer de crainte: c'était un silence affreux, l'image de la mort s'y présentait partout, et ce n'était que des corps étendus d'hommes et d'animaux, qui paraissaient morts. Il reconnut pourtant bien au nez bourgeonné et à la face vermeille des suisses, qu'ils n'étaient qu'endormis, et leurs tasses où il y avait encore quelques gouttes de vin montraient assez qu'ils s'étaient endormis en buvant.

Il passe une grande cour pavée de marbre, il monte l'escalier, il entre dans la salle des gardes qui étaient rangés en haie, la carabine sur l'épaule, et ronflants de leur mieux. Il traverse plusieurs chambres pleines de gentilshommes et de dames, dormants tous, les uns debout, les autres assis; il entre dans une chambre toute dorée, et il vit sur un lit, dont les rideaux étaient ouverts de tous côtés, le plus beau specta-

of the fairy's bag of tricks, so that, while the princess slept, she would have nothing to fear from prying visitors.

A hundred years later, the son of the king who was then reigning, and who was of a different family than the sleeping princess, having gone hunting in the vicinity, asked what those towers were which he saw over the top of a large, very dense forest; people replied in accordance with the stories each of them had heard. Some said it was an old castle haunted by ghosts; others, that all the wizards in the region held their sabbath there. The most widespread opinion was that an ogre lived there, and carried off to that castle all the children he was able to catch, so he could eat them in peace and quiet without being followed, since he alone had the power of creating a passage through the woods.

The prince didn't know what to make of all this, when an old peasant spoke up in his turn, saying:

"Prince, over fifty years ago I heard my father say that in that castle there was a princess, the most beautiful in the world, that she was to sleep there for a hundred years, and that she would be awakened by a king's son, for whom she was destined." Hearing this, the young prince felt all aflame; he unhesitatingly became convinced that he would achieve that wonderful exploit; and, prompted by love and glory, he resolved to learn the truth of it immediately. Scarcely had he proceeded toward the woods when all those tall trees, brambles, and thorns spontaneously parted to let him pass: he walked toward the castle, which he could see at the end of a long, tree-lined walk, which he entered; what surprised him somewhat was finding that none of his retinue had been able to follow him, because the trees had closed in again the moment he had passed through them. That didn't discourage him from proceeding onward: a young prince in love is always valiant. He entered a large forecourt, in which everything that first met his eyes was of a nature to chill him with fear: there was a terrible silence, the image of death was offered everywhere, and he saw nothing but recumbent bodies of men and animals, seemingly dead. Yet he could tell from the pimpled noses and flushed faces of the porters that they were only asleep, and their cups, still containing a few drops of wine, were sufficient evidence that they had fallen asleep while drinking.

He crossed a large marble-paved courtyard, he climbed the stairs, and he entered the guardroom, where the men were lined up on either side, their carbines on their shoulders, snoring as loud as they could. He walked through several rooms full of noblemen and ladies, all asleep, some standing, others seated; he entered a completely gilded room, and he saw on a bed, the curtains of which were open all

cle qu'il eût jamais vu: une princesse qui paraissait avoir quinze ou seize ans, et dont l'éclat resplendissant avait quelque chose de lumineux et de divin. Il s'approcha en tremblant et en admirant, et se mit à genoux auprès d'elle.

Alors comme la fin de l'enchantement était venue, la princesse s'éveilla; et le regardant avec des yeux plus tendres qu'une première vue ne semblait le permettre:

«Est-ce vous, mon prince? lui dit-elle, vous vous êtes bien fait attendre.»

Le prince charmé de ces paroles, et plus encore de la manière dont elles étaient dites, ne savait comment lui témoigner sa joie et sa reconnaissance; il l'assura qu'il l'aimait plus que lui-même. Ses discours furent mal rangés, ils en plurent davantage; peu d'éloquence, beaucoup d'amour. Il était plus embarrassé qu'elle, et l'on ne doit pas s'en étonner; elle avait eu le temps de songer à ce qu'elle aurait à lui dire, car il y a apparence (l'histoire n'en dit pourtant rien) que la bonne fée, pendant un si long sommeil, lui avait procuré le plaisir des songes agréables. Enfin il y avait quatre heures qu'ils se parlaient, et ils ne s'étaient pas encore dit la moitié des choses qu'ils avaient à se dire.

Cependant tout le palais s'était réveillé avec la princesse; chacun songeait à faire sa charge, et comme ils n'étaient pas tous amoureux, ils mouraient de faim; la dame d'honneur, pressée comme les autres, s'impatienta, et dit tout haut à la princesse que la viande était servie. Le prince aida à la princesse à se lever; elle était tout habillée et fort magnifiquement; mais il se garda bien de lui dire qu'elle était habillée comme ma mère-grand, et qu'elle avait un collet monté; elle n'en était pas moins belle.

Ils passèrent dans un salon de miroirs, et y soupèrent, servis par les officiers de la princesse; les violons et les hautbois jouèrent de vieilles pièces, mais excellentes, quoiqu'il y eût près de cent ans qu'on ne les jouât plus; et après soupé, sans perdre de temps, le grand aumônier les maria dans la chapelle du château, et la dame d'honneur leur tira le rideau: ils dormirent peu, la princesse n'en avait pas grand besoin, et le prince la quitta dès le matin pour retourner à la ville, où son père devait être en peine de lui.

Le prince lui dit qu'en chassant il s'était perdu dans la forêt, et qu'il avait couché dans la hutte d'un charbonnier, qui lui avait fait manger du pain noir et du fromage. Le roi son père, qui était bon homme, le crut, mais sa mère n'en fut pas bien persuadée, et voyant qu'il allait presque tous les jours à la chasse, et qu'il avait toujours une raison en main pour s'excuser, quand il avait couché deux ou trois nuits dehors,

around, the loveliest sight he had ever seen: a princess who seemed to be fifteen or sixteen, and whose radiant beauty had something luminous and divine about it. Trembling and marveling, he came nearer and knelt beside her.

Then, since the end of the spell had come, the princess awoke; looking at him with eyes more loving than a first glance might justify, she said:

"Is it you, prince? You've kept me waiting a long, long time."

The prince, charmed by those words, and even more by the manner in which they were spoken, was at a loss as how to demonstrate his joy and gratitude; he assured her that he loved her more than himself. His speech was incoherent, but she liked it all the better for that: not much eloquence, lots of love. He was more embarrassed than she was, which is not surprising: she had had the time to think about what to say to him, because there's every reason to believe (though history gives us no firm information) that the kind fairy had provided her with the enjoyment of pleasant dreams during that very long slumber. In short, they spoke to each other for four hours, and hadn't even said half the things on their mind.

Meanwhile, the whole palace had awakened along with the princess; everyone thought about getting on with his work, and since they weren't all in love, they were dying of hunger; the maid of honor, just as starved as the rest, grew impatient and informed the princess aloud that supper was served. The prince helped the princess get up; she was completely dressed, and with great magnificence; but he took care not to tell her that she was dressed like my grandmother, and was wearing a stand-up collar; that didn't make her less beautiful.

They went to a mirrored salon and ate there, served by the princess's staff; the violins and oboes played old pieces, but excellent ones even though no one had been playing them for nearly a hundred years; after supper, without wasting time, the chief chaplain married them in the castle chapel, and the maid of honor drew their bed curtains: they didn't sleep much (the princess really didn't need to), and the prince left her in the morning to return to town, where his father must surely be worrying about him.

The prince told him that, while hunting, he had lost his way in the forest, and that he had slept in the hut of a charcoal burner, who had given him black bread and cheese to eat. His father the king, who was a simple soul, believed him, but his mother was very suspicious; seeing him go out hunting nearly every day with always some new pretext for staying away, after he had slept away from home two or three nights

elle ne douta plus qu'il n'eût quelque amourette: car il vécut avec la princesse plus de deux ans entiers, et en eut deux enfants, dont le premier, qui fut une fille, fut nommée l'Aurore, et le second un fils, qu'on nomma le Jour, parce qu'il paraissait encore plus beau que sa sœur.

La reine dit plusieurs fois à son fils, pour le faire expliquer, qu'il fallait se contenter dans la vie, mais il n'osa jamais se fier à elle de son secret; il la craignait quoiqu'il l'aimât, car elle était de race ogresse, et le roi ne l'avait épousée qu'à cause de ses grands biens; on disait même tout bas à la cour qu'elle avait les inclinations des ogres, et qu'en voyant passer de petits enfants, elle avait toutes les peines du monde à se retenir de se jeter sur eux; ainsi le prince ne voulut jamais rien dire.

Mais quand le roi fut mort, ce qui arriva au bout de deux ans, et qu'il se vit le maître, il déclara publiquement son mariage, et alla en grande cérémonie querir la reine sa femme dans son château. On lui fit une entrée magnifique dans la ville capitale, où elle entra au milieu de ses deux enfants.

Quelque temps après le roi alla faire la guerre à l'empereur Cantalabutte son voisin. Il laissa la régence du royaume à la reine sa mère, et lui recommanda fort sa femme et ses enfants: il devait être à la guerre tout l'été, et dès qu'il fut parti, la reine-mère envoya sa bru et ses enfants à une maison de campagne dans les bois, pour pouvoir plus aisément assouvir son horrible envie. Elle y alla quelques jours après, et dit un soir à son maître d'hôtel:

«Je veux manger demain à mon dîner la petite Aurore.

—Ah! madame, dit le maître d'hôtel.

—Je le veux, dit la reine (et elle le dit d'un ton d'ogresse qui a envie de manger de la chair fraîche), et je la veux manger à la sauce Robert.»

Ce pauvre homme voyant bien qu'il ne fallait pas se jouer à une ogresse, prit son grand couteau, et monta à la chambre de la petite Aurore: elle avait pour lors quatre ans, et vint en sautant et en riant se jeter à son col, et lui demander du bonbon. Il se mit à pleurer, le couteau lui tomba des mains, et il alla dans la basse-cour couper la gorge à un petit agneau, et lui fit une si bonne sauce que sa maîtresse l'assura qu'elle n'avait jamais rien mangé de si bon. Il avait emporté en même temps la petite Aurore, et l'avait donnée à sa femme pour la cacher dans le logement qu'elle avait au fond de la basse-cour.

she no longer doubted that he was having an affair: indeed, he lived with the princess more than two full years, and they had two children; the first, a girl, they named Aurora (Dawn), and the second, a boy, they named Day, because he looked even more beautiful than his sister.

The queen, in order to make her son own up, remarked to him several times that people had to seek pleasure in their lives, but he never dared to entrust his secret to her; though he loved her, he was afraid of her, because she was of ogre ancestry, and the king had married her solely for her large dowry; it was even whispered in the court that she had an ogre's propensities, and that when she saw little children go by, it was all that she could do to keep from pouncing on them; and so, the prince never wanted to confess.

But after the king died, which happened two years later, and he found himself in command, he publicly declared his marriage, and set out in great pomp to fetch his wife, now queen, from her castle. He was given a magnificent public reception in his capital, where she entered flanked by her two children.

Not long afterward, the new king went to wage war on his neighbor, the emperor Cantalabutte. He left the governance of the kingdom to the queen mother, urging her warmly to look after his wife and children; his campaign was to last all summer. As soon as he was gone, the queen mother sent her daughter-in-law and her children to a country house in the woods, in order to assuage her unspeakable desire more easily. She went there a few days later, and one evening she said to her majordomo:

"Tomorrow for dinner I want to eat little Aurora."

"Oh, madam!" the majordomo exclaimed.

"I insist," said the queen (and she said it with the tone of an ogress yearning to eat fresh meat), "and I want to eat her with sauce Robert."[20]

Seeing that it was unsafe to stand up to an ogress, the poor man took his big knife and went upstairs to little Aurora's room; at the time, she was four; she ran over to hug him, skipping and laughing, and asked him for candy. He started to cry, the knife slipped from his hands, and he went into the farmyard to cut a little lamb's throat; he made such a good sauce for it that his mistress assured him she had never eaten anything so good. At the same time he had taken away little Aurora, giving her to his wife to hide in the lodge she lived in at the end of the farmyard.

---

[20]Made with butter, onions, and spices; an accompaniment for roast pork and other meats.

Huit jours après la méchante reine dit à son maître d'hôtel:

«Je veux manger à mon souper le petit Jour.»

Il ne répliqua pas, résolu de la tromper comme l'autre fois; il alla chercher le petit Jour, et le trouva avec un petit fleuret à la main, dont il faisait des armes avec un gros singe; il n'avait pourtant que trois ans. Il le porta à sa femme qui le cacha avec la petite Aurore, et donna à la place du petit Jour un petit chevreau fort tendre, que l'ogresse trouva admirablement bon.

Cela était fort bien allé jusque-là; mais un soir cette méchante reine dit au maître d'hôtel:

«Je veux manger la reine à la même sauce que ses enfants.»

Ce fut alors que le pauvre maître d'hôtel désespéra de la pouvoir encore tromper. La jeune reine avait vingt ans passés, sans compter les cent ans qu'elle avait dormi: sa peau était un peu dure, quoique belle et blanche; et le moyen de trouver dans la ménagerie une bête aussi dure que cela? Il prit la résolution, pour sauver sa vie, de couper la gorge à la reine, et monta dans sa chambre, dans l'intention de n'en pas faire à deux fois; il s'excitait à la fureur, et entra le poignard à la main dans la chambre de la jeune reine. Il ne voulut pourtant point la surprendre, et il lui dit avec beaucoup de respect l'ordre qu'il avait reçu de la reine-mère.

«Faites votre devoir, lui dit-elle, en lui tendant le col; exécutez l'ordre qu'on vous a donné; j'irai revoir mes enfants, mes pauvres enfants que j'ai tant aimés»; car elle les croyait morts depuis qu'on les avait enlevés sans lui rien dire.

«Non, non, madame, lui répondit le pauvre maître d'hôtel tout attendri, vous ne mourrez point, et vous ne laisserez pas d'aller revoir vos chers enfants, mais ce sera chez moi où je les ai cachés, et je tromperai encore la reine, en lui faisant manger une jeune biche en votre place.»

Il la mena aussitôt à sa chambre, où la laissant embrasser ses enfants et pleurer avec eux, il alla accommoder une biche, que la reine mangea à son soupé, avec le même appétit que si c'eût été la jeune reine. Elle était bien contente de sa cruauté, et elle se préparait à dire au roi, à son retour, que les loups enragés avaient mangé la reine sa femme et ses deux enfants.

Un soir qu'elle rôdait à son ordinaire dans les cours et basses-cours du château pour y halener quelque viande fraîche, elle entendit dans une salle basse le petit Jour qui pleurait, parce que la reine sa mère le voulait faire fouetter, à cause qu'il avait été méchant, et elle entendit aussi la petite Aurore qui demandait pardon pour son frère. L'ogresse

A week later, the evil queen said to her majordomo:

"For supper I want to eat little Day."

He didn't answer back, since he was resolved to deceive her like the previous time; he went to get little Day and found him with a little fencing foil in his hand, practicing with a big monkey as his adversary; and he was only three! He took him to his wife, who hid him with little Aurora, and, in place of little Day, he served up a very tender kidling, which the ogress found extremely tasty.

Up till then, things had gone very well; but one evening that evil queen said to the majordomo:

"I want to eat the queen with the same sauce as her children."

It was then that the poor majordomo despaired of being able to fool her again. The young queen was over twenty, not counting the hundred years that she had slept: her skin was a little tough, though it was beautiful and white; and how could he find in the farmyard an animal as tough as that? To save his own life, he determined to cut the young queen's throat, and went up to her room with the intention of getting it over with at once; he was working himself up into a frenzy, and entered the young queen's room dagger in hand. And yet he didn't wantn to kill her unawares, and with great respect he reported to her the orders he had received from the queen mother.

"Do your duty," she said to him, extending her neck toward him; "execute the orders you have been given; I shall see my children again, those poor children I loved so much" (for she thought they were dead, after they had been taken away with no word to her).

"No, no, my lady," the poor majordomo replied with great emotion, "you shall not die, and you *will* see your dear children again, but at my house, where I've hidden them; and I'll deceive the queen again by serving her a young doe instead of you."

Immediately he brought her to his room, where he left her embracing her children and weeping with them, while he went to dress a doe, which the queen ate for her supper with just as much appetite as if it had been the young queen. She was very satisfied with her cruelty, and she was preparing to tell the king on his return that maddened wolves had eaten his wife the queen and her two children.

One evening, while she was roaming through the château's courtyards and farmyards, as was her wont, in order to scent some fresh meat, she heard little Day crying in a downstairs room because his mother the queen wanted to whip him for doing something naughty; and she also heard little Aurora begging forgiveness for her brother. The ogress recognized the voices of the queen and her children, and,

reconnut la voix de la reine et de ses enfants, et furieuse d'avoir été trompée, elle commande dès le lendemain au matin, avec une voix épouvantable qui faisait trembler tout le monde, qu'on apportât au milieu de la cour une grande cuve, qu'elle fit remplir de crapauds, de vipères, de couleuvres et de serpents, pour y faire jeter la reine et ses enfants, le maître d'hôtel, sa femme et sa servante: elle avait donné ordre de les amener les mains liées derrière le dos.

Ils étaient là, et les bourreaux se préparaient à les jeter dans la cuve, lorsque le roi, qu'on n'attendait pas si tôt, entra dans la cour à cheval; il était venu en poste, et demanda tout étonné ce que voulait dire cet horrible spectacle; personne n'osait l'en instruire, quand l'ogresse, engragée de voir ce qu'elle voyait, se jeta elle-même la tête la première dans la cuve, et fut dévorée en un instant par les vilaines bêtes qu'elle y avait fait mettre. Le roi ne laissa pas d'en être fâché: elle était sa mère; mais il s'en consola bientôt avec sa belle femme et ses enfants.

Moralité

Attendre quelque temps pour avoir un époux,
    Riche, bien fait, galant et doux,
    La chose es assez naturelle,
Mais l'attendre cent ans, et toujours en dormant,
    On ne trouve plus de femelle,
    Qui dormît si tranquillement.

La fable semble encor vouloir nous faire entendre,
Que souvent de l'hymen les agréables nœuds,
Pour étre différés, n'en sont pas moins heureux,
    Et qu'on ne perd rien pour attendre;
    Mais le sexe avec tant d'ardeur,
    Aspire à la foi conjugale,
Que je n'ai pas la force ni le cœur,
    De lui prêcher cette morale.

furious at having been fooled, the very next morning, with a frightening voice that made everyone tremble, she ordered a large vat to be placed in the middle of the courtyard, and had it filled with toads, vipers, snakes, and serpents, intending to throw into it the queen and her children, and the majordomo with his wife and their maid: she had given orders to bring them with their hands tied behind their backs.

There they were, and the executioners were preparing to throw them into the vat, when the king, who wasn't expected so soon, rode into the courtyard; he had made the journey with post horses. Amazed, he asked what was the meaning of that awful sight; no one dared enlighten him, until the ogress, furious at what she saw, dived into the vat head first, and was instantly devoured by the vile animals she had had put in it. The king was grieved all the same: after all, she was his mother. But he soon consoled himself with his beautiful wife and his children.

Moral

To wait awhile for a husband
 who is rich, handsome, gallant, and tender,
 is something quite natural.
But to wait for him a hundred years, asleep the whole time:
 nowadays there are no longer any women
 who would sleep that calmly.

It seems that the story also wants to give us to understand
that frequently, though the pleasant bonds of matrimony
may be deferred, they are no less enjoyable for that,
 and nothing is lost by waiting;
 but women yearn for the nuptial state
 with so much ardor
that I have neither the strength nor the heart
 to preach such a moral to them.

Le Petit Chaperon Rouge

Il était une fois une petite fille de village, le plus jolie qu'on eût su voir; sa mère en était folle, et sa mère-grand plus folle encore. Cette bonne femme lui fit faire un petit chaperon rouge, qui lui seyait si bien, que partout on l'appelait le Petit Chaperon Rouge.

Un jour sa mère, ayant cuit et fait des galettes, lui dit:

«Va voir comme se porte ta mère-grand, car on m'a dit qu'elle était malade, porte-lui une galette et ce petit pot de beurre.»

Le Petit Chaperon Rouge partit aussitôt pour aller chez sa mère-grand, qui demeurait dans un autre village. En passant dans un bois elle rencontra compère le loup, qui eut bien envie de la manger; mais il n'osa, à cause de quelques bûcherons qui étaient dans la forêt. Il lui demanda où elle allait; la pauvre enfant, qui ne savait pas qu'il est dangereux de s'arrêter à écouter un loup, lui dit:

«Je vais voir ma mère-grand, et lui porter une galette avec un petit pot de beurre que ma mère lui envoie.

—Demeure-t-elle bien loin? lui dit le loup.

—Oh! oui, dit le Petit Chaperon Rouge, c'est par-delà le moulin que vous voyez tout là-bas, là-bas, à la première maison du village.

—Hé bien, dit le loup, je veux l'aller voir aussi; je m'y en vais par ce chemin ici, et toi par ce chemin-là, et nous verrons qui plus tôt y sera.»

Le loup se mit à courir de toute sa force par le chemin qui était le plus court, et la petite fille s'en alla par le chemin le plus long, s'amusant à cueillir des noisettes, à courir après des papillons, et à faire des bouquets des petites fleurs qu'elle rencontrait.

Le loup ne fut pas longtemps à arriver à la maison de la mère-grand; il heurte: Toc, toc.

«Qui est là?

—C'est votre fille le Petit Chaperon Rouge (dit le loup, en contre-

Little Red Hood [Little Red Riding Hood]

There was once a little village girl, the prettiest you could get to see; her mother doted on her, and her grandmother even more so. That good woman had a little red hood[21] made for her which was so becoming to her that she was universally called Little Red Hood.

One day, her mother having baked and made some round, flat biscuits, said to her:

"Go see how your grandmother is feeling, because I've been told she was ill; take her a biscuit and this little pot of butter."

Little Red Hood set out immediately to visit her grandmother, who lived in another village. While crossing a forest, she met Godfather Wolf, who had a real urge to eat her, but didn't dare to, because there were a few woodcutters in the forest. He asked her where she was going; the poor girl, who didn't know that it's dangerous to stop and listen to a wolf, said:

"I'm going to see my grandmother and bring her a biscuit with a little pot of butter that my mother is sending her."

"Does she live very far away?" the wolf asked.

"Oh, yes," said Little Red Hood, "it's past the mill you see way over there, the first house in the village."

"All right," said the wolf, "I want to visit her, too; I'll take this path here, and you take that path there, and we'll see who gets there first."

The wolf started running as fast as he could down the shorter path, and the little girl took the longer path, killing time by gathering hazelnuts, chasing butterflies, and making bouquets from the little flowers she came across.

The wolf soon arrived at her grandmother's house; he knocked: "Rap, rap."

"Who is it?"

"It's your granddaughter, Little Red Hood," said the wolf, dis-

---

[21]On the nature of this headgear, and theories about it, see the Introduction.

133

faisant sa voix) qui vous apporte une galette et un petit pot de beurre que ma mère vous envoie.»

La bonne mère-grand, qui était dans son lit à cause qu'elle se trouvait un peu mal, lui cria:

«Tire la chevillette, la bobinette cherra.»

Le loup tira le chevillette, et la porte s'ouvrit. Il se jeta sur la bonne femme, et la dévora en moins de rien; car il y avait plus de trois jours qu'il n'avait mangé. Ensuite il ferma la porte, et s'alla coucher dans le lit de la mère-grand, en attendant le Petit Chaperon Rouge, qui quelque temps après vint heurter à la porte. Toc, toc.

«Qui est là?»

Le Petit Chaperon Rouge, qui entendit la grosse voix du loup, eut peur d'abord, mais croyant que sa mère-grand était enrhumée, répondit:

«C'est votre fille le Petit Chaperon Rouge, qui vous apporte une galette et un petit pot de beurre que ma mère vous envoie.»

Le loup lui cria en adoucissant un peu sa voix:

«Tire la chevillette, la bobinette cherra.»

Le Petit Chaperon Rouge tira la chevillette, et la porte s'ouvrit.

Le loup, la voyant entrer, lui dit en se cachant dans le lit sous la couverture:

«Mets la galette et le petit pot de beurre sur la huche, et viens te coucher avec moi.»

Le Petit Chaperon Rouge se déshabille, et va se mettre dans le lit, où elle fut bien étonnée de voir comment sa mère-grand était faite en son déshabillé. Elle lui dit:

«Ma mère-grand, que vous avez de grands bras!

—C'est pour mieux t'embrasser, ma fille.

—Ma mère-grand, que vous avez de grandes jambes!

—C'est pour mieux courir, mon enfant.

—Ma mère-grand, que vous avez de grandes oreilles!

—C'est pour mieux écouter, mon enfant.

—Ma mère-grand, que vous avez de grands yeux!

—C'est pour mieux voir, mon enfant.

—Ma mère-grand, que vous avez de grandes dents!

—C'est pour te manger.»

Et en disant ces mots, ce méchant loup se jeta sur le Petit Chaperon Rouge, et la mangea.

guising his voice, "bringing you a biscuit and a little pot of butter that my mother is sending you."

Her good grandmother, who was in bed because she felt somewhat poorly, shouted:

"Pull the little peg, and the little latch will open."

The wolf pulled on the peg, and the door opened. He pounced on the good woman and devoured her in no time at all, for he hadn't eaten for over three days. Then he locked the door and lay down in the grandmother's bed to wait for Little Red Hood, who knocked at the door, "Rap, rap," not long afterward.

"Who is it?"

Little Red Hood, hearing the wolf's husky voice, was frightened at first, but, thinking that her grandmother had a cold, answered:

"It's your granddaughter, Little Red Hood, bringing you a biscuit and a little pot of butter that my mother is sending you."

The wolf shouted to her, softening his voice a little:

"Pull the little peg, and the little latch will open."

Little Red Hood pulled on the peg, and the door opened.

The wolf, seeing her come in, hid under the blanket in bed, saying:

"Put the biscuit and the little pot of butter on the bread bin, and come in bed with me."

Little Red Hood got undressed and climbed into bed, where she was very surprised at the way her grandmother looked in her night clothes. She said:

"Grandmother, what big arms you have!"

"The better to hug you with, granddaughter."

"Grandmother, what big legs you have!"

"The better to run with, child."

"Grandmother, what big ears you have!"

"The better to hear with, child."

"Grandmother, what big eyes you have!"

"The better to see with, child."

"Grandmother, what big teeth you have!"

"The better to eat you with!"

And saying that, the wicked wolf pounced on Little Red Hood and ate her.

Moralité

> On voit ici que de jeunes enfants,
>> Surtout de jeunes filles
>> Belles, bien faites, et gentilles,
> Font très mal d'écouter toute sorte de gens,
>> Et que ce n'est pas chose étrange,
>> S'il en est tant que le loup mange.
>> Je dis le loup, car tous les loups
>> Ne sont pas de la même sorte;
>> Il en est d'une humeur accorte,
>> Sans bruit, sans fiel et sans courroux,
>> Qui privés, complaisants et doux,
>> Suivent les jeunes demoiselles
> Jusque dans les maisons, jusque dans les ruelles;
>> Mais hélas! qui ne sait que ces loups doucereux,
>> De tous les loups sont les plus dangereux.

Moral

It is seen here that young children,
    especially young girls
    who are beautiful, shapely, and pretty,
are in the wrong when they listen to just anybody,
    and that it is not strange
    if so many are eaten by the wolf.
    I say "the wolf," because not all wolves
    are of the same type;
    there are some with affable manners,
    quiet, free of spite and anger,
    who, tame, obliging, and gentle,
    follow young ladies
even into their homes, even into their alcoves;
    but alas! everyone knows that these soft-spoken wolves
    are the most dangerous wolves of all.

La Barbe-Bleue

Il était une fois un homme qui avait de belles maisons à la ville et à la campagne, de la vaisselle d'or et d'argent, des meubles en broderie, et des carrosses tout dorés; mais par malheur cet homme avait la barbe bleue: cela le rendait si laid et si terrible, qu'il n'était ni femme ni fille qui ne s'enfuît de devant lui.

Une de ses voisines, dame de qualité, avait deux filles parfaitement belles. Il lui en demanda une en mariage, et lui laissa le choix de celle qu'elle voudrait lui donner. Elles n'en voulaient point toutes deux, et se le renvoyaient l'une à l'autre, ne pouvant se résoudre à prendre un homme qui eût la barbe bleue. Ce qui les dégoûtait encore, c'est qu'il avait déjà épousé plusieurs femmes, et qu'on ne savait ce que ces femmes étaient devenues.

La Barbe-Bleue, pour faire connaissance, les mena avec leur mère, et trois ou quatre de leurs meilleures amies, et quelques jeunes gens du voisinage, à une de ses maisons de campagne, où on demeura huit jours entiers. Ce n'était que promenades, que parties de chasse et de pêche, que danses et festins, que collations: on ne dormait point, et on passait toute la nuit à se faire des malices les uns aux autres; enfin tout alla si bien, que la cadette commença à trouver que le maître du logis n'avait plus la barbe si bleue, et que c'était un fort honnête homme. Dès qu'on fut de retour à la ville, le mariage se conclut.

Au bout d'un mois la Barbe-Bleue dit à sa femme qu'il était obligé de faire un voyage en province, de six semaines au moins, pour une affaire de conséquence; qu'il la priait de se bien divertir pendant son absence, qu'elle fît venir ses bonnes amies, qu'elle les menât à la campagne si elle voulait, que partout elle fît bonne chère.

«Voilà, lui dit-il, les clefs des deux grands garde-meubles, voilà celles de la vaisselle d'or et d'argent qui ne sert pas tous les jours, voilà

Bluebeard

There was once a man who owned beautiful town and country houses, gold and silver plate, embroidered furniture, and coaches gilded all over; but unfortunately that man had a blue beard: that made him so ugly and frightening that there was no woman or girl who didn't shun his company.

One of his neighbors, a lady of distinction, had two perfectly lovely daughters. He asked for the hand of one of them, leaving her the choice of which one she agreed to let him marry. Neither of them was the least bit willing, and each one tried to palm him off on her sister, unable to consent to marry a man with a blue beard. A fact that repelled them even more was that he had already wed several women, and no one knew what had become of them.

To bolster their acquaintance, Bluebeard brought them with their mother, and three or four of their best girlfriends, as well as several young men from the vicinity, to one of his country houses, where they spent a whole week. All they did was go riding, hunting, and fishing, attend dances and banquets, and eat late suppers: they didn't sleep, but spent the whole night playing friendly jokes on one another; in short, all went so well that the younger sister began to think that the master of the house no longer had such a blue beard, and that he was a thoroughly respectable man. As soon as they were back in town, the wedding was celebrated.

A month later, Bluebeard told his wife that he was compelled to take a trip to the provinces, for at least six weeks, on important business; he urged her to have a good time while he was away, to invite her close girlfriends, to take them to the country if she wished, but, wherever she was, to enjoy herself thoroughly.

"Here," he said to her, "are the keys to the two big furniture store-rooms;[22] here are those to the gold and silver plate that we don't use

---

[22]Containing furniture, suitable for other seasons, not in current use.

celles de mes coffres-forts, où est mon or et mon argent, celles des cassettes où sont mes pierreries, et voilà le passe-partout de tous les appartements. Pour cette petite clef-ci, c'est la clef du cabinet au bout de la grande galerie de l'appartement bas; ouvrez tout, allez partout, mais pour ce petit cabinet, je vous défends d'y entrer, et je vous le défends de telle sorte, que s'il vous arrive de l'ouvrir, il n'y a rien que vous ne deviez attendre de ma colère.»

Elle promit d'observer exactement tout ce qui lui venait d'être ordonné; et lui, après l'avoir embrassée, il monte dans son carrosse, et part pour son voyage.

Les voisines et les bonnes amies n'attendirent pas qu'on les envoyât quérir pour aller chez la jeune mariée, tant elles avaient d'impatience de voir toutes les richesses de sa maison, n'ayant osé y venir pendant que le mari y était, à cause de sa barbe bleue qui leur faisait peur. Les voilà aussitôt à parcourir les chambres, les cabinets, les garde-robes, toutes plus belles et plus riches les unes que les autres. Elles montèrent ensuite aux garde-meubles, où elles ne pouvaient assez admirer le nombre et la beauté des tapisseries, des lits, des sofas, des cabinets, des guéridons, des tables et des miroirs, où l'on se voyait depuis les pieds jusqu'à la tête, et dont les bordures, les unes de glace, les autres d'argent et de vermeil doré, étaient les plus belles et les plus magnifiques qu'on eût jamais vues. Elles ne cessaient d'exagérer et d'envier le bonheur de leur amie, qui cependant ne se divertissait point à voir toutes ces richesses, à cause de l'impatience qu'elle avait d'aller ouvrir le cabinet de l'appartement bas.

Elle fut si pressée de sa curiosité, que sans considérer qu'il était malhonnête de quitter sa compagnie, elle y descendit par un petit escalier dérobé, et avec tant de précipitation, qu'elle pensa se rompre le cou deux ou trois fois. Étant arrivée à la porte du cabinet, elle s'y arrêta quelque temps, songeant à la défense que son mari lui avait faite, et considérant qu'il pourrait lui arriver malheur d'avoir été désobéissante; mais la tentation était si forte qu'elle ne put la surmonter: elle prit donc la petite clef, et ouvrit en tremblant la porte du cabinet.

D'abord elle ne vit rien, parce que les fenêtres étaient fermées; après quelques moments elle commença à voir que le plancher était tout couvert de sang caillé, et que dans ce sang se miraient les corps de plusieurs femmes mortes et attachées le long des murs (c'était toutes les femmes que la Barbe-Bleue avait épousées et qu'il avait égorgées l'une après l'autre). Elle pensa mourir de peur, et la clef du cabinet qu'elle venait de retirer de la serrure lui tomba de la main. Après avoir un peu repris ses esprits, elle ramassa la clef, referma la

every day; here are those to my strongboxes, which contains my gold and silver, and those to the cases with my precious stones, and here is the master key to all the apartments. As for this little key, it's the key to the little room at the end of the long gallery in the downstairs apartment; open anything, go anywhere, but as for that little room, I forbid you to enter it, and my prohibition is such that, if you happen to open it, nothing I may do in my anger should surprise you."

She promised to obey faithfully all the orders she had just received from him; he, after embracing her, got into his coach and left on his trip.

The young wife's female neighbors and close friends didn't wait to be sent for to visit her, so impatient were they to see all the riches of her mansion; they hadn't ventured to come while her husband was there, because of his blue beard, which frightened them. Immediately they began examining the bedrooms, boudoirs, and wardrobes, each one more beautiful and sumptuous than the one before. Then they went upstairs to the furniture storerooms, where they couldn't marvel enough at the quantity and beauty of the tapestries, beds, sofas, chests of drawers, pedestal tables, dinner tables, and mirrors in which they could see themselves from head to foot, and whose frames, some of plate glass and some of silver and silver-gilt, were the most beautiful and magnificent they had ever seen. They didn't stop exaggerating and envying the happiness of their friend, who nevertheless wasn't enjoying herself in the least at the sight of all that wealth, because of her impatience to go and open the little room in the downstairs apartment.

She was so overcome by curiosity that, not stopping to reflect that it was impolite to leave her company, she ran down a little hidden staircase, and so impetuously that, two or three times, she almost broke her neck. Reaching the door to the little room, she halted there for awhile, recalling her husband's prohibition, and reflecting that a misfortune could result from her disobedience; but the temptation was so strong that she couldn't resist it: so she took the little key and, all a-tremble, opened the door to the room.

At first she saw nothing because the windows were shut; in a few moments she began to notice that the floor was all covered with clotted blood, and that the blood mirrored the bodies of several dead women hanging against the walls (they were all the women Bluebeard had married and killed one after the other). She thought she would die of fear, and the key to the room, which she had just removed from the lock, fell out of her hand. After pulling herself together somewhat, she picked up the key, locked the door again, and went up to her room

porte, et monta à sa chambre pour se remettre un peu; mais elle n'en pouvait venir à bout, tant elle était émue.

Ayant remarqué que la clef du cabinet était tachée de sang, elle l'essuya deux ou trois fois, mais le sang ne s'en allait point; elle eut beau la laver, et même la frotter avec du sablon et avec du grès, il y demeura toujours du sang, car la clef était fée, et il n'y avait pas moyen de la nettoyer tout à fait: quand on ôtait le sang d'un côté, il revenait de l'autre.

La Barbe-Bleue revint de son voyage dès le soir même, et dit qu'il avait reçu des lettres dans le chemin, qui lui avaient appris que l'affaire pour laquelle il était parti venait d'être terminée à son avantage. Sa femme fit tout ce qu'elle put pour lui témoigner qu'elle était ravie de son prompt retour.

Le lendemain il lui redemanda les clefs, et elle les lui donna, mais d'une main si tremblante, qu'il devina sans peine tout ce qui s'était passé.

«D'où vient, lui dit-il, que la clef du cabinet n'est point avec les autres?

—Il faut, dit-elle, que je l'aie laissée là-haut sur ma table.

—Ne manquez pas, dit la Barbe-Bleue, de me la donner tantôt.»

Après plusieurs remises, il fallut apporter la clef. La Barbe-Bleue, l'ayant considérée, dit à sa femme:

«Pourquoi y a-t-il du sang sur cette clef?

—Je n'en sais rien, répondit la pauvre femme, plus pâle que la mort.

—Vous n'en savez rien, reprit la Barbe-Bleue, je le sais bien, moi; vous avez voulu entrer dans le cabinet! Hé bien, madame, vous y entrerez, et irez prendre votre place auprès des dames que vous y avez vues.»

Elle se jeta aux pieds de son mari, en pleurant et en lui demandant pardon, avec toutes les marques d'un vrai repentir de n'avoir pas été obéissante. Elle aurait attendri un rocher, belle et affligée comme elle était; mais la Barbe-Bleue avait le cœur plus dur qu'un rocher.

«Il faut mourir, madame, lui dit-il, et tout à l'heure.

—Puisqu'il faut mourir, répondit-elle, en le regardant les yeux baignés de larmes, donnez-moi un peu de temps pour prier Dieu.

—Je vous donne un demi-quart d'heure, reprit la Barbe-Bleue, mais pas un moment davantage.»

Lorsqu'elle fut seule, elle appela sa sœur, et lui dit:

«Ma sœur Anne (car elle s'appelait ainsi), monte, je te prie, sur le haut de la tour, pour voir si mes frères ne viennent point; ils m'ont

to recover for awhile; but she didn't succeed in doing so, her shock being too great.

Noticing that the key to the little room was stained with blood, she wiped it two or three times, but the blood wouldn't go away; it was in vain that she washed it, and even scoured it with sand and grit; a little blood remained on it, because the key was enchanted, and there was no way to clean it altogether: whenever the blood was removed on one side, it reappeared on the other.

Bluebeard returned from his trip that very evening, saying he had received letters on the way informing him that his law case, the reason for his journey, had just been settled to his advantage. His wife did all she could to assure him she was delighted by his speedy return.

The next day, he asked to have the keys back again, and she gave them to him, but her hand was trembling so hard that he easily guessed all that had happened.

"How is it," he said, "that the key to the little room isn't with the others?"

She replied: "I must have left it upstairs on my table."

"Don't fail to give it to me later," said Bluebeard.

After several intentional delays, she had to bring the key. Upon studying it, Bluebeard asked his wife:

"Why is there blood on this key?"

"I have no idea," replied the poor woman, paler than death.

"You have no idea," countered Bluebeard, "but I have a very good idea: you decided to enter the little room! Very well, ma'am, you shall enter it and take your place alongside the ladies you saw there."

She threw herself at her husband's feet, weeping and begging his forgiveness, with every sign of true repentance for her disobedience. She would have softened a stone, she was so beautiful and sorrowful; but Bluebeard's heart was harder than a stone.

"You must die, ma'am," he said, "and at once."

"Since I must die," she replied, looking at him with tear-filled eyes, "grant me a little time in which to pray to God."

"I grant you ten minutes," Bluebeard replied, "but not a moment more."

When she was alone, she called over her sister and said to her:

"Sister Anne" (that was her name), "please climb to the top of the tower and see whether my brothers are coming; they promised to visit me today, and if you see them, wave to them to put on speed."

promis qu'ils me viendraient voir aujourd'hui, et si tu les vois, fais-leur signe de se hâter.»

La sœur Anne monta sur le haut de la tour, et la pauvre affligée lui criait de temps en temps:

«Anne, ma sœur Anne, ne vois-tu rien venir?»

Et la sœur Anne lui répondait:

«Je ne vois rien que le soleil qui poudroie, et l'herbe qui verdoie.»

Cependant la Barbe-Bleue, tenant un grand coutelas à sa main, criait de toute sa force à sa femme:

«Descends vite, ou je monterai là-haut.

—Encore un moment, s'il vous plaît», lui répondait sa femme; et aussitôt elle criait tout bas:

«Anne, ma sœur Anne, ne vois-tu rien venir?»

Et la sœur Anne répondait:

«Je ne vois rien que le soleil qui poudroie, et l'herbe qui verdoie.»

«Descends donc vite, criait la Barbe-Bleue, ou je monterai là-haut.

—Je m'en vais» répondait sa femme, et puis elle criait:

«Anne, ma sœur Anne, ne vois-tu rien venir?

—Je vois, répondit la sœur Anne, une grosse poussière qui vient de ce côté-ci.

—Sont-ce mes frères?

—Hélas! non ma sœur, c'est un troupeau de moutons.

—Ne veux-tu pas descendre? criait la Barbe-Bleue.

—Encore un moment», répondait sa femme; et puis elle criait:

«Anne, ma sœur Anne, ne vois-tu rien venir?

—Je vois, répondit-elle, deux cavaliers qui viennent de ce côté-ci, mais ils sont bien loin encore . . . Dieu soit loué, s'écria-t-elle un moment après, ce sont mes frères; je leur fais signe tant que je puis de se hâter.»

La Barbe-Bleue se mit à crier si fort que toute la maison en trembla. La pauvre femme descendit, et alla se jeter à ses pieds toute éplorée et toute échevelée.

«Cela ne sert de rien, dit la Barbe-Bleue, il faut mourir.»

Puis la prenant d'une main par les cheveux, et de l'autre levant le coutelas en l'air, il allait lui abattre la tête. La pauvre femme se tournant vers lui, et le regardant avec des yeux mourants, le pria de lui donner un petit moment pour se recueillir.

«Non, non, dit-il, recommande-toi bien à Dieu»; et levant son bras . . . Dans ce moment on heurta si fort à la porte, que la Barbe-Bleue s'arrêta tout court: on ouvrit, et aussitôt on vit entrer deux cavaliers, qui mettant l'épée à la main, coururent droit à la Barbe-Bleue.

Sister Anne climbed to the top of the tower, while her poor, sorrowful sister called to her from time to time:

"Anne, sister Anne, don't you see anything coming?"

And sister Anne would reply:

"All I see is the sun raising dust and the grass growing green."

Meanwhile, Bluebeard, holding a big cutlass in his hand, kept shouting to his wife as loud as he could:

"Come right down, or I'm coming up there!"

"Just another moment, please," his wife would reply; and at once she would call quietly:

"Anne, sister Anne, don't you see anything coming?"

And sister Anne would reply:

"All I see is the sun raising dust and the grass growing green."

"Come down, I say," Bluebeard was calling, "or I'm coming up there!"

"I'll be right there," his wife would reply, and then she would call:

"Anne, sister Anne, don't you see anything coming?"

"I see," replied sister Anne, "a cloud of dust coming in this direction."

"Is it my brothers?"

"Alas, no, sister, it's a flock of sheep."

"Aren't you coming down?" Bluebeard was yelling.

"Another moment," his wife replied; then she called:

"Anne, sister Anne, don't you see anything coming?"

"I see," she replied, "two horsemen coming in this direction, but they're still very far away. . . . Praised be God!" she exclaimed a moment later, "it's my brothers; I'm beckoning to them the best I can to make haste."

Bluebeard began shouting so loud that it made the whole house shake. The poor woman came downstairs and threw herself at his feet, all in tears and disheveled.

"That will do you no good," said Bluebeard; "you must die." Then, grasping her hair with one hand and lifting up his cutlass with the other, he prepared to cut off her head. The poor woman, turning toward him and looking at him with eyes that were glazing over, begged him to grant her a brief moment for religious meditation.

"No, no," he said, "commend your spirit to God," and, raising his arm. . . . At that moment, there was such a loud knock at the door that Bluebeard stopped short: the door was opened, and immediately two horsemen were seen to come in, who drew their swords and ran straight over to Bluebeard.

Il reconnut que c'était les frères de sa femme, l'un dragon et l'autre mousquetaire, de sorte qu'il s'enfuit aussitôt pour se sauver; mais les deux frères le poursuivirent de si près, qu'ils l'attrapèrent avant qu'il pût gagner le perron. Ils lui passèrent leur épée au travers du corps, et le laissèrent mort. La pauvre femme était presque aussi morte que son mari, et n'avait pas la force de se lever pour embrasser ses frères.

Il se trouva que la Barbe-Bleue n'avait point d'héritiers, et qu'ainsi sa femme demeura maîtresse de tous ses biens. Elle en employa une partie à marier sa sœur Anne avec un jeune gentilhomme, dont elle était aimée depuis longtemps; une autre partie à acheter des charges de capitaine à ses deux frères; et le reste à se marier elle-même à un fort honnête homme, qui lui fit oublier le mauvais temps qu'elle avait passé avec la Barbe-Bleue.

Moralité

La curiosité malgré tous ses attraits,
    Coûte souvent bien des regrets;
On en voit tous les jours mille exemples paraître.
C'est, n'en déplaise au sexe, un plaisir bien léger;
    Dès qu'on le prend il cesse d'être,
    Et toujours il coûte trop cher.

Autre moralité

    Pour peu qu'on ait l'esprit sensé,
Et que du monde on sache le grimoire,
    On voit bientôt que cette histoire
    Est un conte du temps passé;
    Il n'est plus d'époux si terrible,
    Ni qui demande l'impossible,
    Fût-il malcontent et jaloux.
Près de sa femme on le voit filer doux;
Et de quelque couleur que sa barbe puisse être,
On a peine à juger qui des deux est le maître.

He recognized them as his wife's brothers, one a dragoon and the other a musketeer, so that he instantly fled to save his life; but the two brothers pursued him so closely that they caught him before he could reach the front steps. They pierced his body with their swords and left him lying there dead. The poor woman was nearly as dead as her husband, and didn't have the strength to get up and embrace her brothers.

It turned out that Bluebeard had no heirs, and so his wife became the owner of all his assets. She used some of the money to marry her sister Anne to a young nobleman who had long loved her; another sum to purchase commissions[23] as captain for her two brothers; and the rest to remarry with a most respectable man, who made her forget the bad days she had spent with Bluebeard.

Moral

Despite all its attractions, curiosity
*   often leads to regrets;*
every day a thousand examples come to our notice.
May this not displease the ladies: it is a very unsubstantial pleasure;
*   the moment you indulge it, it ceases to exist,*
*   and it is always too costly.*

Second Moral

*   Anyone who has the least bit of common sense,*
and is familiar with the ways of the world,
*   will soon see that this story*
*   is a tale of days long gone by;*
*   such a fearsome husband no longer exists,*
*   or one who asks the impossible,*
*   even though he may be disgruntled and jealous.*
*   In his wife's company he is meek and mild;*
and whatever color his beard may be,
it is hard to tell which of the two is the master.

---

[23]This was not only legal, but normal practice at the time.

Le Maître Chat ou Le Chat Botté

Un meunier ne laissa pour tous biens à trois enfants qu'il avait, que son moulin, son âne, et son chat. Les partages furent bientôt faits, ni le notaire, ni le procureur n'y furent point appelés. Ils auraient eu bientôt mangé tout le pauvre patrimoine. L'aîné eut le moulin, le second eut l'âne, et le plus jeune n'eut que le chat.

Ce dernier ne pouvait se consoler d'avoir un si pauvre lot:

«Mes frères, disait-il, pourront gagner leur vie honnêtement en se mettant ensemble; pour moi, lorsque j'aurai mangé mon chat, et que je me serai fait un manchon de sa peau, il faudra que je meure de faim.»

Le chat qui entendait ce discours, mais qui n'en fit pas semblant, lui dit d'un air posé et sérieux:

«Ne vous affligez point, mon maître, vous n'avez qu'à me donner un sac, et me faire faire une paire de bottes pour aller dans les broussailles, et vous verrez que vous n'êtes pas si mal partagé que vous croyez.»

Quoique le maître du chat ne fît pas grand fond là-dessus, il lui avait vu faire tant de tours de souplesse, pour prendre des rats et des souris, comme quand il se pendait par les pieds, ou qu'il se cachait dans la farine pour faire le mort, qu'il ne désespéra pas d'en être secouru dans sa misère.

Lorsque le chat eut ce qu'il avait demandé, il se botta bravement, et mettant son sac à son cou, il en prit les cordons avec ses deux pattes de devant, et s'en alla dans une garenne où il y avait grand nombre de lapins. Il mit du son et des lacerons dans son sac, et s'étendant comme s'il eût été mort, il attendit que quelque jeune lapin, peu instruit encore des ruses de ce monde, vînt se fourrer dans son sac pour manger ce qu'il y avait mis.

The Capable[24] Cat; or, Puss in Boots

To the three children he had, a miller left, as his entire property, his mill, his donkey, and his cat. The division of goods didn't take long, and no notary or attorney had to be called in; they would have soon consumed the whole skimpy patrimony. The eldest received the mill, the second son received the donkey, and the youngest was left with nothing but the cat.

He couldn't console himself for ending up with such a miserable share, and he often said:

"My brothers will be able to make a decent living by pooling their resources; as for me, once I've eaten my cat and made a muff out of its fur, I'll have to die of hunger."

The cat, hearing that soliloquy but pretending not to, said to him in a sedate, serious manner:

"Don't fret, master, all you need to do is give me a pouch and have a pair of boots made for me so I can walk in the underbrush, and you'll see that your share isn't as bad as you think."

Though the cat's master placed no great reliance on that, he had seen the cat perform so many ruses in order to catch rats and mice—for instance, hanging by his paws, or hiding in the flour and playing dead—that he didn't despair of being aided by him in his poverty.

After the cat received what he had requested, he put on the boots elegantly and, throwing the pouch over his shoulder, he grasped its strings in his two front paws and went to a warren where there were rabbits in plenty. He put bran and wild lettice in his sack and, stretching out as if he were dead, he waited until some young rabbit, still unfamiliar with this world's sharp practices, should come and burrow in his pouch to eat what he had placed in it.

---

[24]See the Introduction for further possible connotations of *maître* in this title.

A peine fut-il couché, qu'il eut contentement; un jeune étourdi de lapin entra dans son sac et le Maître Chat tirant aussitôt les cordons le prit et le tua sans miséricorde.

Tout glorieux de sa proie, il s'en alla chez le roi et demanda à lui parler. On le fit monter à l'appartement de Sa Majesté, où étant entré il fit une grande révérence au roi, et lui dit:

«Voilà, sire, un lapin de garenne que monsieur le marquis de Carabas (c'était le nom qu'il lui prit en gré de donner à son mâitre) m'a chargé de vous présenter de sa part.

—Dis à ton maître, répondit le roi, que je le remercie, et qu'il me fait plaisir.»

Une autre fois, il alla se cacher dans un blé, tenant toujours son sac ouvert; et lorsque deux perdrix y furent entrées, il tira les cordons, et les prit toutes deux. Il alla ensuite les présenter au roi, comme il avait fait le lapin de garenne. Le roi reçut encore avec plaisir les deux perdrix, et lui fit donner pour boire.

Le chat continua ainsi pendant deux ou trois mois à porter de temps en temps au roi du gibier de la chasse de son maître. Un jour qu'il sut que le roi devait aller à la promenade sur le bord de la rivière avec sa fille, la plus belle princesse du monde, il dit à son maître:

«Si vous voulez suivre mon conseil, votre fortune est faite: vous n'avez qu'à vous baigner dans la rivière à l'endroit que je vous montrerai, et ensuite me laisser faire.»

Le marquis de Carabas fit ce que son chat lui conseillait, sans savoir à quoi cela serait bon. Dans le temps qu'il se baignait, le roi vint à passer, et le chat se mit à crier de toute sa force:

«Au secours, au secours, voilà monsieur le marquis de Carabas qui se noie!»

A ce cri le roi mit la tête à la portière, et reconnaissant le chat qui lui avait apporté tant de fois du gibier, il ordonna à ses gardes qu'on allât vite au secours de monsieur le marquis de Carabas.

Pendant qu'on retirait le pauvre marquis de la rivière, le chat s'approcha du carrosse, et dit au roi que dans le temps que son maître se baignait, il était venu des voleurs qui avaient emporté ses habits, quoiqu'il eût crié au voleur de toute sa force; le drôle les avait cachés sous une grosse pierre.

Le roi ordonna aussitôt aux officiers de sa garde-robe d'aller querir un de ses plus beaux habits pour monsieur le marquis de Carabas. Le roi lui fit mille caresses, et comme les beaux habits qu'on venait de lui donner relevaient sa bonne mine (car il était beau, et bien fait de sa personne), la fille du roi le trouva fort à son gré, et le comte de

Scarcely had he lain down when he was gratified; a silly young rabbit entered his pouch, and the Capable Cat immediately drew the strings, captured it, and killed it without mercy.

Beaming over his success, he went to the king's palace and asked to speak to him. He was led upstairs to His Majesty's apartment; on entering he made a low bow to the king and said:

"Sire, here is a wild rabbit that the Marquess of Carabas [that was the name he took into his head to give his master] has commissioned me to offer you on his behalf."

"Tell your master," the king replied, "that I thank him, and that he has given me pleasure."

On another occasion, the cat hid in a wheatfield, keeping his pouch open; and after two partridges had entered it, he drew the strings and caught them both. Then he went to offer them to the king, as he had done with the wild rabbit. Again, the king was pleased to receive the two partridges, and had him given a gratuity.

The cat continued in that way for two or three months to bring the king occasionally some of the game his master had bagged. One day, on which he had found out that the king was to go out for a coach ride along the riverbank with his daughter, the most beautiful princess in the world, he said to his master:

"If you want to take my advice, your fortune is made: all you have to do is bathe in the river in the spot I'll show you, and then leave the rest to me."

The Marquess of Carabas did what his cat advised, though he didn't know the purpose of it. While he was bathing, the king passed by, and the cat started to shout with all his might:

"Help! Help! The Marquess of Carabas is drowning!"

At that outcry the king put his head out of the coach window; recognizing the cat that had brought him game so many times, he ordered his guards to hasten to the rescue of the Marquess of Carabas.

While they were pulling the poor marquess out of the river, the cat approached the coach and told the king that, during the time that his master was bathing, thieves had come and made off with his clothes, even though he had shouted "Stop thief!" at the top of his voice; actually, the rascally cat had hidden them under a big rock.

The king immediately ordered his masters of the robes to go and fetch one of his most beautiful outfits for the Marquess of Carabas. The king was extremely solicitous about him; and since the beautiful clothes he had just been given set off his good looks (for he was handsome and well built physically), the king's daughter found him greatly to her liking, and

Carabas ne lui eut pas jeté deux ou trois regards fort respectueux, et un peu tendres, qu'elle en devint amoureuse à la folie.

Le roi voulut qu'il montât dans son carrosse, et qu'il fût de la promenade. Le chat ravi de voir que son dessein commençait à réussir, prit les devants, et ayant rencontré des paysans qui fauchaient un pré, il leur dit:

«Bonnes gens qui fauchez, si vous ne dites au roi que le pré que vous fauchez appartient à monsieur le marquis de Carabas, vous serez tous hachés menu comme chair à pâté.»

Le roi ne manqua pas à demander aux faucheux à qui était ce pré qu'ils fauchaient.

«C'est à monsieur le marquis de Carabas», dirent-ils tous ensemble, car la menace du chat leur avait fait peur.

«Vous avez là un bel héritage, dit le roi au marquis de Carabas.

—Vous voyez, sire, répondit le marquis, c'est un pré qui ne manque point de rapporter abondamment toutes les années.»

Le Maître Chat, qui allait toujours devant, rencontra des moissonneurs, et leur dit:

«Bonnes gens qui moissonnez, si vous ne dites pas que tous ces blés appartiennent à monsieur le marquis de Carabas, vous serez tous hachés menu comme chair à pâté.»

Le roi, qui passa un moment après, voulut savoir à qui appartenaient tous les blés qu'il voyait.

«C'est à monsieur le marquis de Carabas», répondirent les moissonneurs, et le roi s'en réjouit encore avec le marquis. Le chat, qui allait devant le carrosse, disait toujours la même chose à tous ceux qu'il rencontrait; et le roi était étonné des grands biens de monsieur le marquis de Carabas.

Le Maître Chat arriva enfin dans un beau château dont le maître était un ogre, le plus riche qu'on ait jamais vu, car toutes les terres par où le roi avait passé étaient de la dépendance de ce château. Le chat, qui eut soin de s'informer qui était cet ogre, et ce qu'il savait faire, demanda à lui parler, disant qu'il n'avait pas voulu passer si près de son château, sans avoir l'honneur de lui faire la révérence.

L'ogre le reçut aussi civilement que le peut un ogre, et le fit reposer.

«On m'a assuré, dit le chat, que vous aviez le don de vous changer en toute sorte d'animaux, que vous pouviez par exemple vous transformer en lion, en éléphant?

the Count[25] of Carabas had only cast two or three very respectful, but somewhat warm, glances at her when she fell madly in love with him.

The king insisted on his getting into the coach to join them on their ride. The cat, delighted to see that his plan was beginning to succeed, went out ahead of them; coming across some peasants who were mowing a meadow, he said to them:

"Good folk who are mowing, unless you tell the king that the meadow you're mowing belongs to the Marquess of Carabas, you'll all be chopped up fine like meat for a pâté."

The king didn't fail to ask the mowers who owned the meadow they were mowing.

"It belongs to the Marquess of Carabas," they all said at the same time, because the cat's threat had frightened them.

"That's a fine piece of land you have there," the king said to the Marquess of Carabas.

"You see, sire," the marquess replied, "it's a meadow that never fails to supply me with a substantial profit every year."

The Capable Cat, continuing to precede them, came across some harvesters, and told them:

"Good folk who are harvesting, unless you say that all this wheat belongs to the Marquess of Carabas, you'll all be chopped up fine like meat for a pâté."

When the king passed by a moment later, he asked who owned all the wheat he saw.

"It belongs to the Marquess of Carabas," the harvesters replied, and the king was even more pleased with the marquess. The cat, who preceded the coach, kept saying the same thing to everyone he met; and the king was amazed at the great extent of the Marquess of Carabas's property.

The Capable Cat finally reached a beautiful château, the owner of which was an ogre, the richest ever known, for all the land the king had passed through was part of that château's domain. The cat, who had taken care to learn who that ogre was, and what his powers were, asked to speak with him, saying that he hadn't wanted to pass so close to his château without having the honor of paying him his respects.

The ogre welcomed him as civilly as an ogre can, and asked him to sit down.

"I've been assured," the cat said, "that you have the gift of turning into any kind of animal; that, for example, you can transform yourself into a lion, or an elephant."

---

[25]This lapse (if it is one) is in the original.

—Cela est vrai, répondit l'ogre brusquement, et pour vous le montrer, vous m'allez voir devenir lion.»

Le chat fut si effrayé de voir un lion devant lui, qu'il gagna aussitôt les gouttières, non sans peine et sans péril, à cause de ses bottes qui ne valaient rien pour marcher sur les tuiles.

Quelque temps après, le chat, ayant vu que l'ogre avait quitté sa première forme, descendit, et avoua qu'il avait eu bien peur.

«On m'a assuré encore, dit le chat, mais je ne saurais le croire, que vous aviez aussi le pouvoir de prendre la forme des plus petits animaux, par exemple, de vous changer en un rat, en une souris; je vous avoue que je tiens cela tout à fait impossible.

—Impossible? reprit l'ogre, vous allez voir», et en même temps il se changea en une souris, qui se mit à courir sur le plancher. Le chat ne l'eut pas plus tôt aperçue qu'il se jeta dessus, et la mangea.

Cependant le roi, qui vit en passant le beau château de l'ogre, voulut entrer dedans. Le chat, qui entendit le bruit du carrosse qui passait sur le pont-levis, courut au-devant, et dit au roi:

«Votre Majesté soit la bienvenue dans le château de monsieur le marquis de Carabas.

—Comment, monsieur le marquis, s'écria le roi, ce château est encore à vous! il ne se peut rien de plus beau que cette cour et que tous ces bâtiments qui l'environnent; voyons les dedans, s'il vous plaît.»

Le marquis donna la main à la jeune princesse, et suivant le roi qui montait le premier, ils entrèrent dans une grande salle où ils trouvèrent une magnifique collation que l'ogre avait fait préparer pour ses amis qui le devaient venir voir ce même jour-là, mais qui n'avaient pas osé entrer, sachant que le roi y était. Le roi charmé des bonnes qualités de monsieur le marquis de Carabas, de même que sa fille qui en était folle, et voyant les grands biens qu'il possédait, lui dit, après avoir bu cinq ou six coups:

«Il ne tiendra qu'à vous, monsieur le marquis, que vous ne soyez mon gendre.»

Le marquis, faisant de grandes révérences, accepta l'honneur que lui faisait le roi; et dès le même jour épousa la princesse. Le chat devint grand seigneur, et ne courut plus après les souris, que pour se divertir.

Moralité

Quelque grand que soit l'avantage
De jouir d'un riche héritage

"It's true," the ogre replied curtly, "and to prove it to you, you'll see me become a lion."

The cat was so frightened to see a lion in front of him that he was up on the eaves in a twinkling, and not without difficulty and danger, because of his boots, which hadn't been designed for strolling on the tiles.

After awhile, seeing that the ogre had abandoned his latest shape, the cat came down and admitted that he had been thoroughly scared.

"I've also been assured," the cat said, "though I can't believe it, that you have the additional power to take the shape of the smallest animals, to change into a rat, for example, or a mouse; I confess to you that I consider that altogether impossible."

"Impossible?" the ogre countered. "You'll see!" And at that very moment he turned into a mouse, which began to scurry across the floor. No sooner had the cat caught sight of it than he pounced on it and ate it up.

Meanwhile, the king, seeing the ogre's beautiful château as he passed by, insisted on going in. The cat, hearing the rattle of the coach crossing the drawbridge, ran to meet him, and said:

"Your Majesty is welcome in the château of the Marquess of Carabas."

"What, marquess!" the king exclaimed, "you own this château as well! There can't be anything more beautiful than this courtyard and all the buildings surrounding it; let me see the inside, please."

The marquess gave his hand to the young princess and, following the king, who climbed the front steps first, they entered a spacious hall, where they found a splendid meal that the ogre had had prepared for his friends, who were due to visit him on that very day but hadn't dared to come in when they learned the king was there. The king, delighted with the Marquess of Carabas's good qualities, just like his daughter, who was madly in love with him, and seeing all the property he owned, said to him, after five or six cups of wine:

"It's completely up to you, marquess, whether or not you wish to be my son-in-law."

The marquess, making low bows, accepted the honor the king was showing him, and he married the princess that very day. The cat became a great lord and no longer chased mice, except to amuse himself.

Moral

*However great the benefits may be
of enjoying a rich inheritance*

Venant à nous de père en fils,
Aux jeunes gens pour l'ordinaire,
L'industrie et le savoir-faire
Valent mieux que des biens acquis.

Autre moralité

Si le fils d'un meunier, avec tant de vitesse,
　　Gagne le cœur d'une princesse,
Et s'en fait regarder avec des yeux mourants,
　　C'est que l'habit, la mine et la jeunesse,
　　　Pour inspirer de la tendresse,
N'en sont pas des moyens toujours indifférents.

that comes to us from father to son,
usually for young men
diligence and skill
are more valuable than inherited property.

Second Moral

If a miller's son can so rapidly
win the heart of a princess,
and is gazed at by her with amorous eyes,
it is because clothes, looks, and youth
are not always negligible means
of inspiring love.

Les fées

Il était une fois une veuve qui avait deux filles; l'aînée lui ressemblait si fort et d'humeur et de visage, que qui la voyait voyait la mère. Elles étaient toutes deux si désagréables et si orgueilleuses qu'on ne pouvait vivre avec elles. La cadette, qui était le vrait portrait de son père pour la douceur et pour l'honnêteté, était avec cela une des plus belles filles qu'on eût su voir. Comme on aime naturellement son semblable, cette mère était folle de sa fille aînée, et en même temps avait une aversion effroyable pour la cadette. Elle la faisait manger à la cuisine et travailler sans cesse.

Il fallait entre autre chose que cette pauvre enfant allât deux fois le jour puiser de l'eau à une grande demi-lieue du logis, et qu'elle en rapportât plein une grande cruche. Un jour qu'elle était à cette fontaine, il vint à elle une pauvre femme qui la pria de lui donner à boire.

«Oui-da, ma bonne mère», dit cette belle fille; et rinçant aussitôt sa cruche, elle puisa de l'eau au plus bel endroit de la fontaine, et la lui présenta, soutenant toujours la cruche afin qu'elle bût plus aisément.

La bonne femme, ayant bu, lui dit:

«Vous êtes si belle, si bonne, et si honnête, que je ne puis m'empêcher de vous faire un don (car c'était une fée qui avait pris la forme d'une pauvre femme de village, pour voir jusqu'où irait l'honnêteté de cette jeune fille). Je vous donne pour don, poursuivit la fée, qu'à chaque parole que vous direz, il vous sortira de la bouche ou une fleur, ou une pierre précieuse.»

Lorsque cette belle fille arriva au logis, sa mère la gronda de revenir si tard de la fontaine.

«Je vous demande pardon, ma mère, dit cette pauvre fille, d'avoir tardé si longtemps»; et en disant ces mots, il lui sortit de la bouche deux roses, deux perles, et deux gros diamants.

«Que vois-je là! dit sa mère toute étonnée; je crois qu'il lui sort de la bouche des perles et des diamants; d'où vient cela, ma fille?» (ce fut là la première fois qu'elle l'appela sa fille). La pauvre enfant lui

The Fairies

There was once a widow who had two daughters; the older one resembled her so greatly in character and in looks that whoever saw her, saw her mother. Both of them were so unpleasant and haughty that there was no living with them. The younger girl, who was the exact image of her father in gentleness and courtesy, was, besides, one of the most beautiful girls you could hope to see. Since people naturally like those who resemble them, this mother doted on her older daughter, and, at the same time, had a terrible aversion to the younger one. She made her eat in the kitchen and toil ceaselessly.

Among her other chores, that poor child had to go out twice a day to draw water a full mile and a half from the house and bring back a big pitcherful. One day, while she was at that spring, a poor woman came to her and asked for a drink.

"Yes, my dear lady," that beautiful girl said; and, immediately rinsing out her pitcher, she drew water from the loveliest part of the spring and offered it to her, holding up the pitcher the whole time so she could drink more easily.

The good woman, after drinking, said to her:

"You are so beautiful, good, and polite that I can't help giving you a gift" (for she was a fairy who had assumed the guise of a poor village woman in order to test the extent of that girl's courtesy). "The gift I give you," the fairy continued, "is that, with every word you speak, either a flower or a precious stone will fall from your lips."

When that beautiful girl arrived home, her mother scolded her for coming back from the spring so late.

"I beg your pardon, mother," the poor girl said, "for having lingered so long"; and, as she spoke those words, two roses, two pearls, and two big diamonds fell from her lips.

"What's this I see!" said her astonished mother; "I think pearls and diamonds are falling from her lips; how can that be, daughter?" (That was the first time she had ever called her her daughter.) The poor girl

raconta naïvement tout ce qui lui était arrivé, non sans jeter une infinité de diamants.

«Vraiment, dit la mère, il faut que j'y envoie ma fille; tenez, Fanchon, voyez ce qui sort de la bouche de votre sœur quand elle parle; ne seriez-vous pas bien aise d'avoir le même don? Vous n'avez qu'à aller puiser de l'eau à la fontaine, et quand une pauvre femme vous demandera à boire, lui en donner bien honnêtement.

—Il me ferait beau voir, répondit la brutale, aller à la fontaine.

—Je veux que vous y alliez, reprit la mère, et tout à l'heure.»

Elle y alla, mais toujours en grondant. Elle prit le plus beau flacon d'argent qui fût dans le logis. Elle ne fut pas plus tôt arrivée à la fontaine qu'elle vit sortir du bois une dame magnifiquement vêtue qui vint lui demander à boire: c'était la même fée qui avait apparu à sa sœur, mais qui avait pris l'air et les habits d'une princesse, pour voir jusqu'où irait la malhonnêteté de cette fille.

«Est-ce que je suis ici venue, lui dit cette brutale orgueilleuse, pour vous donner à boire? Justement j'ai apporté un flacon d'argent tout exprès pour donner à boire à Madame! J'en suis d'avis, buvez à même si vous voulez.

—Vous n'êtes guère honnête, reprit la fée, sans se mettre en colère; hé bien! puisque vous êtes si peu obligeante, je vous donne pour don qu'à chaque parole que vous direz, il vous sortira de la bouche ou un serpent ou un crapaud.»

D'abord que sa mère l'aperçut, elle lui cria:

«Hé bien, ma fille!

—Hé bien, ma mère! lui répondit la brutale, en jetant deux vipères, et deux crapauds.

—O Ciel! s'écria la mère, que vois-je là? C'est sa sœur qui en est cause, elle me le paiera»; et aussitôt elle courut pour la battre. La pauvre enfant s'enfuit, et alla se sauver dans la forêt prochaine. Le fils du roi qui revenait de la chasse la rencontra et la voyant si belle, lui demanda ce qu'elle faisait là toute seule et ce qu'elle avait à pleurer.

«Hélas! monsieur, c'est ma mère qui m'a chassée du logis.»

Le fils du roi, qui vit sortir de sa bouche cinq ou six perles, et autant de diamants, la pria de lui dire d'où cela lui venait. Elle lui conta toute son aventure. Le fils du roi en devint amoureux, et considérant qu'un tel don valait mieux que tout ce qu'on pouvait donner en mariage à une autre, l'emmena au palais du roi son père, où il l'épousa.

told her, with childish simplicity, all that had befallen her, not without emitting a huge number of diamonds.

"Really," her mother said, "I've got to send my daughter there; come, Fanny, see what falls from your sister's lips when she talks; wouldn't you be happy to have the same gift? All you need to do is draw water from the spring, and when a poor woman asks you for a drink, give her one very politely."

"I'd really look like something," replied the coarse girl, "going to the spring."

"I want you to go there," her mother countered, "and right this minute."

She went, but grumbling all the way. She took along the most beautiful silver flagon they had in the house. As soon as she reached the spring, she saw a magnificently attired lady emerging from the woods, who asked her for a drink: it was the same fairy that had appeared to her sister, but had now assumed the appearance and garb of a princess, in order to test the extent of that girl's discourtesy.

"Did I come here," that coarse, haughty girl said to her, "to give you a drink? Naturally, I brought along a silver flagon just for the purpose of giving *you* a drink! My opinion is that, if you're really thirsty, you can drink directly from the spring."

"You're not very polite," the fairy replied, without becoming angry. "Very well, since you are so disobliging, my gift to you is that, with every word you speak, either a serpent or a toad will fall from your lips."

As soon as her mother caught sight of her, she called out to her:

"Well, daughter?"

"It's like this, mother," the coarse girl replied, emitting two vipers and two toads.

"Oh, heavens!" her mother exclaimed; "what's this I see? It's your sister who's to blame for this, and she'll pay me for it!" And immediately she ran over to beat her. The poor child escaped and went to hide in the nearby forest. The king's son, returning from the hunt, met her and, seeing how beautiful she was, asked her what she was doing there all alone, and what reason she had to be crying.

"Alas, sir, my mother has driven me out of the house."

The king's son, seeing five or six pearls, and the same number of diamonds, falling from her lips, asked her to tell him how she had acquired that gift. She narrated her entire adventure to him. The king's son fell in love with her, and deeming a gift of that nature to be more valuable than any amount of dowry that could come with another girl, he brought her to the palace of his father the king, where he married her.

Pour sa sœur, elle se fit tant haïr, que sa propre mère la chassa de chez elle; et la malheureuse, après avoir bien couru sans trouver personne qui voulût la recevoir, alla mourir au coin d'un bois.

Moralité

> *Les diamants et les pistoles,*
> *Peuvent beaucoup sur les esprits;*
> *Cependant les douces paroles*
> *Ont encor plus de force, et sont d'un plus grand prix.*

Autre moralité

> *L'honnêteté coûte des soins,*
> *Et veut un peu de complaisance,*
> *Mais tôt ou tard elle a sa récompense,*
> *Et souvent dans le temps qu'on y pense le moins.*

As for her sister, she made herself so hated that her own mother drove her out of the house; and the wretched girl, after wandering far without finding anyone willing to take her in, went to the corner of a forest to die.

Moral

> Diamonds and ten-franc pieces
> exert great influence over people's minds;
> and yet, soft words
are even more powerful, and more valuable.

Second Moral

> Courtesy calls for taking pains
> and being somewhat indulgent,
> but sooner or later it receives its reward,
and often at the time one least expects it to.

Cendrillon ou La petite pantoufle de verre

Il était une fois un gentilhomme qui épousa en secondes noces une femme, le plus hautaine et la plus fière qu'on eût jamais vue. Elle avait deux filles de son humeur, et qui lui ressemblaient en toutes choses. Le mari avait de son côté une jeune fille, mais d'une douceur et d'une bonté sans exemple; elle tenait cela de sa mère, qui était la meilleure personne du monde.

Les noces ne furent pas plus tôt faites, que la belle-mère fit éclater sa mauvaise humeur; elle ne put souffrir les bonnes qualités de cette jeune enfant, qui rendaient ses filles encore plus haïssables. Elle la chargea des plus viles occupations de la maison: c'était elle qui nettoyait la vaisselle et les montées, qui frottait la chambre de Madame, et celles de Mesdemoiselles ses filles; elle couchait tout au haut de la maison, dans un grenier, sur une méchante paillasse, pendant que ses sœurs étaient dans des chambres parquetées, où elles avaient des lits des plus à la mode, et des miroirs où elles se voyaient depuis les pieds jusqu'à la tête. La pauvre fille souffrait tout avec patience, et n'osait s'en plaindre à son père qui l'aurait grondée, parce que sa femme le gouvernait entièrement.

Lorsqu'elle avait fait son ouvrage, elle s'allait mettre au coin de la cheminée, et s'asseoir dans les cendres, ce qui faisait qu'on l'appelait communément dans le logis Cucendron. La cadette, qui n'était pas si malhonnête que son aînée, l'appelait Cendrillon; cependant Cendrillon, avec ses méchants habits, ne laissait pas d'être cent fois plus belle que ses sœurs, quoique vêtues très magnifiquement.

Il arriva que le fils du roi donna un bal, et qu'il en pria toutes les personnes de qualité: nos deux demoiselles en furent aussi priées, car elles faisaient grande figure dans le pays. Les voilà bien aises et bien occupées à choisir les habits et les coiffures qui leur siéraient le mieux; nouvelle peine pour Cendrillon, car c'était elle qui repassait le

Cinderella; or, The Little Glass Slipper

There was once a distinguished gentleman whose second marriage was to a woman as haughty and proud as any ever known. She had two daughters who shared her character and resembled her in every way. From his first marriage, her husband had a young daughter, too, but one who was incomparably gentle and kind; in that respect she took after her mother, who had been the most agreeable woman in the world.

No sooner was the wedding over than the girl's stepmother revealed her nasty character; she couldn't abide the child's good qualities, which made her own daughters even more hateful. She assigned her the lowliest household chores: it was she who washed the dishes and scrubbed the steps, and who cleaned the bedroom of the lady of the house and those of her two misses; her own bed was all the way up in the house, in a garret, on a wretched straw mattress, while her step-sisters slept in rooms with parquet floors, where they had beds of the latest fashion and mirrors in which they could view themselves from head to foot. The poor girl endured all this patiently, never daring to complain about it to her father, who would only have scolded her, because his wife had him completely under her thumb.

After the girl had finished her work, she would go to the corner of the fireplace and sit down in the ashes, so that in the house she was generally called Cinder-Ass.[26] Her younger stepsister, who wasn't as vulgar as the older one, used to call her Cinderella; all the same, Cinderella, bad clothes and all, was still a hundred times more beautiful than her sisters, even though they dressed superbly.

It came about that the king's son gave a ball, to which he invited all people of rank: our two misses were invited, also, because they were prominent figures in that country. They were very glad and very busy selecting the clothes and hair styles that would be most becoming to them; this created new trouble for Cinderella, because it was she who

---

[26]The first syllable of *Cucendron* no doubt represents *cul* (in which the *l* is silent).

linge de ses sœurs et qui godronnait leurs manchettes. On ne parlait que de la manière dont on s'habillerait.

«Moi, dit l'aînée, je mettrai mon habit de velours rouge et ma garniture d'Angleterre.

—Moi, dit la cadette, je n'aurai que ma jupe ordinaire; mais en récompense, je mettrai mon manteau à fleurs d'or, et ma barrière de diamants, qui n'est pas des plus indifférentes.»

On envoya querir la bonne coiffeuse, pour dresser les cornettes à deux rangs, et on fit acheter des mouches de la bonne faiseuse: elles appelèrent Cendrillon pour lui demander son avis, car elle avait le goût bon. Cendrillon les conseilla le mieux du monde, et s'offrit même à les coiffer; ce qu'elles voulurent bien.

En les coiffant, elles lui disaient:

«Cendrillon, serais-tu bien aise d'aller au bal?

«Hélas, mesdemoiselles, vous vous moquez de moi, ce n'est pas là ce qu'il me faut.

—Tu as raison, on rirait bien si on voyait un Cucendron aller au bal.»

Une autre que Cendrillon les aurait coiffées de travers; mais elle était bonne, et elle les coiffa parfaitement bien. Elles furent près de deux jours sans manger, tant elles étaient transportées de joie. On rompit plus de douze lacets à force de les serrer pour leur rendre la taille plus menue, et elles étaient toujours devant leur miroir.

Enfin l'heureux jour arriva, on partit, et Cendrillon les suivit des yeux le plus longtemps qu'elle put; lorsqu'elle ne les vit plus, elle se mit à pleurer. Sa marraine, qui la vit toute en pleurs, lui demanda ce qu'elle avait.

«Je voudrais bien . . . je voudrais bien . . .»

Elle pleurait si fort qu'elle ne put achever. Sa marraine, qui était fée, lui dit:

«Tu voudrais bien aller au bal, n'est-ce pas?

—Hélas oui, dit Cendrillon en soupirant.

—Hé bien, seras-tu bonne fille? dit sa marraine, je t'y ferai aller.»

Elle la mena dans sa chambre, et lui dit:

«Va dans le jardin et apporte-moi une citrouille.»

Cendrillon alla aussitôt cueillir la plus belle qu'elle put trouver, et la porta à sa marraine, ne pouvant deviner comment cette citrouille la pourrait faire aller au bal. Sa marraine la creusa, et n'ayant laissé que l'écorce, la frappa de sa baguette, et la citrouille fut aussitôt changée en un beau carrosse tout doré.

Ensuite elle alla regarder dans sa souricière, où elle trouva six souris

ironed her sisters' linen and pleated their cuffs. They spoke of nothing but what they would wear.

"As for me," the older one said, "I'll put on my red velvet gown and my English lace trim."

"As for me," said the younger one, "I'll wear only my ordinary skirt, but, to compensate for that, I'll put on my gold-flowered cloak, and my diamond brooch, which is nothing to look down on."

They sent for the most fashionable milliner to make them two-tiered bonnets, and they bought beauty spots from the most fashionable maker: they summoned Cinderella to ask her opinion, because she had good taste. Cinderella gave them the very best advice, and even offered her own services to do their hair; and they were very willing to accept.

While she was arranging their hair, they said to her:

"Cinderella, would you like to go to the ball?"

"Alas, young ladies, you're making fun of me; that's no place for me."

"You're right, people would have a good laugh seeing a cinder-ass attending the ball."

Anyone else but Cinderella would have spoiled their hairdo; but she was kind, and she did a perfectly good job. They remained without eating for nearly two days, they were in such raptures of joy. More than twelve bodice laces snapped while being tightened to give them a narrower waist, and they were constantly in front of their mirrors.

Finally the happy day arrived, they left, and Cinderella watched them go as long as she could; when they were no longer visible, she started to cry. Her godmother, seeing her soaked with tears, asked her what was wrong.

"Oh, how I'd like . . . oh, how I'd like. . . ."

She was crying so hard that she couldn't finish. Her godmother, who had magic powers, said to her:

"You'd like to go to the ball, isn't that it?"

"Oh, yes," Cinderella said with a sigh.

"Well, then, will you be a good girl?" her godmother said; "I'll see to it that you go."

She led her to her room and said to her:

"Go out to the garden and bring me a pumpkin."

Instantly Cinderella went and picked the most beautiful one she could find and took it to her godmother, unable to guess how that pumpkin would help her get to the ball. Her godmother hollowed it out, leaving only the shell, and struck it with her wand, and the pumpkin was immediately changed into a beautiful coach, gilded all over.

Then she went to take a look at her mousetrap, in which she found

toutes en vie; elle dit à Cendrillon de lever un peu la trappe de la souricière, et à chaque souris qui sortait, elle lui donnait un coup de sa baguette, et la souris était aussitôt changée en un beau cheval; ce qui fit un bel attelage de six chevaux, d'un beau gris de souris pommelé.

Comme elle était en peine de quoi elle ferait un cocher:

«Je vais voir, dit Cendrillon, s'il n'y a point quelque rat dans la ratière, nous en ferons un cocher.

—Tu as raison, dit sa marraine, va voir.»

Cendrillon lui apporta la ratière, où il y avait trois gros rats. La fée en prit un d'entre les trois, à cause de sa maîtresse barbe, et l'ayant touché, il fut changé en un gros cocher, qui avait une des plus belles moustaches qu'on ait jamais vues.

Ensuite elle lui dit:

«Va dans le jardin, tu y trouveras six lézards derrière l'arrosoir, apporte-les-moi.»

Elle ne les eut pas plus tôt apportés que la marraine les changea en six laquais, qui montèrent aussitôt derrière le carrosse avec leurs habits chamarrés, et qui s'y tenaient attachés, comme s'ils n'eussent fait autre chose toute leur vie.

La fée dit alors à Cendrillon:

«Hé bien, voilà de quoi aller au bal, n'es-tu pas bien aise?

—Oui, mais est-ce que j'irai comme cela avec mes vilains habits?»

Sa marraine ne fit que la toucher avec sa baguette, et en même temps ses habits furent changés en des habits de drap d'or et d'argent tout chamarrés de pierreries; elle lui donna ensuite une paire de pantoufles de verre, les plus jolies du monde. Quand elle fut ainsi parée, elle monta en carrosse; mais sa marraine lui recommanda sur toutes choses de ne pas passer minuit, l'avertissant que si elle demeurait au bal un moment davantage, son carrosse redeviendrait citrouille, ses chevaux des souris, ses laquais des lézards, et que ses vieux habits reprendraient leur première forme.

Elle promit à sa marraine qu'elle ne manquerait pas de sortir du bal avant minuit. Elle part, ne se sentant pas de joie. Le fils du roi, qu'on alla avertir qu'il venait d'arriver une grande princesse qu'on ne connaissait point, courut la recevoir; il lui donna la main à la descente du carrosse, et la mena dans la salle où était la compagnie. Il se fit alors un grand silence; on cessa de danser et les violons ne jouèrent plus, tant on était attentif à contempler les grandes beautés de cette inconnue. On n'entendait qu'un bruit confus:

«Ah, qu'elle est belle!»

six live mice; she told Cinderella to raise the door to the trap slightly, and every time a mouse came out, she struck it with her wand, and the mouse was immediately changed into a beautiful horse; that composed a fine team of six horses, of a beautiful dappled mouse-gray.

Since she was at a loss for providing a coachman, Cinderella said:

"I'll go see whether there's a rat in the rattrap, and we'll make a coachman out of it."

"You're right," said her godmother, "go see."

Cinderella brought her the rattrap, in which there were three big rats. The fairy chose one of them on account of its marvelous whiskers and, when she touched it, it was changed into a fat coachman who had one of the most beautiful mustaches ever seen.

Then she said to her:

"Go out to the garden, where you'll find six lizards behind the watering can; bring them to me."

As soon as the girl brought them, her godmother changed them into six lackeys, who immediately climbed in back of the coach in their braid-adorned uniforms and held on tightly, as if they had never done anything else all their lives.

Then the fairy said to Cinderella:

"Well, then, this is how you'll get to the ball. Aren't you satisfied?"

"Yes, but am I to go like this, with my ugly clothes?"

Her godmother had only to touch her with her wand, and at once her clothes were changed into an outfit of cloth of gold and silver, all bedecked with precious stones; she then gave her a pair of glass slippers, the prettiest in the world. When she was thus adorned, she got into the coach; but her godmother urged her above all not to remain past midnight, warning her that if she lingered at the ball one moment longer, her coach would turn back into a pumpkin, her horses into mice, and her lackeys into lizards, and that her old clothes would assume their original appearance.

She promised her godmother that she'd leave the ball before midnight, without fail. She departed, beside herself with joy. The king's son, upon being informed that a great princess whom no one knew had just arrived, ran out to welcome her; he gave her his hand to help her out of the coach, and led her into the great hall, where the company was assembled. A great silence then fell; people stopped dancing and the musicians stopped playing, everyone was so intent on observing the great beauty of that unknown young lady. All that could be heard was a confused murmur:

"Oh, how beautiful she is!"

Le roi même, tout vieux qu'il était, ne laissait pas de la regarder, et de dire tout bas à la reine qu'il y avait longtemps qu'il n'avait vu une si belle et si aimable personne. Toutes les dames étaient attentives à considérer sa coiffure et ses habits, pour en avoir dès le lendemain de semblables, pourvu qu'il se trouvât des étoffes assez belles, et des ouvriers assez habiles.

Le fils du roi la mit à la place la plus honorable, et ensuite la prit pour la mener danser. Elle dansa avec tant de grâce, qu'on l'admira encore davantage. On apporta une fort belle collation, dont le jeune prince ne mangea point, tant il était occupé à la considérer. Elle alla s'asseoir auprès de ses sœurs, et leur fit mille honnêtetés: elle leur fit part des oranges et des citrons que le prince lui avait donnés, ce qui les étonna fort, car elles ne la connaissaient point.

Lorsqu'elles causaient ainsi, Cendrillon entendit sonner onze heures trois quarts: elle fit aussitôt une grande révérence à la compagnie, et s'en alla le plus vite qu'elle put. Dès qu'elle fut arrivée, elle alla trouver sa marraine, et après l'avoir remerciée, elle lui dit qu'elle souhaiterait bien aller encore le lendemain au bal, parce que le fils du roi l'en avait priée. Comme elle était occupée à raconter à sa marraine tout ce qui s'était passé au bal, les deux sœurs heurtèrent à la porte; Cendrillon leur alla ouvrir.

«Que vous êtes longtemps à revenir!» leur dit-elle en bâillant, en se frottant les yeux, et en s'étendant comme si elle n'eût fait que de se réveiller; elle n'avait cependant pas eu envie de dormir depuis qu'elles s'étaient quittées.

«Si tu étais venue au bal, lui dit une de ses sœurs, tu ne t'y serais pas ennuyée: il y est venu la plus belle princesse, la plus belle qu'on puisse jamais voir; elle nous a fait mille civilités, elle nous a donné des oranges et des citrons.»

Cendrillon ne se sentait pas de joie: elle leur demanda le nom de cette princesse; mais elles lui répondirent qu'on ne la connaissait pas, que le fils du roi en était fort en peine, et qu'il donnerait toutes choses au monde pour savoir qui elle était. Cendrillon sourit et leur dit:

«Elle était donc bien belle? Mon Dieu, que vous êtes heureuses, ne pourrais-je point la voir? Hélas! Mademoiselle Javotte, prêtez-moi votre habit jaune que vous mettez tous les jours.

—Vraiment, dit mademoiselle Javotte, je suis de cet avis! Prêter votre habit à un vilain Cucendron comme cela: il faudrait que je fusse bien folle.»

Cendrillon s'attendait bien à ce refus, et elle en fut bien aise, car elle aurait été grandement embarrassée si sa sœur eût bien voulu lui prêter son habit.

The king himself, old as he was, kept gazing at her, and kept whispering to the queen that for a long time he hadn't seen such a beautiful and lovable girl. All the ladies paid great attention to her hairdo and clothes, so they could get ones just like them the very next day, supposing that they could find fabrics sufficiently beautiful and seamstresses equally skillful.

The king's son gave her the seat of honor, and then led her out to the dance floor. She danced so gracefully that she was wondered at even more. A beautiful supper was brought in, but the prince didn't eat a thing, he was so busy studying her. She sat down next to her stepsisters, and showed them every courtesy: she gave them some of the oranges and citrons the prince had given her; this surprised them greatly, because they didn't recognize her.

While they were chatting that way, Cinderella heard the clock strike eleven forty-five; at once she made a low curtsey to one and all, and left as quickly as she could. As soon as she got home, she went to see her godmother and, after thanking her, told her that she'd very much like to return to the ball the next evening, because the king's son had asked her to. While she was busy telling her godmother everything that had occurred at the ball, her two stepsisters knocked at the door; Cinderella went to open it for them.

"My, you took your time getting back!" she said with a yawn, rubbing her eyes and stretching as if she had just awakened, though she hadn't felt sleepy from the moment they had taken leave.

"If you had come to the ball," one of her stepsisters told her, "you wouldn't have been bored: the most beautiful princess came there, the most beautiful you could ever hope to see; she paid us all sorts of kind attentions; she gave us oranges and citrons."

Cinderella was beside herself with joy; she asked them that princess's name, but they replied that no one was acquainted with her, that the king's son was in perplexity, and would give anything in the world to know who she was. Cinderella smiled and said:

"So she was really beautiful? Heavens, how lucky you two are! Couldn't I get to see her? Alas! Miss Javotte, lend me that yellow dress you wear every day."

"Really!" said Miss Javotte, "what are you thinking of? To lend a dress to an ugly cinder-ass like you: I'd have to be crazy!"

Cinderella fully expected that refusal, and was glad about it, because she would have been in a great quandary if her stepsister had consented to lend her dress.

Le lendemain les deux sœurs furent au bal, et Cendrillon aussi, mais encore plus parée que la première fois. Le fils du roi fut toujours auprès d'elle, et ne cessa de lui conter des douceurs; la jeune demoiselle ne s'ennuyait point, et oublia ce que sa marraine lui avait recommandé; de sorte qu'elle entendit sonner le premier coup de minuit, lorsqu'elle ne croyait pas qu'il fût encore onze heures: elle se leva et s'enfuit aussi légèrement qu'aurait fait une biche. Le prince la suivit, mais il ne put l'attraper; elle laissa tomber une de ses pantoufles de verre, que le prince ramassa bien soigneusement. Cendrillon arriva chez elle bien essoufflée, sans carrosse, sans laquais, et avec ses méchants habits, rien ne lui étant resté de toute sa magnificence qu'une de ses petites pantoufles, la pareille de celle qu'elle avait laissé tomber. On demanda aux gardes de la porte du palais s'ils n'avaient point vu sortir une princesse; ils dirent qu'ils n'avaient vu sortir personne, qu'une jeune fille fort mal vêtue, et qui avait plus l'air d'une paysanne que d'une demoiselle.

Quand ses deux sœurs revinrent du bal, Cendrillon leur demanda si elles s'étaient encore bien diverties, et si la belle dame y avait été; elles lui dirent que oui, mais qu'elle s'était enfuie lorsque minuit avait sonné, et si promptement qu'elle avait laissé tomber une de ses petites pantoufles de verre, la plus jolie du monde; que le fils du roi l'avait ramassée, et qu'il n'avait fait que la regarder pendant tout le reste du bal, et qu'assurément il était fort amoureux de la belle personne à qui appartenait la petite pantoufle.

Elles dirent vrai, car peu de jours après, le fils du roi fit publier à son de trompe qu'il épouserait celle dont le pied serait bien juste à la pantoufle. On commença à l'essayer aux princesses, ensuite aux duchesses, et à toute la Cour, mais inutilement. On l'apporta chez les deux sœurs, qui firent tout leur possible pour faire entrer leur pied dans la pantoufle, mais elles ne purent en venir à bout. Cendrillon qui les regardait, et qui reconnut sa pantoufle, dit en riant:

«Que je voie si elle ne me serait pas bonne!»

Ses sœurs se mirent à rire et à se moquer d'elle. Le gentilhomme qui faisait l'essai de la pantoufle, ayant regardé attentivement Cendrillon, et la trouvant fort belle, dit que cela était juste, et qu'il avait ordre de l'essayer à toutes les filles. Il fit asseoir Cendrillon, et approchant la pantoufle de son petit pied, il vit qu'elle y entrait sans peine, et qu'elle y était juste comme de cire. L'étonnement des deux sœurs fut grand, mais plus grand encore quand Cendrillon tira de sa poche l'autre petite pantoufle qu'elle mit à son pied. Là-dessus arriva la marraine, qui ayant donné un coup de sa baguette sur les habits de

The next day, the two stepsisters went to the ball, and so did Cinderella, but wearing even finer clothes than the first time. The king's son was constantly at her side and never stopped saying sweet nothings to her; the young lady was far from bored, and she forgot her godmother's injunctions, so that when she heard the first stroke of midnight chiming, she hadn't thought it was eleven yet: she got up and ran out as nimbly as a doe. The prince followed her, but couldn't catch her; she lost one of her glass slippers, which the prince picked up with great care. Cinderella arrived home all out of breath, without her coach, without her lackeys, and dressed in her wretched clothes, with nothing remaining to her of all her magnificence but one of her little slippers, the mate to the one she had lost. The guards at the palace gate were asked whether they hadn't seen a princess leaving; they said they hadn't seen anyone leave except a girl in awful clothes who looked more like a peasant than a fine young lady.

When her two stepsisters returned from the ball, Cinderella asked them if they had had a good time again, and whether the beautiful lady had been there; they said yes, but that she had run out when midnight sounded, and so hastily that she had lost one of her little glass slippers, the prettiest thing in the world; that the king's son had picked it up and had done nothing but stare at it for the remainder of the ball; he was surely very much in love with the beautiful girl to whom the little slipper belonged.

They were telling the truth, because only a few days later the king's son issued a proclamation, heralded by trumpets, that he would marry the girl whose foot the slipper would fit exactly. The fittings began with the princesses, then the duchesses, and all the court ladies, but in vain. The slipper was brought to the home of the two stepsisters, who tried as hard as they could to get their foot into the slipper, but unsuccessfully. Cinderella, who was watching them, and who recognized her slipper, said with a laugh:

"Let me see whether it won't fit me!"

Her stepsisters began to laugh and make fun of her. The courtier who was conducting the slipper fittings, after observing Cinderella closely and finding her extremely beautiful, said that it was only fair, and that his orders were to try it on every girl. He had Cinderella sit down and, bringing the slipper up to her small foot, he saw that it went in without difficulty and the fit was as perfect as if it had been molded in wax on her foot. The astonishment of the two stepsisters was great, but it was greater yet when Cinderella drew out of her pocket the other little slipper and put it on. At that moment her godmother arrived;

Cendrillon, les fit devenir encore plus magnifiques que tous les autres.

Alors ses deux sœurs la reconnurent pour la belle personne qu'elles avaient vue au bal. Elles se jetèrent à ses pieds pour lui demander pardon de tous les mauvais traitements qu'elles lui avaient fait souffrir. Cendrillon les releva, et leur dit, en les embrassant, qu'elle leur pardonnait de bon cœur, et qu'elle les priait de l'aimer bien toujours. On la mena chez le jeune prince, parée comme elle était: il la trouva encore plus belle que jamais, et peu de jours après, il l'épousa. Cendrillon, qui était aussi bonne que belle, fit loger ses deux sœurs au palais, et les maria dès le jour même à deux grands seigneurs de la cour.

Moralité

La beauté pour le sexe est un rare trésor,
  De l'admirer jamais on ne se lasse;
    Mais ce qu'on nomme bonne grâce
    Est sans prix, et vaut mieux encor.

C'est ce qu'à Cendrillon fit avoir sa marraine,
    En la dressant, en l'instruisant,
  Tant et si bien qu'elle en fit une reine:
(Car ainsi sur ce conte on va moralisant.)

Belles, ce don vaut mieux que d'être bien coiffées,
Pour engager un cœur, pour en venir à bout,
  La bonne grâce est le vrai don des fées;
Sans elle on ne peut rien, avec elle, on peut tout.

Autre moralité

    C'est sans doute un grand avantage,
    D'avoir de l'esprit, du courage,
    De la naissance, du bon sens,
    Et d'autres semblables talents,
    Qu'on reçoit du Ciel en partage;
    Mais vous aurez beau les avoir,
Pour votre avancement ce seront choses vaines,
    Si vous n'avez, pour les faire valoir,
    Ou des parrains ou des marraines.

touching Cinderella's clothing with her wand, she caused it to become even more splendid than any of her previous outfits.

Then her two stepsisters recognized her as the beautiful girl they had seen at the ball. They threw themselves at her feet to beg forgiveness for all the bad treatment she had endured at their hands. Cinderella raised them up and, embracing them, said that she forgave them wholeheartedly and asked them to love her always. She was brought to the young prince, dressed just as she was: he found her more beautiful than ever, and only a few days later he married her. Cinderella, who was as good-hearted as she was beautiful, had her two stepsisters given rooms in the palace, and that very day she married them off to two great lords of the court.

Moral

Beauty is a rare treasure for the fair sex,
*   and people never tire of admiring it;*
*   but the quality known as graciousness*
*   is beyond price, and is worth even more.*

That is what Cinderella's godmother bestowed on her
*   when she was training and instructing her,*
*   with the result that she made her a queen*
(for that is the moral drawn from this tale).

Beauties, that gift is more valuable than a fine hairdo
to entice a man's heart and to capture it;
*   graciousness is the true gift of the fairies:*
without it you are powerless; with it, all-powerful.

Second Moral

*   It is no doubt a great advantage*
*   to have wit, pluck,*
*   high birth, good sense,*
*   and other similar talents*
*   that Heaven allots to you;*
*   but you will possess all this in vain,*
and they will do nothing for your advancement,
*   unless, to turn them to account, you have*
*   either godfathers or godmothers.*

Riquet à la Houppe

Il était une fois une reine qui accoucha d'un fils, si laid et si mal fait, qu'on douta longtemps s'il avait forme humaine. Une fée qui se trouva à sa naissance assura qu'il ne laisserait pas d'être aimable, parce qu'il aurait beaucoup d'esprit; elle ajouta même qu'il pourrait, en vertu du don qu'elle venait de lui faire, donner autant d'esprit qu'il en aurait à la personne qu'il aimerait le mieux.

Tout cela consola un peu la pauvre reine, qui était bien affligée d'avoir mis au monde un si vilain marmot. Il est vrai que cet enfant ne commença pas plus tôt à parler qu'il dit mille jolies choses, et qu'il avait dans toutes ses actions je ne sais quoi de si spirituel, qu'on en était charmé. J'oubliais de dire qu'il vint au monde avec une petite houppe de cheveux sur la tête, ce qui fit qu'on le nomma Riquet à la Houppe, car Riquet était le nom de la famille.

Au bout de sept ou huit ans la reine d'un royaume voisin accoucha de deux filles. La première qui vint au monde était plus belle que le jour: la Reine en fut si aise, qu'on appréhenda que la trop grande joie qu'elle en avait ne lui fît mal. La même fée qui avait assisté à la naissance du petit Riquet à la Houppe était présente, et pour modérer la joie de la reine, elle lui déclara que cette petite princesse n'aurait point d'esprit, et qu'elle serait aussi stupide qu'elle était belle. Cela mortifia beaucoup la reine; mais elle eut quelques moments après un bien plus grand chagrin, car la seconde fille dont elle accoucha se trouva extrêmement laide.

«Ne vous affligez point tant, madame, lui dit la fée; votre fille sera récompensée d'ailleurs, et elle aura tant d'esprit, qu'on ne s'apercevra presque pas qu'il lui manque de la beauté.

—Dieu le veuille, répondit la reine; mais n'y aurait-il point moyen de faire avoir un peu d'esprit à l'aînée qui est si belle?

—Je ne puis rien pour elle, madame, du côté de l'esprit, lui dit la fée, mais je puis tout du côté de la beauté; et comme il n'y a rien que

176

Riquet-with-the-Tuft

There was once a queen who gave birth to a son who was so ugly and misshapen that for a long time it was doubted whether he had a human form. A fairy who was present at his birth assured everyone that he wouldn't fail to be lovable, because he'd be very intelligent; she even added that, by virtue of the gift she had just given him, he'd be able to give as much intelligence as he himself had to the woman he loved best.

All this was some consolation to the poor queen, who was in great distress for having given birth to such an ugly ape. It's true that, just as soon as that child began to talk, he said a thousand witty things, and in all his actions there was something so clever that everyone was charmed. I almost forgot to say that he was born with a little tuft of hair on his head, so that he was called Riquet-with-the-Tuft, Riquet being his family name.

Seven or eight years later, the queen of a neighboring realm gave birth to two daughters. The one born first was more beautiful than the daylight: the queen was so pleased with her that people were worried that her excessive joy over the girl might cause her some harm. The same fairy that had been present at the birth of little Riquet-with-the-Tuft was there, as well, and in order to moderate the queen's joy, she informed her that the little princess would have no intelligence; she'd be as stupid as she was beautiful. This hurt the queen's feelings badly, but a few moments later, she received a much greater vexation, because the second girl she gave birth to was extremely ugly.

"Don't take on so, ma'am," the fairy told her; "your daughter will be compensated for it in another way: she'll be so intelligent that people will hardly notice her want of good looks."

"God grant it!" the queen replied. "But isn't there any way to give a little intelligence to the older one, who's so beautiful?"

"I can do nothing for her, ma'am, as far as intelligence goes," replied the fairy, "but I can do everything as far as beauty goes; and

je ne veuille faire pour votre satisfaction, je vais lui donner pour don
de pouvoir rendre beau ou belle la personne qui lui plaira.»

A mesure que ces deux princesses devinrent grandes, leurs perfections crûrent aussi avec elles, et on ne parlait partout que de la beauté
de l'aînée, et de l'esprit de la cadette. Il est vrai aussi que leurs défauts
augmentèrent beaucoup avec l'âge. La cadette enlaidissait à vue d'œil,
et l'aînée devenait plus stupide de jour en jour. Ou elle ne répondait
rien à ce qu'on lui demandait, ou elle disait une sottise. Elle était avec
cela si maladroite qu'elle n'eût pu ranger quatre porcelaines sur le
bord d'une cheminée sans en casser une, ni boire un verre d'eau sans
en répandre la moitié sur ses habits.

Quoique la beauté soit un grand avantage dans une jeune personne,
cependant la cadette l'emportait presque toujours sur son aînée dans
toutes les compagnies. D'abord on allait du côté de la plus belle pour
la voir et pour l'admirer, mais bientôt après, on allait à celle qui avait
le plus d'esprit, pour lui entendre dire mille choses agréables; et on
était étonné qu'en moins d'un quart d'heure l'aînée n'avait plus personne auprès d'elle, et que tout le monde s'était rangé autour de la
cadette. L'aînée, quoique fort stupide, le remarqua bien, et elle eût
donné sans regret toute sa beauté pour avoir la moitié de l'esprit de sa
sœur. La reine, toute sage qu'elle était, ne put s'empêcher de lui reprocher plusieurs fois sa bêtise, ce qui pensa faire mourir de douleur
cette pauvre princesse.

Un jour qu'elle s'était retirée dans un bois pour y plaindre son malheur, elle vit venir à elle un petit homme fort laid et fort désagréable,
mais vêtu très magnifiquement. C'était le jeune prince Riquet à la
Houppe, qui étant devenu amoureux d'elle sur ses portraits qui
couraient par tout le monde, avait quitté le royaume de son père pour
avoir le plaisir de la voir et de lui parler. Ravi de la rencontrer ainsi
toute seule, il l'aborde avec tout le respect et toute la politesse
imaginable. Ayant remarqué, après lui avoir fait les compliments
ordinaires, qu'elle était fort mélancolique, il lui dit:

«Je ne comprends point, madame, comment une personne aussi
belle que vous l'êtes peut être aussi triste que vous le paraissez; car,
quoique je puisse me vanter d'avoir vu une infinité de belles personnes,
je puis dire que je n'en ai jamais vu dont la beauté approche de la vôtre.

—Cela vous plaît à dire, monsieur», lui répondit la princesse, et en
demeure là.

«La beauté, reprit Riquet à la Houppe, est un si grand avantage
qu'il doit tenir lieu de tout le reste; et quand on le possède, je ne vois
pas qu'il y ait rien qui puisse nous affliger beaucoup.

since there's nothing I wouldn't do to gratify you, I shall give her as a gift the power to make anyone she likes handsome or beautiful."

As these two princesses grew up, their good points became perfected as well, and the only topic of conversation anywhere was the older one's beauty and the younger one's intelligence. It is equally true that their defects increased greatly as they got older. The younger one got uglier every minute, and the older one got stupider day by day. Either she made no reply at all when asked a question, or else she said something foolish. Besides that, she was so clumsy that she couldn't arrange four pieces of china on a mantelpiece without breaking one, or drink a glass of water without spilling half of it over her clothes.

Even though beauty is of great benefit to a girl, nevertheless the younger sister nearly always had the advantage over the older one at all gatherings. At first people would flock toward the beautiful one to see her and admire her, but before long they shifted to the one with greater intelligence, to hear her say any number of charming things; and it was surprising to see that, in less than a quarter-hour, the older one had no one left around her, while everyone had taken a place around the younger one. Though the older girl was very stupid, she didn't fail to notice this, and she would have given all her beauty, with no regrets, to have half of her sister's intelligence. The queen, wise as she was, couldn't help scolding her for her stupidity several times, which nearly made that poor princess die of grief.

One day, when she had withdrawn into a forest to bewail her unhappiness there, she saw coming toward her a short man who was very ugly and unpleasant-looking but was dressed in great splendor. It was the young prince Riquet-with-the-Tuft, who having fallen in love with her after seeing her portraits, which were universally circulated, had left his father's realm to have the pleasure of seeing her and speaking with her. Delighted to find her all alone like that, he accosted her with all possible respect and courtesy. After making her the customary compliments, noticing that she was very melancholy, he said:

"I fail to comprehend, ma'am, how a young lady as beautiful as you can be as sad as you appear to be; for, even though I can boast of having seen an infinite number of lovely ladies, I may say that I have never seen one whose beauty comes close to yours."

"You're just saying that, sir," the princess replied, and she stopped there.

"Beauty," Riquet-with-the-Tuft continued, "is such a great advantage that it ought to compensate for everything else; and when someone possesses it, I can't see that there's anything that can distress us very much."

—J'aimerais mieux, dit la princesse, être aussi laide que vous et avoir de l'esprit, que d'avoir de la beauté comme j'en ai, et être bête autant que je le suis.

—Il n'y a rien, madame, qui marque davantage qu'on a de l'esprit, que de croire n'en pas avoir, et il est de la nature de ce bien-là, que plus on en a, plus on croit en manquer.

—Je ne sais pas cela, dit la princesse, mais je sais bien que je suis fort bête, et c'est de là que vient le chagrin qui me tue.

—Si ce n'est que cela, madame, qui vous afflige, je puis aisément mettre fin à votre douleur.

—Et comment ferez-vous? dit la princesse.

—J'ai le pouvoir, madame, dit Riquet à la Houppe, de donner de l'esprit autant qu'on en saurait avoir à la personne que je dois aimer le plus, et comme vous êtes, madame, cette personne, il ne tiendra qu'à vous que vous n'ayez autant d'esprit qu'on en peut avoir, pourvu que vous vouliez bien m'épouser.»

La princesse demeura toute interdite, et ne répondit rien.

«Je vois, reprit Riquet à la Houppe, que cette proposition vous fait de la peine, et je ne m'en étonne pas; mais je vous donne un an tout entier pour vous y résoudre.»

La princesse avait si peu d'esprit, et en même temps une si grande envie d'en avoir, qu'elle s'imagina que la fin de cette année ne viendrait jamais; de sorte qu'elle accepta la proposition qui lui était faite. Elle n'eut pas plus tôt promis à Riquet à la Houppe qu'elle l'épouserait dans un an à pareil jour, qu'elle se sentit tout autre qu'elle n'était auparavant; elle se trouva une facilité incroyable à dire tout ce qui lui plaisait, et à le dire d'une manière fine, aisée et naturelle. Elle commença dès ce moment une conversation galante et soutenue avec Riquet à la Houppe, où elle brilla d'une telle force que Riquet à la Houppe crut lui avoir donné plus d'esprit qu'il ne s'en était réservé pour lui-même.

Quand elle fut retournée au palais, toute la cour ne savait que penser d'un changement si subit et si extraordinaire, car autant qu'on lui avait ouï dire d'impertinences auparavant, autant lui entendait-on dire des choses bien sensées et infiniment spirituelles. Toute la cour en eut une joie qui ne se peut imaginer; il n'y eut que sa cadette qui n'en fut pas bien aise, parce que n'ayant plus sur son aînée l'avantage de l'esprit, elle ne paraissait plus auprès d'elle qu'une guenon fort désagréable.

Le roi se conduisait par ses avis, et allait même quelquefois tenir le conseil dans son appartement. Le bruit de ce changement s'étant répandu, tous les jeunes princes des royaumes voisins firent leurs efforts

The princess said: "I'd rather be as ugly as you, and be intelligent, than to be as beautiful as I am and as stupid as I am."

"There is nothing, ma'am, which indicates more clearly that a person is intelligent than his belief that he isn't, and it's the nature of that asset that, the more one has of it, the less one is conscious of having."

"I don't know about that," the princess said, "but I do know that I'm very stupid; and that's the reason for the grief that's killing me."

"If that's the only thing distressing you, ma'am, I can easily put an end to your sorrow."

"How can you do that?" asked the princess.

"I have the power, ma'am," said Riquet-with-the-Tuft, "to give as much intelligence as anyone could have to the woman I am to love best, and since you are that woman, ma'am, it's completely up to you to have as much intelligence as possible, provided that you're willing to marry me."

The princess was altogether taken aback, and made no reply.

"I see," Riquet-with-the-Tuft resumed, "that this proposal is painful to you, nor am I surprised; but I grant you a whole year to make up your mind to it."

The princes had so little intelligence, but at the same time was so eager to acquire some, that she imagined that that year would never come to an end; and so, she accepted the proposal she had been made. No sooner had she promised Riquet-with-the-Tuft to marry him on that date a year later than she felt completely different from before; she discovered in herself an unbelievable readiness to express any of her thoughts, and to do so in an elegant, easy, and natural manner. That very moment she initiated a long bantering conversation with Riquet-with-the-Tuft, in which she sparkled so brightly that Riquet-with-the-Tuft thought he had given her more wit than he had saved for himself.

When she was back in the palace, the entire court was dumbfounded by that sudden and extraordinary change, because the number of foolish things she had been heard to say previously was now equaled by the number of very sensible and highly witty comments she uttered. The entire court was happier over this than words can tell; only her younger sister was displeased, because, no longer having the advantage of intelligence over her elder, she now appeared next to her merely as a most unpleasant monkey.

The king was guided by his older daughter's advice, and even convened his council in her quarters at times. The news of this transformation having spread, all the young princes from the neighboring

pour s'en faire aimer, et presque tous la demandèrent en mariage; mais elle n'en trouvait point qui eût assez d'esprit, et elle les écoutait tous sans s'engager à pas un d'eux. Cependant il en vint un si puissant, si riche, si spirituel et si bien fait, qu'elle ne put s'empêcher d'avoir de la bonne volonté pour lui. Son père s'en étant aperçu lui dit qu'il la faisait la maîtresse sur le choix d'un époux, et qu'elle n'avait qu'à se déclarer. Comme plus on a d'esprit et plus on a de peine à prendre une ferme résolution sur cette affaire, elle demanda, après avoir remercié son père, qu'il lui donnât du temps pour y penser.

Elle alla par hasard se promener dans le même bois où elle avait trouvé Riquet à la Houppe, pour rêver plus commodément à ce qu'elle avait à faire. Dans le temps qu'elle se promenait, rêvant profondément, elle entendit un bruit sourd sous ses pieds, comme de plusieurs personnes qui vont et viennent et qui agissent. Ayant prêté l'oreille plus attentivement, elle ouït que l'un disait: «Apporte-moi cette marmite»; l'autre: «Donne-moi cette chaudière»; l'autre: «Mets du bois dans ce feu.» La terre s'ouvrit dans le même temps, et elle vit sous ses pieds comme une grande cuisine pleine de cuisiniers, de marmitons et de toutes sortes d'officiers nécessaires pour faire un festin magnifique. Il en sortit une bande de vingt ou trente rôtisseurs, qui allèrent se camper dans une allée du bois autour d'une table fort longue, et qui tous, la lardoire à la main, et la queue de renard sur l'oreille, se mirent à travailler en cadence au son d'une chanson harmonieuse.

La princesse, étonnée de ce spectacle, leur demanda pour qui ils travaillaient.

«C'est, madame, lui répondit le plus apparent de la bande, pour le prince Riquet à la Houppe, dont les noces se feront demain.»

La princesse encore plus surprise qu'elle ne l'avait été, et se ressouvenant tout à coup qu'il y avait un an qu'à pareil jour elle avait promis d'épouser le prince Riquet à la Houppe, elle pensa tomber de son haut. Ce qui faisait qu'elle ne s'en souvenait pas, c'est que, quand elle fit cette promesse, elle était une bête, et qu'en prenant le nouvel esprit que le prince lui avait donné, elle avait oublié toutes ses sottises.

Elle n'eut pas fait trente pas en continuant sa promenade, que Riquet à la Houppe se présenta à elle, brave, magnifique, et comme un prince qui va se marier.

kingdoms made every effort to win her heart, and nearly all of them asked for her hand; but she didn't find any of them sufficiently bright, and heard them all out without committing herself to a single one. Meanwhile, one arrived who was so mighty, wealthy, witty, and handsome that she couldn't help having tender feelings for him. Her father, noticing this, told her that he left the choice of a husband up to her, and that she need only make up her mind. Since the more intelligent a woman is, the harder it is for her to arrive at a firm resolve in such matters, she thanked her father and asked him to give her some time to think it over.

By chance she went for a stroll in the same forest where she had met Riquet-with-the-Tuft, in order to meditate more conveniently over what she should do. While she was walking there, lost in thought, she heard a muffled noise under her feet; it sounded like several people moving to and fro very busily. Lending a more attentive ear, she heard one man saying, "Bring me that cooking pot," another saying, "Give me that kettle," and another saying, "Add wood to that fire." At the same moment, the ground opened up, and she saw below her feet something like a big kitchen full of cooks, kitchen boys, and every kind of servant needed to prepare a magnificent banquet. Out came a troop of twenty or thirty chefs in charge of roasting meats; they took up positions in an avenue of the woods all around a very long table; all of them, larding needles in their hands and foxtails over their ears,[27] began working in cadence to the sound of a melodious song.

The princess, amazed at that sight, asked them whom they were working for.

"Ma'am," replied the most prominent man among the troop, "we're working for Prince Riquet-with-the-Tuft, whose wedding will be celebrated tomorrow."

The princess, even more surprised than before, suddenly remembered that exactly a year had gone by since she had promised to marry Prince Riquet-with-the-Tuft, and she was greatly startled. The reason for her not having recalled this is that, at the time she made the promise, she was a fool; after acquiring the new intelligence the prince had given her, she had forgotten her previous acts of folly.

Before she had taken thirty steps in continuation of her stroll, Riquet-with-the-Tuft appeared before her, elegantly and splendidly dressed, like a prince about to marry.

---

[27]Apparently, an insignia of roasting-chefs in great houses (seemingly not attested elsewhere).

«Vous me voyez, dit-il, madame, exact à tenir ma parole, et je ne doute point que vous ne veniez ici pour exécuter la vôtre, et me rendre, en me donnant la main, le plus heureux de tous les hommes.

—Je vous avouerai franchement, répondit la princesse, que je n'ai pas encore pris ma résolution là-dessus, et que je ne crois pas pouvoir jamais la prendre telle que vous la souhaitez.

—Vous m'étonnez, madame, lui dit Riquet à la Houppe.

—Je le crois, dit la princesse, et assurément si j'avais affaire à un brutal, à un homme sans esprit, je me trouverais bien embarrassée. Une princesse n'a que sa parole, me dirait-il, et il faut que vous m'épousiez, puisque vous me l'avez promis; mais comme celui à qui je parle est l'homme du monde qui a le plus d'esprit, je suis sûre qu'il entendra raison. Vous savez que, quand je n'étais qu'une bête, je ne pouvais néanmoins me résoudre à vous épouser; comment voulez-vous qu'ayant l'esprit que vous m'avez donné, qui me rend encore plus difficile en gens que je n'étais, je prenne aujourd'hui une résolution que je n'ai pu prendre dans ce temps-là? Si vous pensiez tout de bon à m'épouser, vous avez eu grand tort de m'ôter ma bêtise, et de me faire voir plus clair que je ne voyais.

—Si un homme sans esprit, répondit Riquet à la Houppe, serait bien reçu, comme vous venez de le dire, à vous reprocher votre manque de parole, pourquoi voulez-vous, madame, que je n'en use pas de même, dans une chose où il y va de tout le bonheur de ma vie? Est-il raisonnable que les personnes qui ont de l'esprit soient d'une pire condition que ceux qui n'en ont pas? Le pouvez-vous prétendre, vous qui en avez tant, et qui avez tant souhaité d'en avoir? Mais venons au fait, s'il vous plaît. A la réserve de ma laideur, y a-t-il quelque chose en moi qui vous déplaise? Êtes-vous mal contente de ma naissance, de mon esprit, de mon humeur, et de mes manières?

—Nullement, répondit la princesse, j'aime en vous tout ce que vous venez de me dire.

—Si cela est ainsi, reprit Riquet à la Houppe, je vais être heureux, puisque vous pouvez me rendre le plus aimable de tous les hommes.

—Comment cela se peut-il faire? lui dit la princesse.

—Cela se fera, répondit Riquet à la Houppe, si vous m'aimez assez pour souhaiter que cela soit; et afin, madame, que vous n'en doutiez pas, sachez que la même fée qui au jour de ma naissance me fit le don de pouvoir rendre spirituelle la personne qu'il me plairait, vous a aussi fait le don de pouvoir rendre beau celui que vous aimerez, et à qui vous voudrez bien faire cette faveur.

"Here you find me, ma'am," he said, "punctual and ready to keep my word, and I have no doubt that you have come here to fulfill your own promise and, by giving me your hand, to make me the happiest of men."

"I confess to you frankly," the princess replied, "that I have not yet made up my mind on that subject, and that I don't believe I ever will be able to do so in accordance with your wishes."

"You astonish me, ma'am," said Riquet-with-the-Tuft.

"I'm certain I do," the princess said, "and assuredly, if I were dealing with a roughneck or a man without wit, I'd be quite abashed. 'A princess's word is her bond,' he'd tell me, 'and you must marry me because you promised to'; but since the man to whom I am speaking is the most intelligent man in the world, I'm sure he'll listen to reason. You know that, even when I was only a fool, I still couldn't make up my mind to marry you; now that I have the intelligence which you gave me, which makes me even more choosy with men than I was, how do you expect me to make a decision today that I was unable to, back then? If you really intended to marry me, you made a big mistake by taking away my stupidity and making me see things more clearly than before."

"Seeing that even a man without intelligence," Riquet-with-the-Tuft replied, "would have every right to blame you for breaking your word, as you have just said, why, ma'am, do you refuse me the same right in a matter in which the happiness of my entire life is at stake? Does it make sense for people with intelligence to be worse off than those without it? You, who have so much, and wanted so badly to have it, can you make that claim? But let's get down to brass tacks, if you don't mind. With the exception of my ugliness, is there anything about me you don't like? Are you dissatisfied with my birth, my wit, my character, or my manners?"

"Not at all," replied the princess, "I like you for all the things you've just mentioned."

"That being the case," resumed Riquet-with-the-Tuft, "I'm going to be happy, because you can make me the most lovable of men."

"How can that be?" the princess asked.

"It will come about," replied Riquet-with-the-Tuft, "if you love me enough to wish it were so; in order to dispel your doubts, ma'am, let me inform you that the same fairy who, on the day of my birth, gave me as a gift the power to make any woman I liked intelligent, also gave you as a gift the power to make handsome the man you love and to whom you are willing to do that favor."

—Si la chose est ainsi, dit la princesse, je souhaite de tout mon
cœur que vous deveniez le prince du monde le plus beau et le plus
aimable; et je vous en fais le don autant qu'il est en moi.»

La princesse n'eut pas plus tôt prononcé ces paroles, que Riquet à
la Houppe parut à ses yeux l'homme du monde le plus beau, le mieux
fait et le plus aimable qu'elle eût jamais vu. Quelques-uns assurent
que ce ne furent point les charmes de la fée qui opérèrent, mais que
l'amour seul fit cette métamorphose. Ils disent que la princesse ayant
fait réflexion sur la persévérance de son amant, sur sa discrétion, et
sur toutes les bonnes qualités de son âme et de son esprit, ne vit plus
la difformité de son corps, ni la laideur de son visage, que sa bosse ne
lui sembla plus que le bon air d'un homme qui fait le gros dos, et
qu'au lieu que jusqu'alors elle l'avait vu boiter effroyablement, elle ne
lui trouva plus qu'un certain air penché qui la charmait; ils disent encore que ses yeux, qui étaient louches, ne lui en parurent que plus
brillants, que leur dérèglement passa dans son esprit pour la marque
d'un violent excès d'amour, et qu'enfin son gros nez rouge eut pour
elle quelque chose de martial et d'héroïque.

Quoi qu'il en soit, la princesse lui promit sur-le-champ de l'épouser,
pourvu qu'il en obtînt le consentement du roi son père. Le roi ayant
su que sa fille avait beaucoup d'estime pour Riquet à la Houppe, qu'il
connaissait d'ailleurs pour un prince très spirituel et très sage, le reçut
avec plaisir pour son gendre. Dès le lendemain les noces furent faites,
ainsi que Riquet à la Houppe l'avait prévu, et selon les ordres qu'il en
avait donnés longtemps auparavant.

Moralité

Ce que l'on voit dans cet écrit,
Est moins un conte en l'air que la vérité même;
Tout est beau dans ce que l'on aime,
Tout ce qu'on aime a de l'esprit.

Autre moralité

Dans un objet où la nature
Aura mis de beaux traits, et la vive peinture

"If things are that way," the princess said, "I wish with all my heart for you to become the handsomest and most lovable prince in the world; and I give you that gift to the full extent that I can."

No sooner had the princess uttered those words than Riquet-with-the-Tuft appeared to her eyes the handsomest, most well-built, and most lovable man she had ever seen anywhere. Some people insist that it wasn't the fairy's magic working, but love alone that caused this metamorphosis. They say that the princess, having reflected on her suitor's perseverance, his discretion, and all the good qualities of his soul and mind, no longer saw his physical deformity or the ugliness of his face; that his hump now appeared to her as merely the fashionable gesture of making a low bow;[28] that, whereas she had seen him limping terribly up till then, she now merely found that he was affecting a negligently stooped look that was charming; they also say that his squinty eyes merely seemed more brilliant to her, that in her mind their defect was taken to be the mark of impetuous and excessive love; and that, finally, his big red nose had something martial and heroic about it in her eyes.

However that may be, the princess immediately promised to marry him, provided he obtained the consent of her father the king. The king, learning that his daughter had great esteem for Riquet-with-the-Tuft, whom he already knew to be a very intelligent and wise prince, gladly welcomed him as his son-in-law. The very next day, the wedding was celebrated, just as Riquet-with-the-Tuft had foreseen, and in accordance with the instructions he had given long before.

Moral

> What is seen in this piece
> is not so much a baseless tale as the truth itself;
> everything about the person you love is beautiful,
> everyone you love is intelligent.

Second Moral

> In a person to whom nature
> has given fine features and the bright coloring

---

[28]Or, just possibly: "shrugging his shoulders." The phrase *faire le gros dos* is normally applied to a cat and means "to arch the back." There is a similar area of latitude in rendering the expression *air penché,* just below.

D'un teint où jamais l'art ne saurait arriver,
Tous ces dons pourront moins pour rendre un cœur sensible,
    Qu'un seul agrément invisible
    Que l'amour y fera trouver.

of a complexion that art can never match,
all those gifts are less able to soften another's heart
    than the one invisible attraction
    that love will cause to be found in that person.

Le Petit Poucet

Il était une fois un bûcheron et une bûcheronne qui avaient sept enfants tous garçons. L'aîné n'avait que dix ans, et le plus jeune n'en avait que sept. On s'étonnera que le bûcheron ait eu tant d'enfants en si peu de temps; mais c'est que sa femme allait vite en besogne, et n'en faisait pas moins que deux à la fois.

Ils étaient fort pauvres, et leurs sept enfants les incommodaient beaucoup, parce qu'aucun d'eux ne pouvait encore gagner sa vie.

Ce qui les chagrinait encore, c'est que le plus jeune était fort délicat et ne disait mot: prenant pour bêtise ce qui était une marque de la bonté de son esprit. Il était fort petit, et quand il vint au monde, il n'était guère plus gros que le pouce, ce qui fit que l'on l'appela le Petit Poucet.

Ce pauvre enfant était le souffre-douleurs de la maison, et on lui donnait toujours le tort. Cependant il était le plus fin, et le plus avisé de tous ses frères, et s'il parlait peu, il écoutait beaucoup.

Il vint une année très fâcheuse, et la famine fut si grande, que ces pauvres gens résolurent de se défaire de leurs enfants.

Un soir que ces enfants étaient couchés, et que le bûcheron était auprès du feu avec sa femme, il lui dit, le cœur serré de douleur:

«Tu vois bien que nous ne pouvons plus nourrir nos enfants; je ne saurais les voir mourir de faim devant mes yeux, et je suis résolu de les mener perdre demain au bois, ce qui sera bien aisé, car tandis qu'ils s'amuseront à fagoter, nous n'avons qu'à nous enfuir sans qu'ils nous voient.

—Ah! s'écria la bûcheronne, pourrais-tu bien toi-même mener perdre tes enfants?»

Son mari avait beau lui représenter leur grande pauvreté, elle ne pouvait y consentir; elle était pauvre, mais elle était leur mère. Cependant ayant considéré quelle douleur ce lui serait de les voir mourir de faim, elle y consentit, et alla se coucher en pleurant.

Little Thumbling [Tom Thumb]

There were once a woodcutter and his wife who had seven children, all boys. The oldest one was only ten, and the youngest only seven. It may sound odd for the woodcutter to have had that many children in so short a time; it was because his wife was a fast worker, and never produced fewer than two at a time.

They were very poor, and their seven children were a great burden to them, because none of them could earn his own living yet.

But what worried them in addition was that their youngest was very frail and didn't speak; they took for stupidity what was actually a sign of his great intelligence. He was very small, and when he was born, he was hardly bigger than someone's thumb, so that they called him Little Thumbling.

That poor child was the scapegoat of the whole household, and he always received the blame for things. And yet he was the shrewdest and cleverest of all the brothers, and, if he didn't speak much, he listened a great deal.

A very bitter year arrived in which the famine was so great that that poor couple decided to get rid of their children.

One evening, when the children were in bed, and the woodcutter was next to the fire with his wife, he said to her, his heart aching with sorrow:

"You see perfectly well that we can no longer feed our children; I can't watch them starve to death in front of my eyes, and I've decided to take them into the woods tomorrow and lose them there; it will be very easy because, while they're killing time by making bundles of firewood, all we need to do is run away without their seeing us."

"Oh!" his wife exclaimed, "could you really take your own children out and lose them?"

It did her husband no good to depict their great poverty; she couldn't consent; she was poor, but she was their mother. Nevertheless, after reflecting on how sad she would feel to watch them starve to death, she consented, and went to bed weeping.

Le Petit Poucet ouït tout ce qu'ils dirent, car ayant entendu de
dedans son lit qu'ils parlaient d'affaires, il s'était levé doucement, et
s'était glissé sous l'escabelle de son père pour les écouter sans être vu.
Il alla se recoucher et ne dormit point le reste de la nuit, songeant à
ce qu'il avait à faire. Il se leva de bon matin, et alla au bord d'un ruisseau où il emplit ses poches de petits cailloux blancs, et ensuite revint
à la maison. On partit, et le Petit Poucet ne découvrit rien de tout ce
qu'il savait à ses frères.

Ils allèrent dans une forêt fort épaisse, où à dix pas de distance on
ne se voyait pas l'un l'autre. Le bûcheron se mit à couper du bois et
ses enfants à ramasser les broutilles pour faire des fagots. Le père et
la mère, les voyant occupés à travailler, s'éloignèrent d'eux insensible-
ment, et puis s'enfuirent tout à coup par un petit sentier détourné.

Lorsque ces enfants se virent seuls, ils se mirent à crier et à pleurer
de toute leur force. Le Petit Poucet les laissait crier, sachant bien par
où il reviendrait à la maison; car en marchant il avait laissé tomber le
long du chemin les petits cailloux blancs qu'il avait dans ses poches.
Il leur dit donc:

«Ne craignez point, mes frères; mon père et ma mère nous ont lais-
sés ici, mais je vous remènerai bien au logis, suivez-moi seulement.»

Ils le suivirent, et il les mena jusqu'à leur maison par le même
chemin qu'ils étaient venus dans la forêt. Ils n'osèrent d'abord entrer,
mais ils se mirent tous contre la porte pour écouter ce que disaient
leur père et leur mère.

Dans le moment que le bûcheron et la bûcheronne arrivèrent chez
eux, le seigneur du village leur envoya dix écus qu'il leur devait il y
avait longtemps, et dont ils n'espéraient plus rien. Cela leur redonna
la vie, car les pauvres gens mouraient de faim. Le bûcheron envoya
sur l'heure sa femme à la boucherie. Comme il y avait longtemps
qu'elle n'avait mangé, elle acheta trois fois plus de viande qu'il n'en
fallait pour le souper de deux personnes. Lorsqu'ils furent rassasiés, la
bûcheronne dit:

«Hélas! où sont maintenant nos pauvres enfants? Ils feraient bonne
chère de ce qui nous reste là. Mais aussi, Guillaume, c'est toi qui les
as voulu perdre; j'avais bien dit que nous nous en repentirions. Que
font-ils maintenant dans cette forêt? Hélas! mon Dieu, les loups les
ont peut-être déjà mangés! Tu es bien inhumain d'avoir perdu ainsi
tes enfants.»

Le bûcheron s'impatienta à la fin, car elle redit plus de vingt fois
qu'ils s'en repentiraient et qu'elle l'avait bien dit. Il la menaça de la
battre si elle ne se taisait. Ce n'est pas que le bûcheron ne fût peut-

Little Thumbling heard everything they said, because having heard, while in bed, that they were talking business, he had got up quietly and had slipped under his father's stool, in order to listen to them without being seen. He went back to bed, but couldn't sleep a wink all night, thinking about what he needed to do. He arose early in the morning and went to the edge of a brook, where he filled his pockets with small white pebbles; then he returned home. The family departed, but Little Thumbling revealed nothing of what he knew to his brothers.

They entered a very dense forest, where they couldn't see one another at ten paces' distance. The woodcutter began to chop down trees, and his children began to gather twigs to make bundles. Their parents, seeing them busily at work, moved away from them by slow degrees, then suddenly broke into a run down a little bypath.

When the children found themselves alone, they began to shout and weep with all their might. Little Thumbling let them shout, knowing very well how he'd get back home; for, while they were walking, he had dropped the little white pebbles he had in his pockets all along the way. And so he said to them:

"Don't be afraid, brothers; father and mother have left us here, but I'll definitely lead you back home; just follow me."

They followed him, and he led them all the way home along the same route by which they had entered the forest. At first they didn't dare go in, but all took up their stand beside the door, to listen to what their parents were saying.

At the very moment the woodcutter and his wife had reached home, the lord of the domain in which their village was located had sent them thirty francs, which he had long owed them and which they had never expected to receive. That restored them to life, for the poor people were dying of hunger. At once the woodcutter sent his wife to the butcher's. Since she hadn't eaten for some time, she bought three times as much meat as was necessary for two people's supper. When they were full, the woodcutter's wife said:

"Alas! Where are our poor children now? They could make a good meal of our leftovers. But, I tell you, William, you wre the one who wanted to lose them; I told you we'd be sorry we did. What are they doing now in that forest? Oh, Lord, maybe the wolves have eaten them! You're really inhuman, the way you got rid of your own children."

Finally the woodcutter lost his patience, because she repeated more than twenty times that they'd be sorry for it and that she had told him so. He threatened her with a beating if she didn't keep quiet.

être encore plus fâché que sa femme, mais c'est qu'elle lui rompait la tête, et qu'il était de l'humeur de beaucoup d'autres gens, qui aiment fort les femmes qui disent bien, mais qui trouvent très importunes celles qui ont toujours bien dit.

La bûcheronne était toute en pleurs:

«Hélas! où sont maintenant mes enfants, mes pauvres enfants?»

Elle le dit une fois si haut que les enfants qui étaient à la porte, l'ayant entendu, se mirent à crier tous ensemble:

«Nous voilà, nous voilà.»

Elle courut vite leur ouvrir la porte, et leur dit en les embrassant:

«Que je suis aise de vous revoir, mes chers enfants! Vous êtes bien las, et vous avez bien faim; et toi Pierrot, comme te voilà crotté, viens que je te débarbouille.»

Ce Pierrot était son fils aîné qu'elle aimait plus que tous les autres, parce qu'il était un peu rousseau, et qu'elle était un peu rousse.

Ils se mirent à table, et mangèrent d'un appétit qui faisait plaisir au père et à la mère, à qui ils racontaient la peur qu'ils avaient eue dans la forêt en parlant presque toujours tous ensemble. Ces bonnes gens étaient ravis de revoir leurs enfants avec eux, et cette joie dura tant que les dix écus durèrent. Mais lorsque l'argent fut dépensé, ils retombèrent dans leur premier chagrin, et résolurent de les perdre encore, et pour ne pas manquer leur coup, de les mener bien plus loin que la première fois.

Ils ne purent parler de cela si secrètement qu'ils ne fussent entendus par le Petit Poucet, qui fit son compte de sortir d'affaire comme il avait déjà fait; mais quoiqu'il se fût levé de bon matin pour aller ramasser des petits cailloux, il ne put en venir à bout, car il trouva la porte de la maison fermée à double tour. Il ne savait que faire, lorsque la bûcheronne leur ayant donné à chacun un morceau de pain pour leur déjeuner, il songea qu'il pourrait se servir de son pain au lieu de cailloux en le jetant par miettes le long des chemins où ils passeraient; il le serra donc dans sa poche.

Le père et la mère les menèrent dans l'endroit de la forêt le plus épais et le plus obscur, et dès qu'ils y furent, ils gagnèrent un fauxfuyant et les laissèrent là. Le Petit Poucet ne s'en chagrina pas beaucoup, parce qu'il croyait retrouver aisément son chemin par le moyen de son pain qu'il avait semé partout où il avait passé; mais il fut bien surpris lorsqu'il ne put en retrouver une seule miette; les oiseaux étaient venus qui avaient tout mangé.

Les voilà donc bien affligés, car plus ils marchaient, plus ils s'égaraient et s'enfonçaient dans la forêt. La nuit vint, et il s'éleva un

That doesn't mean that the woodcutter wasn't even more grieved than his wife; but she was driving him crazy, and he shared the characteristics of many other men: they appreciate women who are right in what they say, but are annoyed no end by those who are *always* right.

His wife was in tears:

"Alas! Where are my children now, my poor children?"

She said it so loud one time that the children, who were at the door, heard her and they all started calling together:

"Here we are! Here we are!"

She quickly ran over to let them in, and said to them, while embracing them:

"How glad I am to see you again, dear children! You must be very tired and hungry; and you, Petie, how filthy you are; come let me wash you off."

That Petie was her eldest son, whom she liked more than all the rest, because he had somewhat red hair, like hers.

They sat down at the table, and ate with an appetite that gave their parents pleasure; they told them how frightened they had been in the forest; they were nearly always all talking at the same time. Those kind people were delighted to have their children back, and their joy lasted as long as the thirty francs lasted. But when the money was all spent, they relapsed into their former worries, and decided to lose the children again; so as not to fail this time, they would take them out farther than before.

No matter how they tried to keep that conversation a secret, they were overheard by Little Thumbling, who was relying on pulling through as he had done earlier; but even though he got up early in the morning to go out and gather little pebbles, he was unsuccessful, because he found the house door double-locked. He didn't know what to do, until the woodcutter's wife gave each of them a piece of bread for their midday meal, and it occurred to him to use his bread in place of pebbles, crumbling it and scattering it on the paths along which they would walk; so he kept his piece in his pocket.

The boys' parents led them to the densest and darkest spot in the forest, and as soon as they arrived, they took a bypath and abandoned them there. Little Thumbling wasn't too worried, because he thought he could easily find the path again by means of the breadcrumbs he had scattered everywhere he had passed; but he was very surprised when he couldn't find a single crumb; the birds had come and had eaten everything.

So there they were, in great distress, because the more they walked, the more lost they got, and the deeper into the forest. Night came and

grand vent qui leur faisait des peurs épouvantables. Ils croyaient n'entendre de tous côtés que des hurlements de loups qui venaient à eux pour les manger. Ils n'osaient presque se parler ni tourner la tête. Il survint une grosse pluie qui les perça jusqu'aux os; ils glissaient à chaque pas et tombaient dans la boue, d'où ils se relevaient tout crottés, ne sachant que faire de leurs mains.

Le Petit Poucet grimpa au haut d'un arbre pour voir s'il ne découvrirait rien; ayant tourné la tête de tous côtés, il vit une petite lueur comme d'une chandelle, mais qui était bien loin par-delà la forêt. Il descendit de l'arbre; et lorsqu'il fut à terre, il ne vit plus rien; cela le désola. Cependant, ayant marché quelque temps avec ses frères du côté qu'il avait vu la lumière, il la revit en sortant du bois.

Ils arrivèrent enfin à la maison où était cette chandelle, non sans bien des frayeurs, car souvent ils la perdaient de vue, ce qui leur arrivait toutes les fois qu'ils descendaient dans quelques fonds. Ils heurtèrent à la porte, et une bonne femme vint leur ouvrir. Elle leur demanda ce qu'ils voulaient; le Petit Poucet lui dit qu'ils étaient de pauvres enfants qui s'étaient perdus dans la forêt, et qui demandaient à coucher par charité. Cette femme les voyant tous si jolis se mit à pleurer, et leur dit:

«Hélas! mes pauvres enfants, où êtes-vous venus? Savez-vous bien que c'est ici la maison d'un ogre qui mange les petits enfants?

—Hélas! madame, lui répondit le Petit Poucet, qui tremblait de toute sa force aussi bien que ses frères, que ferons-nous? Il est bien sûr que les loups de la forêt ne manqueront pas de nous manger cette nuit, si vous ne voulez pas nous retirer chez vous. Et cela étant, nous aimons mieux que ce soit Monsieur qui nous mange; peut-être qu'il aura pitié de nous, si vous voulez bien l'en prier.»

La femme de l'ogre qui crut qu'elle pourrait les cacher à son mari jusqu'au lendemain matin, les laissa entrer et les mena se chauffer auprès d'un bon feu; car il y avait un mouton tout entier à la broche pour le souper de l'ogre.

Comme ils commençaient à se chauffer, ils entendirent heurter trois ou quatre grands coups à la porte: c'était l'ogre qui revenait. Aussitôt sa femme les fit cacher sous le lit et alla ouvrir la porte. L'ogre demanda d'abord si le souper était prêt, et si on avait tiré du vin, et aussitôt se mit à table. Le mouton était encore tout sanglant, mais il ne lui en sembla que meilleur. Il flairait à droite et à gauche, disant qu'il sentait la chair fraîche.

a strong wind sprang up, frightening them terribly. They thought they heard all around them nothing but the howling of wolves coming to eat them up. They hardly dared to talk to one another or look behind them. In addition, a heavy rain came and soaked them to the skin; at every step, they were slipping and falling in the mud, from which they got up all filthy, not knowing what to do with their hands.

Little Thumbling climbed to the top of a tree to see whether he could catch sight of anything; after turning his head in all directions, he made out a little gleam, like that of a candle, but it was far away, beyond the forest. He climbed down from the tree, but when he reached the ground, he saw nothing anymore; this discouraged him. Nevertheless, after walking with his brothers for awhile in the direction in which he had seen the light, he caught sight of it again as they were leaving the woods.

They finally reached the house where that candle was burning, but not without many a scare, because they frequently lost sight of it; this happened every time they descended into some hollow. They knocked at the door, and a kindly woman came to open it. She asked them what they wanted; Little Thumbling told her that they were poor children who had gotten lost in the forest and were seeking a place to sleep as a favor. Seeing how good-looking they all were, the woman started to cry, saying:

"Alas, you poor children, where have you arrived? Do you know that this is the house of an ogre who eats little children?"

"Alas, ma'am," Little Thumbling replied, trembling all over, like his brothers, "what are we to do? Sure as anything, the wolves in the forest won't fail to eat us up tonight if you refuse to take us in. That being the case, we prefer to be eaten by the gentleman of the house; maybe he'll take pity on us, if you're good enough to ask him to."

The ogre's wife, who thought she could hide them from her husband until the next morning, let them in and brought them to a good fire to get warm; for there was an entire sheep on the spit for the ogre's supper.

When they were beginning to feel warmer, they heard three or four loud knocks at the door; it was the ogre returning home. Immediately his wife hid them under the bed and went to let him in. The first thing the ogre did was to ask whether his supper was ready and whether the wine had been drawn; he sat down at the table instantly. The sheep was still so rare it bled, but it only tasted all the better to him that way. He sniffed around to the right and to the left, saying that he smelled fresh meat.

«Il faut, lui dit sa femme, que ce soit ce veau que je viens d'habiller que vous sentez.

—Je sens la chair fraîche, te dis-je encore une fois, reprit l'ogre, en regardant sa femme de travers, et il y a ici quelque chose que je n'entends pas.»

En disant ces mots, il se leva de table, et alla droit au lit.

«Ah, dit-il, voilà donc comme tu veux me tromper, maudite femme! Je ne sais à quoi il tient que je ne te mange aussi; bien t'en prend d'être une vieille bête. Voilà du gibier qui me vient bien à propos pour traiter trois ogres de mes amis qui doivent me venir voir ces jours ici.»

Il les tira de dessous le lit l'un après l'autre. Ces pauvres enfants se mirent à genoux en lui demandant pardon; mais ils avaient à faire au plus cruel de tous les ogres, qui bien loin d'avoir de la pitié les dévorait déjà des yeux, et disait à sa femme que ce serait là de friands morceaux lorsqu'elle leur aurait fait une bonne sauce.

Il alla prendre un grand couteau, et en approchant de ces pauvres enfants, il l'aiguisait sur une longue pierre qu'il tenait à sa main gauche. Il en avait déjà empoigné un, lorsque sa femme lui dit:

«Que voulez-vous faire à l'heure qu'il est? n'aurez-vous pas assez de temps demain matin?

—Tais-toi, reprit l'ogre, ils en seront plus mortifiés.

—Mais vous avez encore là tant de viande, reprit sa femme; voilà un veau, deux moutons et la moitié d'un cochon!

—Tu as raison, dit l'ogre; donne-leur bien à souper, afin qu'ils ne maigrissent pas, et va les mener coucher.»

La bonne femme fut ravie de joie, et leur porta bien à souper, mais ils ne purent manger tant ils étaient saisis de peur. Pour l'ogre, il se remit à boire, ravi d'avoir de quoi si bien régaler ses amis. Il but une douzaine de coups plus qu'à l'ordinaire, ce qui lui donna un peu dans la tête, et l'obligea de s'aller coucher.

L'ogre avait sept filles, qui n'étaient encore que des enfants. Ces petites ogresses avaient toutes le teint fort beau, parce qu'elles mangeaient de la chair fraîche comme leur père; mais elles avaient de petits yeux gris et tout ronds, le nez crochu et une fort grande bouche avec de longues dents fort aiguës et fort éloignées l'une de l'autre. Elles n'étaient pas encore fort méchantes; mais elles promettaient beaucoup, car elles mordaient déjà les petits enfants pour en sucer le sang.

On les avait fait coucher de bonne heure, et elles étaient toutes sept dans un grand lit, ayant chacune une couronne d'or sur la tête. Il y avait dans la même chambre un autre lit de la même grandeur; ce fut

His wife said, "That must be this calf, which I just dressed, that you smell."

"I smell fresh meat, I tell you," the ogre insisted, giving his wife a funny look, "and there's something going on here that I don't understand."

Saying this, he got up from the table and headed straight for the bed.

"Aha!" he said, "that's how you're trying to fool me, accursed woman! I don't know what's keeping me from eating you, too; you're lucky you're an old animal. Here's some game that comes right in handy for entertaining three of my ogre friends whom I expect to visit me some day soon."

He pulled them out from under the bed, one after another. The poor children knelt before him, begging him to spare them; but they were dealing with the cruelest of all ogres; far from feeling pity for them, he was already devouring them with his eyes, telling his wife they'd make tasty morsels once she had made a good sauce for them.

He went to get a large knife and, approaching the poor children, he sharpened it on a long stone that he held in his left hand. He had already seized one boy when his wife said:

"What are you up to at this time of night? Won't tomorrow morning be time enough?"

"Be still," the ogre countered, "this will make them gamier."

"But you still have so much meat left," his wife insisted; "here's a calf, two sheep, and half a pig!"

"You're right," said the ogre; "give them a good supper so they don't get thin, and put them to bed."

The good woman was overjoyed and brought them a big meal, but they were so overcome with fear that they couldn't eat. As for the ogre, he resumed his drinking, delighted to have such a fine treat for his friends. He had a dozen cups of wine more than usual; this went to his head somewhat and compelled him to go to bed.

The ogre had seven daughters, who were still children. All these little ogresses had a very lovely complexion, because they ate fresh meat like their father; but they had small eyes, gray and round, a hooked nose, and a very big mouth with teeth that were very sharp and very far apart. They were not yet extremely wicked, but showed enormous promise, because they were already biting little children to suck out their blood.

They had been put to bed early, and all seven were in one big bed, each one wearing a gold crown on her head. In the same room there was another bed of the same size; it was in that bed that the ogre's wife

dans ce lit que la femme de l'ogre mit coucher les sept petits garçons; après quoi, elle s'alla coucher auprès de son mari.

Le Petit Poucet qui avait remarqué que les filles de l'ogre avaient des couronnes d'or sur la tête, et qui craignait qu'il ne prît à l'ogre quelque remords de ne les avoir pas égorgés dès le soir même, se leva vers le milieu de la nuit, et prenant les bonnets de ses frères et le sien, il alla tout doucement les mettre sur la tête des sept filles de l'ogre, après leur avoir ôté leurs couronnes d'or qu'il mit sur la tête de ses frères et sur la sienne, afin que l'ogre les prît pour ses filles, et ses filles pour les garçons qu'il voulait égorger. La chose réussit comme il l'avait pensé; car l'ogre s'étant éveillé sur le minuit eut regret d'avoir différé au lendemain ce qu'il pouvait exécuter la veille; il se jeta donc brusquement hors du lit, et prenant son grand couteau:

«Allons voir, dit-il, comment se portent nos petits drôles; n'en faisons pas à deux fois.»

Il monta donc à tâtons à la chambre de ses filles et s'approcha du lit où étaient les petits garçons, qui dormaient tous, excepté le Petit Poucet, qui eut bien peur lorsqu'il sentit la main de l'ogre qui lui tâtait la tête, comme il avait tâté celles de tous ses frères. L'ogre, qui sentit les couronnes d'or:

«Vraiment, dit-il, j'allais faire là un bel ouvrage; je vois bien que je bus trop hier au soir.»

Il alla ensuite au lit de ses filles, où ayant senti les petits bonnets des garçons:

«Ah! les voilà, dit-il, nos gaillards! travaillons hardiment.»

En disant ces mots, il coupa sans balancer la gorge à ses sept filles. Fort content de cette expédition, il alla se recoucher auprès de sa femme.

Aussitôt que le Petit Poucet entendit ronfler l'ogre, il réveilla ses frères, et leur dit de s'habiller promptement et de le suivre. Ils descendirent doucement dans le jardin, et sautèrent par-dessus les murailles. Ils coururent presque toute la nuit, toujours en tremblant et sans savoir où ils allaient.

L'ogre s'étant éveillé dit à sa femme:

«Va-t'en là-haut habiller ces petits drôles d'hier au soir.»

L'ogresse fut fort étonnée de la bonté de son mari, ne se doutant point de la manière qu'il entendait qu'elle les habillât, et croyant qu'il lui ordonnait de les aller vêtir, elle monta en haut où elle fut bien surprise lorsqu'elle aperçut ses sept filles égorgées et nageant dans leur sang.

put the seven little boys; after that, she joined her husband in their own bed.

Little Thumbling, having noticed that the ogre's daughters had gold crowns on their heads, and fearing that the ogre might regret not having slaughtered the boys that very night, got up around the middle of the night, took his brothers' caps and his own, and very quietly put them on the heads of the ogre's seven daughters, after removing their gold crowns, which he placed on his brothers' heads and his own, so that the ogre would mistake them for his daughters, and his daughters for the boys he wished to slaughter. Matters turned out as he had thought; for the ogre, awakening at midnight, was sorry he had postponed for the next day what he could accomplish right away; so he jumped briskly out of bed and, taking his big knife, he said:

"Let's see how our little scamps are doing; let's get it over with all at once."

So he groped his way up to his daughters' room and approached the bed in which the little boys were lying; they were all asleep except for Little Thumbling, who was terribly frightened when he felt the ogre's hand touching his head, just as he had touched those of all his brothers. The ogre, feeling the gold crowns, said:

"I was just about to do something really smart! I can tell I had too much to drink last night."

Then he went to his daughters' bed; there, feeling the boys' little caps, he said:

"Ah, there they are, our rascals! Now, to work with a will!"

Saying this, without hesitating he cut his seven daughters' throats. Mightily pleased with this exploit,[29] he went back to bed, rejoining his wife.

As soon as Little Thumbling heard the ogre snoring, he woke up his brothers and told them to get dressed quickly and follow him. They quietly went down to the garden, and jumped over the walls. They ran nearly all night, constantly trembling and not knowing where they were going.

Upon awakening, the ogre said to his wife:

"Go upstairs and dress those little scamps from last night."

The ogress was quite surprised at her husband's kindness, not at all suspecting his use of the word "dress"; thinking he meant her to go and put on their clothes, she went upstairs, where she was shocked to find her seven daughters slaughtered and awash in their own blood.

---

[29]Or, possibly: "diligence; expeditiousness."

Elle commença par s'évanouir (car c'est le premier expédient que trouvent presque toutes les femmes en pareilles rencontres). L'ogre, craignant que sa femme ne fût trop longtemps à faire la besogne dont il l'avait chargée, monta en haut pour lui aider. Il ne fut pas moins étonné que sa femme lorsqu'il vit cet affreux spectacle.

«Ah! qu'ai-je fait là? s'écria-t-il. Ils me le payeront, les malheureux, et tout à l'heure.»

Il jeta aussitôt une potée d'eau dans le nez de sa femme et l'ayant fait revenir:

«Donne-moi vite mes bottes de sept lieues, lui dit-il, afin que j'aille les attraper.»

Il se mit en campagne, et après avoir couru bien loin de tous côtés, enfin il entra dans le chemin où marchaient ces pauvres enfants qui n'é-taient plus qu'à cent pas du logis de leur père. Ils virent l'ogre qui allait de montagne en montagne, et qui traversait des rivières aussi aisément qu'il aurait fait le moindre ruisseau. Le Petit Poucet, qui vit un rocher creux proche le lieu où ils étaient, y fit cacher ses six frères, et s'y fourra aussi, regardant toujours ce que l'ogre deviendrait. L'ogre qui se trou-vait fort las du long chemin qu'il avait fait inutilement (car les bottes de sept lieues fatiguent fort leur homme), voulut se reposer, et par hasard il alla s'asseoir sur la roche où les petits garçons s'étaient cachés.

Comme il n'en pouvait plus de fatigue, il s'endormit après s'être reposé quelque temps, et vint à ronfler si effroyablement que les pau-vres enfants n'en eurent pas moins de peur que quand il tenait son grand couteau pour leur couper la gorge. Le Petit Poucet en eut moins de peur, et dit à ses frères de s'enfuir promptement à la maison pendant que l'ogre dormait bien fort, et qu'ils ne se missent point en peine de lui. Ils crurent son conseil, et gagnèrent vite la maison.

Le Petit Poucet s'étant approché de l'ogre lui tira doucement ses bottes, et les mit aussitôt. Les bottes étaient fort grandes et fort larges; mais comme elles étaient fées, elles avaient le don de s'agrandir et de s'apetisser selon la jambe de celui qui les chaussait, de sorte qu'elles se trouvèrent aussi justes à ses pieds et à ses jambes que si elles avaient été faites pour lui.

Il alla droit à la maison de l'ogre où il trouva sa femme qui pleurait auprès de ses filles égorgées.

«Votre mari, lui dit le Petit Poucet, est en grand danger; car il a été pris par une troupe de voleurs qui ont juré de le tuer s'il ne leur donne tout son or et tout son argent. Dans le moment qu'ils lui tenaient le poignard sur la gorge, il m'a aperçu et m'a prié de vous venir avertir de l'état où il est, et de vous dire de me donner tout ce qu'il a vaillant

The first thing she did was to faint (for that's the first recourse of nearly all women in such occurrences). The ogre, fearing that his wife might take too long with the chore he had given her, went upstairs to help her. He was no less stunned than his wife when he saw that terrible sight.

"Oh, what have I done?" he exclaimed. "They'll pay for this, those scum, and right away, too!"

Immediately he dashed a pitcherful of water in his wife's face and, after bringing her to, he said:

"Quick, give me my seven-league boots, so I can go and catch them!"

He set out and, after a long run in all directions, he finally found the path taken by the poor children, who were now only a hundred paces from their father's house. They saw the ogre striding from mountain to mountain, and crossing rivers as easily as if they were the smallest brooks. Little Thumbling, who saw a hollow boulder near the spot they were at, hid his six brothers in it and burrowed his own way in, always keeping an eye out for the ogre. The ogre, very weary from the long march he had made to no purpose (because seven-league boots tire out their wearer), felt like resting, and by chance he sat down on the rock in which the little boys were hiding.

Since he was too worn out to go on, he fell asleep after a brief rest period, and began snoring so fearfully that the poor children were just as afraid as they had been when he was wielding his big knife to cut their throats. Little Thumbling was less afraid, and told his brothers to run away home quickly while the ogre was fast asleep, and not to worry on his account. They thrusted his advice, and were quickly safe at home.

Little Thumbling went up to the ogre, gently drew off his boots, and put them on at once. The boots were extremely big and wide, but since they were enchanted, they had the power to get bigger or smaller to fit the leg of the wearer, so that they were just as snug on his feet and legs as if they had been made for him.

He went straight to the ogre's house, where he found his wife weeping beside her massacred daughters.

"Your husband," Little Thumbling told her, "is in great danger: he's been captured by a gang of thieves, who have sworn to kill him unless he gives them all his gold and silver. Just as they were holding the dagger to his throat, he caught sight of me and begged me to come and inform you of the plight he's in, and to tell you to give me all his

sans en rien retenir, parce qu'autrement ils le tueront sans miséricorde. Comme la chose presse beaucoup, il a voulu que je prisse ses
bottes de sept lieues que voilà pour faire diligence, et aussi afin que
vous ne croyiez pas que je sois un affronteur.»

La bonne femme fort effrayée lui donna aussitôt tout ce qu'elle
avait: car cet ogre ne laissait pas d'être fort bon mari, quoiqu'il
mangeât les petits enfants. Le Petit Poucet étant donc chargé de
toutes les richesses de l'ogre s'en revint au logis de son père, où il fut
reçu avec bien de la joie.

Il y a bien des gens qui ne demeurent pas d'accord de cette
dernière circonstance, et qui prétendent que le Petit Poucet n'a jamais fait ce vol à l'ogre; qu'à la vérité, il n'avait pas fait conscience de
lui prendre ses bottes de sept lieues, parce qu'il ne s'en servait que
pour courir après les petits enfants. Ces gens-là assurent le savoir de
bonne part, et même pour avoir bu et mangé dans la maison du
bûcheron. Ils assurent que lorsque le Petit Poucet eut chaussé les
bottes de l'ogre, il s'en alla à la cour, où il savait qu'on était fort en
peine d'une armée qui était à deux cents lieues de là, et du succès
d'une bataille qu'on avait donnée. Il alla, disent-ils, trouver le roi, et
lui dit que s'il le souhaitait, il lui rapporterait des nouvelles de l'armée
avant la fin du jour. Le roi lui promit une grosse somme d'argent s'il
en venait à bout. Le Petit Poucet rapporta des nouvelles dès le soir
même, et cette première course l'ayant fait connaître, il gagnait tout
ce qu'il voulait; car le roi le payait parfaitement bien pour porter ses
ordres à l'armée, et une infinité de dames lui donnaient tout ce qu'il
voulait pour avoir des nouvelles de leurs amants, et ce fut là son plus
grand gain.

Il se trouvait quelques femmes qui le chargeaient de lettres pour
leurs maris, mais elles le payaient si mal, et cela allait à si peu de
chose, qu'il ne daignait mettre en ligne de compte ce qu'il gagnait de
ce côté-là.

Après avoir fait pendant quelque temps le métier de courrier, et y
avoir amassé beaucoup de bien, il revint chez son père, où il n'est pas
possible d'imaginer la joie qu'on eut de le revoir. Il mit toute sa famille
à son aise. Il acheta des offices de nouvelle création pour son père et
pour ses frères; et par là il les établit tous, et fit parfaitement bien sa
cour en même temps.

wealth, holding nothing back, because otherwise they'll kill him without mercy. Since it's a very urgent matter, he insisted on my taking these seven-league boots of his, which you see here, in order to save time, and also in order to prove to you that I'm no swindler."

The good woman, very frightened, immediately gave him everything she had: because that ogre was still a very good husband even though he ate little children. And so, Little Thumbling, laden down with all the ogre's valuables, returned to his father's house, where he was welcomed with great joy.

Many people disagree with regard to this last episode, asserting that Little Thumbling never robbed the ogre in that manner; the truth is, they say, that he had no scruples about taking away his seven-league boots because the ogre used them only to pursue little children. These people insist that they have this from a good source, even claiming that they ate and drank in the woodcutter's house. They assure us that, after Little Thumbling put on the ogre's boots, he went to the royal court, where he knew that the people were greatly concerned about an army of theirs located two hundred leagues away, and in suspense over the outcome of a battle that had been waged there. He went (these people say) to see the king and told him that, if he wished, he'd report back to him about the army's doings before the day was over. The king promised him a large sum of money if he succeeded. Little Thumbling returned with the news that evening; after that first trip had made him well known, he earned all the money he wanted, because the king gave him a good salary for conveying his orders to the army, and a huge number of ladies gave him anything he asked in return for news from their lovers: that was his chief profit.

There were a few women who entrusted him with letters to their husbands, but they were such bad payers, and it amounted to so little, that he scorned to take into account the money he made from that services.

After plying the trade of courier for awhile and accumulating much wealth at it, he returned to his father's home, where you can't imagine the family's joy at seeing him again. He placed every member of it in comfortable circumstances. He purchased newly created positions for his father and brothers, and by so doing, he not only settled them in life, but also substantially improved his own standing at court.

Moralité

On ne s'afflige point d'avoir beaucoup d'enfants,
   Quand ils sont tous beaux, bien faits et bien grands,
      Et d'un extérieur qui brille;
   Mais si l'un d'eux est faible ou ne dit mot,
   On le méprise, on le raille, on le pille.
Quelquefois cependant c'est ce petit marmot
Qui fera le bonheur de toute la famille.

Moral

It is not distressing to have a lot of children
  when they are all good-looking, well built, and tall,
    with a brilliant exterior;
  but if one of them is sickly or doesn't speak,
  he is scorned, mocked, and attacked.
And yet at times it is that same little monkey
who will bring good luck to the whole family.

"Peau d'Ane" en prose (1781)

Il était une fois un roi si grand, si aimé de ses peuples, si respecté de tous ses voisins et de ses alliés, qu'on pouvait dire qu'il était le plus heureux de tous les monarques. Son bonheur était encore confirmé par le choix qu'il avait fait d'une princesse aussi belle que vertueuse; et les heureux époux vivaient dans une union parfaite. De leur chaste hymen était née une fille, douée de tant de grâces et de charmes, qu'ils ne regrettaient pas de n'avoir pas une plus ample lignée.

La magnificence, le goût et l'abondance régnaient dans son palais; les ministres étaient sages et habiles; les courtisans, vertueux et attachés; les domestiques fidèles et laborieux; les écuries, vastes et remplies des plus beaux chevaux du monde, couverts de riches caparaçons: mais ce qui étonnait les étrangers qui venaient admirer ces belles écuries, c'est qu'au lieu le plus apparent un maître âne étalait de longues et grandes oreilles. Ce n'était pas par fantaisie, mais avec raison, que le roi lui avait donné une place particulière et distinguée. Les vertus de ce rare animal méritaient cette distinction, puisque la nature l'avait formé si extraordinaire que sa litière, au lieu d'être malpropre, était couverte, tous les matins, avec profusion, de beaux écus au soleil et de louis d'or de toute espèce qu'on allait recueillir à son réveil.

Or, comme les vicissitudes de la vie s'étendent aussi bien sur les rois que sur les sujets, et que toujours les biens sont mêlés de quelques maux, le Ciel permit que la reine fût tout à coup attaquée d'une âpre maladie pour laquelle, malgré la science et l'habileté des médecins, on ne put trouver aucun secours. La désolation fut générale. Le roi, sensible et amoureux, malgré le proverbe fameux qui dit que l'hymen est le tombeau de l'amour, s'affligeait sans modération, faisait des vœux ardents à tous les temples de son royaume, offrait sa vie pour celle d'une épouse si chère; mais les dieux et les fées étaient évoqués en vain. La reine, sentant sa dernière heure approcher, dit à son époux qui fondait en larmes:

210

"Donkey-Skin" in Prose (1781)

There was once a king so great, so beloved by his subjects, and so respected by all his neighbors and allies, that he could be said to be the most fortunate of all monarchs. His good fortune was further consolidated by the choice he had made of a princess who was as beautiful as she was virtuous; and the happy pair lived in perfect harmony. From their chaste matrimony was born a daughter endowed with so much grace and charm that they weren't sorry about having no other children.

Magnificence, good taste, and plenty reigned in his palace; his ministers were wise and skillful; his courtiers, virtuous and devoted; his servants, loyal and industrious; his stables, huge and filled with the most beautiful horses in the world, covered with sumptuous caparisons; but the greatest surprise for the foreigners who came to admire those fine stables was that, in the most prominent spot, stood an egregious donkey with big, long ears. It wasn't through caprice, but for a solid reason, that the king had granted him a special place of honor. The powers of that rare animal merited this distinction, because nature had created him so extraordinary that his litter, instead of being soiled, was abundantly covered every morning with beautiful three-franc pieces, with a sun mint-mark, and with gold twenty-franc pieces of all sorts, which the grooms collected when he awoke.

Now, since the ups and downs of life apply to kings as well as to their subjects, and the good things are always mingled with some troubles, Heaven allowed the queen to be suddenly stricken with a severe illness for which, despite the knowledge and skill of the physicians, no remedy could be found. There was universal consternation. The king, sensitive and in love, despite the notorious proverb to the effect that marriage is the grave of love, showed no moderation in his sorrow; he made heartfelt vows in every church in his realm, offering his own life to save that of so dear a wife; but the gods and the fairies were invoked in vain. The queen, feeling her final hour approaching, said to her husband, who was dissolved in tears:

«Trouvez bon, avant que je meure, que j'exige une chose de vous: c'est que s'il vous prenait envie de vous remarier . . .»

A ces mots, le roi fit des cris pitoyables, prit les mains de sa femme, les baigna de pleurs et, l'assurant qu'il était superflu de lui parler d'un second hyménée:

«Non, non, dit-il enfin, ma chère reine, parlez-moi plutôt de vous suivre.

—L'État, reprit la reine avec une fermeté qui augmentait les regrets de ce prince, l'État doit exiger des successeurs et, comme je ne vous ai donné qu'une fille, vous presser d'avoir des fils qui vous ressemblent; mais je vous demande instamment, par tout l'amour que vous avez eu pour moi, de ne céder à l'empressement de vos peuples que lorsque vous aurez trouvé une princesse plus belle et mieux faite que moi; j'en veux votre serment et alors je mourrai contente.»

On présume que la reine, qui ne manquait pas d'amour-propre, avait exigé ce serment, ne croyant pas qu'il fût au monde personne qui pût l'égaler, pensant bien que c'était s'assurer que le roi ne se remarierait jamais. Enfin elle mourut. Jamais mari ne fit tant de vacarme: pleurer, sangloter jour et nuit, menus droits du veuvage furent son unique occupation.

Les grandes douleurs ne durent pas. D'ailleurs, les grands de l'État s'assemblèrent et vinrent en corps prier le roi de se remarier. Cette première proposition lui parut dure et lui fit répandre de nouvelles larmes. Il allégua le serment qu'il avait fait à la reine, défiant tous ses conseillers de pouvoir trouver une princesse plus belle et mieux faite que feu sa femme, pensant que cela était impossible. Mais le conseil traita de babiole une telle promesse et dit qu'il importait peu de la beauté, pourvu qu'une reine fût vertueuse et point stérile; que l'État demandait des princes pour son repos et sa tranquillité; qu'à la vérité l'infante avait toutes les qualités requises pour faire une grande reine, mais qu'il fallait lui choisir un étranger pour époux; et qu'alors, ou cet étranger l'emmènerait chez lui ou que, s'il régnait avec elle, ses enfants ne seraient plus réputés du même sang; et que, n'y ayant point de prince de son nom, les peuples voisins pourraient leur susciter des guerres qui entraîneraient la ruine du royaume. Le roi frappé de ces considérations, promit qu'il songerait à les contenter.

Effectivement, il chercha, parmi les princesses à marier, qui serait celle qui pourrait lui convenir. Chaque jour on lui apportait des portraits charmants, mais aucun n'avait les grâces de la feue reine; ainsi, il ne se déterminait point. Malheureusement il s'avisa de trouver que

"Please permit me, before I die, to exact one favor from you: namely, that if you should feel the urge to remarry. . . ."

When she said this, the king uttered pitiful cries, seized his wife's hands, bathed them with tears, and, assuring her that it was pointless to speak to him about a second marriage, he finally said:

"No, no, my dear queen, rather than that, speak to me about following you to the grave."

"The nation," continued the queen with a firmness that only increased the monarch's regret, "the nation will surely demand a successor and, since I have borne you only a daughter, you will be urged to have sons like yourself; but I ask you earnestly, by all the love you have had for me, not to yield to your subjects' insistence until you find a princess more comely and shapely than I; I want your oath on it, and then I can die in peace."

It is presumed that the queen, who wasn't lacking in self-love, had exacted that oath in the belief that she had no equal in the world and that this was an assurance that the king would never remarry. Finally she died. Never did a husband raise such a hubbub, weeping and sobbing day and night; the little privileges of being a widower were his sole occupation.

His major sorrows were soon over. Besides, the grandees of the nation assembled and came en masse to urge the king to remarry. This first request struck him as being severe, and caused him to shed further tears. He cited the oath he had sworn to the queen, and defied all his advisers to find a princess more comely and shapely than his late wife, believing it an impossibility. But the council considered that sort of promise to be devoid of significance, saying that a queen's beauty was of little account, just as long as she was virtuous and not barren; that the nation demanded princes for its peace of mind and tranquility; that, indeed, his daughter the princess had all the qualities requisite to become a great queen, but a foreigner would have to be selected as her husband, and, on that occasion, either that foreigner would take her back home with him, or else, if she reigned alongside him, her children would no longer be considered as being of the same blood, and, there being no prince bearing his name, the neighboring peoples might make war on them, entailing the ruin of the kingdom. Moved by these reflections, the king promised to consider gratifying the petitioners.

And, indeed, he inquired into all marriageable princesses to see which one might suit him. Daily he was brought charming portraits, but none had the graces of the late queen; and so, he wouldn't make up his mind. Unfortunately, he took it into his head that his daughter

l'infante, sa fille, était non seulement belle et bien faite à ravir, mais qu'elle surpassait encore de beaucoup la reine sa mère en esprit et en agréments. Sa jeunesse, l'agréable fraîcheur de son beau teint enflamma le roi d'un feu si violent qu'il ne put le cacher à l'infante, et il lui dit qu'il avait résolu de l'épouser, puisqu'elle seule pouvait le dégager de son serment.

La jeune princesse, remplie de vertu et de pudeur, pensa s'évanouir à cette horrible proposition. Elle se jeta aux pieds du roi son père et le conjura, avec toute la force qu'elle put trouver dans son esprit, de ne la pas contraindre à commettre un tel crime.

Le roi, qui s'était mis en tête ce bizarre projet, avait consulté un vieux druide pour mettre la conscience de la princesse en repos. Ce druide, moins religieux qu'ambitieux, sacrifia à l'honneur d'être confident d'un grand roi l'intérêt de l'innocence et de la vertu et s'insinua avec tant d'astuce dans l'esprit du roi, lui adoucit tellement le crime qu'il allait commettre qu'il lui persuada même que c'était une œuvre pie que d'épouser sa fille. Le prince, flatté pas les discours de ce scélérat, l'embrassa et revint d'avec lui plus entêté que jamais dans son projet: il fit donc ordonner à l'infante de se préparer à lui obéir.

La jeune princesse, outrée d'une vive douleur, n'imagina rien autre chose que d'aller trouver la fée des Lilas sa marraine. Pour cet effet elle partit la même nuit dans un joli cabriolet attelé d'un gros mouton qui savait tous les chemins. Elle y arriva heureusement. La fée, qui aimait l'infante, lui dit qu'elle savait tout ce qu'elle venait lui dire, mais qu'elle n'eût aucun souci, rien ne pouvant lui nuire si elle exécutait fidèlement ce qu'elle allait lui prescrire.

«Car, ma chère enfant, lui dit-elle, ce serait une grande faute que d'épouser votre père; mais, sans le contredire, vous pouvez l'éviter; dites-lui que, pour remplir une fantaisie que vous avez, il faut qu'il vous donne une robe couleur du temps; jamais, avec tout son amour et son pouvoir, il ne pourra y parvenir.»

La princesse remercia bien sa marraine; et dès le lendemain matin elle dit au roi ce que la fée lui avait conseillé et protesta qu'on ne tirerait d'elle aucun aveu qu'elle n'eût une robe couleur du temps. Le roi, ravi de l'espérance qu'elle lui donnait, assembla les plus fameux ouvriers et leur commanda cette robe, sous la condition que, s'ils ne pouvaient réussir, il les ferait tous pendre. L'empyrée n'est pas d'un plus beau bleu lorsqu'il est ceint de nuages d'or, que cette belle robe lorsqu'elle fut étalée. L'infante en fut toute contristée et ne savait comment se tirer d'embarras. Le roi pressait la conclusion. Il fallut

the princess was not only beautiful and delightfully shapely, but also far exceeded her mother the queen in intelligence and pleasantness. Her youth, and the charming freshness of her fine complexion, kindled such a hot flame in the king that he was unable to conceal it from the princess, and told her he had determined to marry her, since she alone could release him from his oath.

The young princess, full of virtue and modesty, thought she would faint when she heard that fearful proposal. She threw herself at the feet of her father the king and implored him with all the force of her mind not to compel her to commit such a crime.

The king, who had conceived that grotesque idea, had consulted an old druid in order to set the princess's conscience at rest. This druid, less religious than ambitious, sacrificed the interests of innocence and virtue to the honor of being a great king's confidant, working his way into the king's favor so astutely, and so thoroughly playing down the enormity of the crime he wanted to commit, that he actually convinced him that marrying his daughter was an act of piety. The monarch, flattered by this criminal's arguments, embraced him and, when he left him, he was more stubbornly set on his plan than before; so that he sent word to the princess to get ready to obey him.

The young princess, beside herself with bitter sorrow, could think of nothing else to do but to visit her godmother, the Lilac Fairy. To that purpose she departed that very night in a pretty gig drawn by a large sheep that knew all the roads. She arrived there successfully. The fairy, who loved the princess, told her that she already knew everything she had come to tell her, and that she was not to worry, because nothing could harm her if she carried out exactly the instructions she was about to give her.

"For, my dear child," she said, "it would be a grave crime to marry your father; but, without a direct refusal, you can avoid it; tell him that, to gratify a whim of yours, he must give you a gown the color of the sky; despite all his love and his power, he'll never manage it."

The princess thanked her godmother warmly, and the very next morning she requested from the king what her godmother had advised her to, declaring that she would never give her consent before receiving a gown the color of the sky. The king, delighted by the hope she hinted at, convened the most reputable tailors and ordered that gown, adding that, if they didn't succeed, he'd hang them all. The empyrean is not more beautifully blue when encircled by golden clouds than that beautiful gown was when fully spread out. The princess was extremely downcast to see it, and didn't know how to get

recourir encore à la marraine qui, étonnée de ce que son secret n'avait pas réussi, lui dit d'essayer d'en demander une de la couleur de la lune. Le roi, qui ne pouvait lui rien refuser, envoya chercher les plus habiles ouvriers et leur commanda si expressément une robe couleur de la lune qu'entre ordonner et l'apporter il n'y eut pas vingt-quatre heures.

L'infante, plus charmée de cette superbe robe que des soins du roi son père, s'affligea immodérément lorsqu'elle fut avec ses femmes et sa nourrice. La fée des Lilas, qui savait tout, vint au secours de l'affligée princesse et lui dit:

«Ou je me trompe fort, ou je crois que si vous demandez une robe couleur du soleil, ou nous viendrons à bout de dégoûter le roi votre père, car jamais on ne pourra parvenir à faire une pareille robe, ou nous gagnerons au moins du temps.»

L'infante en convint, demanda la robe, et l'amoureux roi donna, sans regret, tous les diamants et les rubis de sa couronne pour aider à ce superbe ouvrage, avec ordre de ne rien épargner pour rendre cette robe égale au soleil. Aussi, dès qu'elle parut, tous ceux qui la virent furent obligés de fermer les yeux, tant ils furent éblouis. C'est de ce temps que datent les lunettes vertes et les verres noirs. Que devint l'infante à cette vue? Jamais on n'avait rien vu de si beau et de si artistement ouvré. Elle était confondue; et sous prétexte d'avoir mal aux yeux, elle se retira dans sa chambre où la fée l'attendait, plus honteuse qu'on ne peut dire. Ce fut bien pis: car, en voyant la robe du soleil, elle devint rouge de colère.

«Oh! pour le coup, ma fille, dit-elle à l'infante, nous allons mettre l'indigne amour de votre père à une terrible épreuve. Je le crois bien entêté de ce mariage qu'il croit si prochain, mais je pense qu'il sera un peu étourdi de la demande que je vous conseille de lui faire: c'est la peau de cet âne qu'il aime si passionnément et qui fournit à toutes ses dépenses avec tant de profusion; allez, et ne manquez pas de lui dire que vous désirez cette peau.»

L'infante, ravie de trouver encore un moyen d'éluder un mariage qu'elle détestait, et qui pensait en même temps que son père ne pourrait jamais se résoudre à sacrifier son âne, vint le trouver et lui exposa son désir pour la peau de ce bel animal. Quoique le roi fût étonné de cette fantaisie, il ne balança pas à la satisfaire. Le pauvre âne fut sacrifié et la peau galamment apportée à l'infante qui, ne voyant plus aucun moyen d'éluder son malheur, s'allait désespérer lorsque sa marraine accourut.

out of her difficulty. The king was insisting on an answer. She had to return to her godmother, who, amazed that her secret advice hadn't succeeded, told her to try again and ask for a gown the color of the moon. The king, who could refuse her nothing, sent for the most skillful tailors and gave them so explicit an order for a gown the color of the moon that, from the time he ordered it to the time they delivered it, not even twenty-four hours had elapsed.

The princess, more charmed by that superb gown than by the efforts of her father the king, displayed immoderate grief when she was with her ladies and her nurse. The Lilac Fairy, who knew all that had occurred, came to the aid of the distressed princess, saying:

"I may be greatly mistaken, but I think that if you request a gown the color of the sun, either we'll succeed in discouraging your father the king, because it will never be possible to make such a gown, or at least we'll gain some time."

The princess agreed and asked for the gown, and the lovesick king, with no regrets, gave up all the diamonds and rubies in his crown to contribute to that splendid piece of work, issuing orders to spare no expense to make that gown equal to the sun. And so, as soon as it was delivered, all those who saw it were forced to shut their eyes, they were so dazzled. It's since then that people have used green spectacles and smoked glass. How did the princess feel when she saw it? No one had ever seen anything so beautiful or so artistically crafted. She was thunderstruck; and, under the pretext that it hurt her eyes, she withdrew to her room, where the fairy awaited her, more ashamed than words can tell. Even worse than that: when she saw the sun gown, she turned red with anger.

"Oh! This time, my girl," she said to the princess, "we're going to subject your father's shameful love to a terrible trial. I know how stubborn he is on the subject of this marriage, which he thinks is so imminent, but I think he'll be somewhat taken aback by the request I now advise you to make: the skin of that donkey which he loves so passionately and which covers all his expenses so abundantly; go, and don't fail to tell him that you want its skin."

The princess, delighted to find one more means of avoiding a marriage she detested, and, at the same time, sure that her father would never resolve to sacrifice his donkey, accosted him and declared her desire for the skin of that fine animal. Though the king was surprised at that whim, he didn't hesitate to gratify it. The poor donkey was sacrificed, and its skin lovingly presented to the princess, who, seeing no further way to avoid her misfortune, was about to sink into despair when her godmother came to her aid.

«Que faites-vous, ma fille? dit-elle, voyant la princesse déchirant ses cheveux et meurtrissant ses belles joues; voici le moment le plus heureux de votre vie. Enveloppez-vous de cette peau; sortez de ce palais, et allez tant que terre pourra vous porter. Lorsqu'on sacrifie tout à la vertu, les dieux savent en récompenser. Allez, j'aurai soin que votre toilette vous suive partout; en quelque lieu que vous vous arrêtiez, votre cassette, où seront vos habits et vos bijoux, suivra vos pas sous terre; et voici ma baguette que je vous donne; en frappant la terre, quand vous aurez besoin de cette cassette, elle paraîtra à vos yeux; mais hâtez-vous de partir, et ne tardez pas.»

L'infante embrassa mille fois sa marraine, la pria de ne pas l'abandonner, s'affubla de cette vilaine peau, après s'être barbouillée de suie de cheminée et sortit de ce riche palais sans être reconnue de personne.

L'absence de l'infante causa une grande rumeur. Le roi, au désespoir, qui avait fait préparer une fête magnifique, était inconsolable. Il fit partir plus de cent gendarmes et plus de mille mousquetaires pour aller à la quête de sa fille; mais la fée, qui la protégeait, la rendait invisible aux plus habiles recherches: ainsi il fallut bien s'en consoler.

Pendant ce temps l'infante cheminait. Elle alla bien loin, bien loin, encore plus loin et cherchait partout une place; mais quoique par charité on lui donnât à manger, on la trouvait si crasseuse que personne n'en voulait. Cependant, elle entra dans une belle ville, à la porte de laquelle était une métairie, dont la fermière avait besoin d'une souillon pour laver les torchons, nettoyer les dindons et l'auge des cochons. Cette femme, voyant cette voyageuse si malpropre, lui proposa d'entrer chez elle; ce que l'infante accepta de grand cœur, tant elle était lasse d'avoir tant marché. On la mit dans un coin reculé de la cuisine, où elle fut, les premiers jours, en butte aux plaisanteries grossières de la valetaille, tant sa peau d'âne la rendait sale et dégoûtante. Enfin on s'y accoutuma; d'ailleurs elle était si soigneuse de remplir ses devoirs que la fermière la prit sous sa protection. Elle conduisait les moutons, les faisait parquer au temps où il le fallait; elle menait les dindons paître avec une telle intelligence qu'il semblait qu'elle n'eût jamais fait autre chose: aussi tout fructifiait sous ses belles mains.

Un jour qu'assise près d'une claire fontaine, où elle déplorait souvent sa triste condition, elle s'avisa de s'y mirer, l'effroyable peau d'âne qui faisait sa coiffure et son habillement l'épouvanta. Honteuse de cet ajustement, elle se décrassa le visage et les mains,

"What are you doing, my girl?" she asked, seeing the princess tear out her hair and bruise her beautiful cheeks; "this is the happiest moment of your life. Wrap yourself up in this skin; leave this palace, and go as far as the earth will support you. When people sacrifice everything to virtue, the gods know how to reward them for it. Go; I'll see to it that your cosmetics follow you everywhere; any place you stop at, your casket containing your clothes and jewels will follow you below the ground; and here, I'm giving you my wand; if you strike the ground with it whenever you need this casket, it will appear before you; but hasten to depart, and don't tarry."

The princess hugged her godmother a thousand times, begging her not to desert her; she put on that ugly skin after daubing herself with soot from the fireplace, and she left her sumptuous palace without being recognized by anyone.

The princess's absence created a great stir. The king, who had ordered a magnificent party prepared, was in despair and couldn't be consoled. He sent out over a hundred men-at-arms and over a thousand musketeers to look for his daughter; but her protectress, the fairy, made her invisible to even the most skillful searchers: and so the king had to console himself.

Meanwhile, the princess was proceeding on her way. She traveled very far, very far, and farther still, seeking employment everywhere; but, even though she was given food out of charity, people found her so filthy that no one wanted her. Nevertheless she entered a beautiful city, at the gate of which was a tenant farm, in which the farmer's wife needed a scullion to wash the dishcloths and keep the turkeys and the pigs' trough clean. This woman, seeing that untidy wayfarer, asked her to stay and work for her; this the princess accepted wholeheartedly, she was so weary from her long journey. She was installed in a remote corner of the kitchen, where, at the beginning, she was the butt of the farmhands' coarse jokes, because her donkey-skin made her so dirty and repulsive. Finally people got used to her; besides, she accomplished her duties so diligently that the farmer's wife took her under her protection. She would lead the sheep to pasture and bring them back to the fold at the proper time; she would take the turkeys out to feed with such intelligence that she seemed to have been doing it all her life: and so everything prospered in her lovely hands.

One day, while she was sitting near the clear spring, at which she often lamented her sad state, she took it into her head to look at her reflection, and the fearful donkey-skin, which formed both her headgear and her cloak, frightened her. Ashamed of that attire, she washed

qui devinrent plus blanches que l'ivoire, et son beau teint reprit sa fraîcheur naturelle. La joie de se trouver si belle lui donna envie de s'y baigner, ce qu'elle exécuta; mais il lui fallut remettre son indigne peau pour retourner à la métairie. Heureusement le lendemain était un jour de fête; ainsi elle eut le loisir de tirer sa cassette, d'arranger sa toilette, de poudrer ses beaux cheveux et de mettre sa belle robe couleur du temps. Sa chambre était si petite que la queue de cette belle robe ne pouvait pas s'étendre. La belle princesse se mira et s'admira elle-même avec raison, si bien qu'elle résolut, pour se désennuyer de mettre tour à tour ses belles robes, les fêtes et les dimanches; ce qu'elle exécuta ponctuellement. Elle mêlait des fleurs et des diamants dans ses beaux cheveux avec un art admirable; et souvent elle soupirait de n'avoir pour témoins de sa beauté que ses moutons et ses dindons qui l'aimaient autant avec son horrible peau d'âne, dont on lui avait donné le nom dans cette ferme.

Un jour de fête, que Peau d'Ane avait mis la robe couleur du soleil, le fils du roi, à qui cette ferme appartenait, vint y descendre pour se reposer, en revenant de la chasse. Le prince était jeune, beau et admirablement bien fait, l'amour de son père et de la reine sa mère, adoré des peuples. On offrit à ce jeune prince une collation champêtre, qu'il accepta; puis il se mit à parcourir les basses-cours et tous les recoins. En courant ainsi de lieu en lieu, il entra dans une sombre allée au bout de laquelle il vit une porte fermée. La curiosité lui fit mettre l'œil à la serrure; mais que devint-il en apercevant la princesse si belle et si richement vêtue qu'à son air noble et modeste il la prit pour une divinité! L'impétuosité du sentiment qu'il éprouva dans ce moment l'aurait porté à enfoncer la porte, sans le respect que lui inspira cette ravissante personne.

Il sortit avec peine de cette allée sombre et obscure, mais ce fut pour s'informer qui était la personne qui demeurait dans cette petite chambre. On lui répondit que c'était une souillon, qu'on nommait Peau d'Ane, à cause de la peau dont elle s'habillait, et qu'elle était si sale et si crasseuse que personne ne la regardait ni ne lui parlait; et qu'on ne l'avait prise que par pitié, pour garder les moutons et les dindons.

Le prince, peu satisfait de cet éclaircissement, vit bien que ces gens grossiers n'en savaient pas davantage et qu'il était inutile de les questionner. Il revint au palais du roi son père, plus amoureux qu'on ne peut dire, ayant continuellement devant les yeux la belle image de

the grime from her face and hands, which became whiter than ivory, and her lovely complexion regained its natural freshness. The joy of finding herself so beautiful made her feel like bathing in the spring, and she did so; but she had to put her shameful skin back on before returning to the farm. Fortunately, the next day was a holiday, so she had the time to produce her casket, sort out her cosmetics, powder her beautiful hair, and put on her lovely gown that was the color of the sky. Her room was so small that the train of that lovely gown couldn't be fully displayed. The beautiful princess looked at her reflection and justly admired herself, so that she resolved to relieve her boredom by putting on each of her lovely gowns in turn, on Sundays and holidays; and she did this regularly. She would scatter flowers and diamonds in her beautiful hair with admirable art; and she often sighed because the only witnesses to her beauty were her sheep and her turkeys, who loved her just as much when she was wearing her awful donkey-skin, which provided her nickname on the farm.

On one holiday, when Donkey-Skin had put on the gown that was the color of the sun, the son of the king, to whom that farm belonged, stopped there to rest on his way home from hunting. The prince was young and handsome, with a wonderful physique: the darling of his father and his mother the queen, and beloved by their subjects. This young prince was offered a rustic meal, which he accepted; then he began to stroll through the farmyards, going into every nook and cranny. While he was thus proceeding from one spot to another, he entered a dark lane, at the end of which he saw a closed door. Curiosity caused him to put his eye to the keyhole; and what was his amazement to see the princess, so beautiful and so sumptuously dressed that her noble and modest appearance made him take her for a goddess! The surge of emotion he felt at that moment would have led him to break down the door, had it not been for the respect he felt was due to that ravishing young woman.

It was hard for him to leave that dark, gloomy lane, and he did so only to inquire into the identity of the woman who lived in that small room. The reply was that she was a scullion, called Donkey-Skin because of the skin she wore; that she was so dirty and grimy that no one looked at her or spoke to her; and that she had only been taken in out of pity, to tend the sheep and turkeys.

The prince, not satisfied with that explanation, realized that those bumpkins knew no better, and that it was pointless to question them. He returned to the palace of his father the king, more deeply in love than words can tell, with the lovely vision of the goddess he had seen

cette divinité qu'il avait vue par le trou de la serrure. Il se repentit de n'avoir pas heurté à la porte et se promit bien de n'y pas manquer une autre fois. Mais l'agitation de son sang, causée par l'ardeur de son amour, lui donna, dans la même nuit, une fièvre si terrible que bientôt il fut réduit à l'extrémité. La reine sa mère, qui n'avait que lui d'enfant, se désespérait de ce que tous les remèdes étaient inutiles. Elle promettait en vain les plus grandes récompenses aux médecins; ils y employaient tout leur art, mais rien ne guérissait le prince.

Enfin ils devinèrent qu'un mortel chagrin causait tout ce ravage; ils en avertirent la reine qui, toute pleine de tendresse pour son fils, vint le conjurer de dire la cause de son mal; et que, quand il s'agirait de lui céder la couronne, le roi son père descendrait de son trône sans regret pour l'y faire monter; que s'il désirait quelque princesse, quand même on serait en guerre avec le roi son père, et qu'on eût de justes sujets pour s'en plaindre, on sacrifierait tout pour obtenir ce qu'il désirait; mais qu'elle le conjurait de ne pas se laisser mourir, puisque de sa vie dépendait la leur.

La reine n'acheva pas ce touchant discours sans mouiller le visage du prince d'un torrent de larmes.

«Madame, lui dit enfin le prince avec une voix très faible, je ne suis pas assez dénaturé pous désirer la couronne de mon père; plaise au Ciel qu'il vive de longues années et qu'il veuille bien que je sois longtemps le plus fidèle et le plus respectueux de ses sujets! Quant aux princesses que vous m'offrez, je n'ai point encore pensé à me marier; et vous pensez bien que, soumis comme je le suis à vos volontés, je vous obéirai toujours, quoi qu'il m'en coûte.

«Ah! mon fils, reprit la reine, rien ne me coûtera pour lui sauver la vie; mais, mon cher fils, sauve la mienne et celle du roi ton père, en me déclarant ce que tu désires, et sois bien assuré qu'il te sera accordé.

—Hé bien, madame, dit-il, puisqu'il faut vous déclarer ma pensée, je vais vous obéir; je me ferais un crime de mettre en danger deux êtres qui me sont chers. Oui, ma mère, je désire que Peau d'Ane me fasse un gâteau, et que, dès qu'il sera fait, elle me l'apporte.»

La reine, étonnée de ce nom bizarre, demanda qui était cette Peau d'Ane.

«C'est, madame, reprit un de ses officiers qui par hasard avait vu cette fille, c'est la plus vilaine bête après le loup; une peau noire, une crasseuse, qui loge dans votre métairie et garde vos dindons.

through the keyhole constantly before his eyes. He regretted not having knocked at the door, and resolved not to fail to do so the next time. But that very night, the turmoil in his circulation caused by the intensity of his love made him so terribly feverish that he was soon in an extremely serious condition. His mother the queen, whose only child he was, was in despair because no remedy could help him. It was in vain that she promised the physicians the greatest rewards; they expended all their skill on the case, but the prince wouldn't get well.

Finally they surmised that all this damage was due to a deadly sorrow; they informed the queen of this, and she, full of love for her son, implored him to reveal the cause of his illness; she said that, if it was a question of yielding the crown to him, his father the king would gladly step down from the throne and let him ascend it; that if he was yearning for some princess, even though they were at war with her royal father and had good reasons to complain of him, they would sacrifice everything to obtain what he wanted; but that she implored him not to let himself die, since their life depended on his.

The queen didn't bring this touching speech to its close without bathing the prince's face in a torrent of tears.

"Madam," the prince finally said in a very feeble voice, "I am not so unnatural as to long for my father's crown; may it please Heaven to let him live for many years to come and allow me to be his most loyal and respectful subject all that time! As for the princesses you offer me, I haven't thought about marrying yet; and you must know that, subject as I am to your wishes, I shall always obey you, whatever it costs me."

"Oh, my son," the queen resumed, "I'll spare no pains to save your[30] life; but, dear son, save mine and your royal father's by telling me what you want, and you can rest assured that your request will be granted."

"Very well, madam," he said, "since I must tell you what's on my mind, I'll obey; I'd consider it a crime to endanger two people who are dear to me. Yes, mother, I want Donkey-Skin to bake me a cake and bring it to me as soon as it's done."

The queen, astonished at that peculiar name, asked who that Donkey-Skin was.

"Madam," interrupted one of her servants, who had seen the girl by chance, "she's the ugliest animal there is, except for the wolf; a black skin, a filthy thing, who has a room at your farm and tends your turkeys."

---

[30]One would expect the French to have *te* here, rather than *lui*.

—Qu'importe, dit la reine, mon fils, au retour de la chasse, a peut-être mangé de sa pâtisserie; c'est une fantaisie de malade; en un mot, je veux que Peau d'Ane, puisque Peau d'Ane il y a, lui fasse promptement un gâteau.»

On courut à la métairie et l'on fit venir Peau d'Ane, pour lui ordonner de faire de son mieux un gâteau pour le prince.

Quelques auteurs ont assuré que Peau d'Ane, au moment que ce prince avait mis l'œil à la serrure, les siens l'avaient aperçu; et puis que, regardant par sa petite fenêtre, elle avait vu ce prince si jeune, si beau et si bien fait, que l'idée lui en était restée, et que souvent ce souvenir lui avait coûté quelques soupirs. Quoi qu'il en soit, Peau d'Ane l'ayant vu, ou en ayant beaucoup entendu parler avec éloge, ravie de pouvoir trouver un moyen d'être connue, s'enferma dans sa chambre, jeta sa vilaine peau, se décrassa le visage et les mains, se coiffa de ses blonds cheveux, mit un beau corps d'argent brillant, un jupon pareil, et se mit à faire le gâteau tant désiré: elle prit de la plus pure farine, des œufs et du beurre frais. En travaillant, soit de dessein ou autrement, une bague qu'elle avait au doigt tomba dans la pâte, s'y mêla, et dès que le gâteau fut cuit, s'affublant de son horrible peau, elle donna le gâteau à l'officier, à qui elle demanda des nouvelles du prince; mais cet homme, ne diagnant pas lui répondre, courut chez le prince lui porter ce gâteau.

Le prince le prit avidement des mains de cet homme, et le mangea avec une telle vivacité, que les médecins, qui étaient présents, ne manquèrent pas de dire que cette fureur n'était pas un bon signe: effectivement, le prince pensa s'étrangler par la bague qu'il trouva dans un des morceaux du gâteau; mais il la tira adroitement de sa bouche, et son ardeur à dévorer ce gâteau se ralentit, en examinant cette fine émeraude, montée sur un jonc d'or, dont le cercle était si étroit, qu'il jugea ne pouvoir servir qu'au plus joli doigt du monde.

Il baisa mille fois cette bague, la mit sous son chevet, et l'en tirait à tout moment, quand il croyait n'être vu de personne. Le tourment qu'il se donna pour imaginer comment il pourrait voir celle à qui cette bague pouvait aller, et n'osant croire, s'il demandait Peau d'Ane, qui avait fait ce gâteau qu'il avait demandé, qu'on lui accordât de la faire venir, n'osant non plus dire ce qu'il avait vu par le trou de cette serrure, de crainte qu'on se moquât de lui et qu'on le prît pour un visionnaire, toutes ces idées le tourmentant à la fois, la fièvre le reprit fortement; et les médecins ne sachant plus que faire, déclarèrent à la reine que le prince était malade d'amour.

"What's the difference?" said the queen. "Maybe when my son was on his way home from hunting, he ate something she baked; it's a sick person's whim; in short, since Donkey-Skin exists, I want Donkey-Skin to bake him a cake immediately."

They dashed over to the farm and summoned Donkey-Skin, ordering her to bake the best cake she could for the prince.

Some writers have claimed that, when the prince put his eye to the keyhole, Donkey-Skin noticed it; and that then, looking out of her little window, she had seen that the prince was so young, handsome, and well built that his image had remained in her mind, and the memory of him had frequently elicited a few sighs from her. However that may be, whether Donkey-Skin had seen him or had heard him frequently mentioned with praise, she was now delighted to find some means of revealing her identity; she locked herself in her room, threw aside the ugly skin, washed the grime from her face and hands, arranged her blonde hair, put on a beautiful bodice of bright silver, with a skirt to match, and began to bake that longed-for cake: she took the purest flour, eggs, and fresh butter. While she was working, whether intentionally or otherwise, a ring fell from her finger into the dough and was kneaded into it. As soon as the cake was done, she put on the horrible skin and gave the cake to the messenger, asking him for news of the prince; but the fellow, not deigning to reply, dashed back to the prince to bring him the cake.

The prince greedily seized it from the man's hands, and ate it with such vivacity that the physicians who were present didn't fail to declare that such furor wasn't a good sign; and, in fact, the prince almost choked on the ring, which he found in one of the slices of the cake; but he skillfully drew it out of his mouth, and his eagerness to devour the cake abated as he examined that fine emerald set on a golden band that was so narrow, he deemed it could only be worn on the prettiest finger in the world.

He kissed that ring a thousand times, put it under his bolster, and drew it out again every minute, when he thought no one was looking. How he tortured himself to figure out some way to see the young woman whose finger that ring would fit! He didn't dare believe that, if he asked for Donkey-Skin, who had baked the cake he requested, they would allow him to let her come; nor did he dare to reveal what he had seen through the keyhole, fearing that he would be made fun of and taken for a dreamer. With all those thoughts tormenting him at the same time, the fever assailed him again with violence; and the physicians, totally at a loss, declared to the queen that the prince was lovesick.

La reine accourut chez son fils, avec le roi, qui se désolait:

«Mon fils, mon cher fils, s'écria le monarque affligé, nomme-nous celle que tu veux; nous jurons que nous te la donnerons, fût-elle la plus vile des esclaves.»

La reine, en l'embrassant, lui confirma le serment du roi. Le prince, attendri par les larmes et les caresses des auteurs de ses jours:

«Mon père et ma mère, leur dit-il, je n'ai point dessein de faire une alliance qui vous déplaise; et, pour preuve de cette vérité, dit-il en tirant l'émeraude de dessous son chevet, c'est que j'épouserai la personne à qui cette bague ira, telle qu'elle soit; et il n'y a pas d'apparence que celle qui aura ce joli doigt soit une rustaude ou une paysanne.»

Le roi et la reine prirent la bague, l'examinèrent curieusement, et jugèrent, ainsi que le prince, que cette bague ne pouvait aller qu'à quelque fille de bonne maison. Alors le roi, ayant embrassé son fils en le conjurant de guérir, sortit, fit donner les tambours, les fifres et les trompettes par toute la ville, et crier par ses hérauts, que l'on n'avait qu'à venir au palais essayer une bague, et que celle à qui elle irait juste épouserait l'héritier du trône.

Les princesses d'abord arrivèrent, puis les duchesses, les marquises et les baronnes; mais elles eurent beau toutes s'amenuiser les doigts, aucune ne put mettre la bague. Il en fallut revenir aux grisettes, qui, toutes jolies qu'elles étaient, avaient toutes les doigts trop gros. Le prince, qui se portait mieux, faisait lui-même l'essai. Enfin on en vint aux filles de chambre; elles ne réussirent pas mieux. Il n'y avait plus personne qui n'eût essayé cette bague sans succès, lorsque le prince demanda les cuisinières, les marmitonnes, les gardeuses de moutons: on amena tout cela; mais leurs gros doigts rouges et courts ne purent seulement aller par-delà l'ongle.

«A-t-on fait venir cette Peau d'Ane qui m'a fait un gâteau ces jours derniers? dit le prince. Chacun se prit à rire, et lui dit que non, tant elle était sale et crasseuse.

—Qu'on l'aille chercher tout à l'heure, dit le roi; il ne sera pas dit que j'aie excepté quelqu'un.»

On courut, en riant et se moquant, chercher la dindonnière.

L'infante, qui avait entendu le tambour et le cri des hérauts d'armes, s'était bien doutée que sa bague faisait ce tintamarre: elle aimait le prince; et, comme le véritable amour est craintif et n'a point de vanité, elle était dans la crainte continuelle que quelque dame n'eût le doigt aussi menu que le sien. Elle eut donc une grande joie

The queen hastened to her son's room, along with the king, who was downcast.

"Son, dear son," exclaimed the sorrowing monarch, "tell us the name of the woman you want; we swear we'll give her to you, even if she were the lowliest of slaves."

The queen hugged him and added her oath to the king's. The prince, softened by the tears and attentions of his parents, said:

"Father, mother, I have no desire to enter into a marriage you won't like; to prove that I'm telling the truth," he said, taking out the emerald ring from under his bolster, "I shall marry the woman whom this ring fits, whoever she may be; it's not very likely that the possessor of such a pretty finger is a rustic or a peasant."

The king and queen took the ring, examined it carefully, and came to the same conclusion as the prince, that such a ring would only fit some girl of good family. Then the king, after embracing his son and imploring him to get better, went out and sent drums, fifes, and trumpets throughout the city, along with heralds proclaiming that the women need only come to the palace to try on a ring, and the one it would fit perfectly would marry the heir to the throne.

First the princesses arrived, then the duchesses, the marchionesses, and the baronesses; but it was in vain that they all tried to make their fingers slenderer; none of them could get the ring on. It was necessary to proceed to the daughters of the commoners, who, pretty as they were, all had fingers that were too thick. The prince, who was feeling better, conducted the fittings himself. Finally they came down to the chambermaids, who had no better luck. There was no one left who hadn't tried on the ring unsuccessfully, when the prince asked for the cooks, the scullions, and the shepherdesses: they were all brought in, but their fat, red, stumpy fingers weren't even able to go into the ring farther than the fingernail.

"Have they sent for Donkey-Skin, who baked me a cake recently?" the prince asked. Everyone started laughing and said they hadn't, because she was so dirty and grimy.

"Let her be brought here at once!" the king said. "I don't want anyone to say that I left someone out."

With laughter and raillery they ran off to fetch the turkey girl.

The princess, who had heard the drumming and the heralds' calls, had a very good idea that her ring was the cause of all that commotion: she loved the prince; and, since true love is timid and free from vanity, she was in constant fear that some great lady might have a finger as slender as hers. Therefore she was overjoyed when they

quand on vint la chercher et quand on heurta à sa porte. Depuis qu'elle avait su qu'on cherchait un doigt propre à mettre sa bague, je ne sais quel espoir l'avait portée à se coiffer plus soigneusement, et à mettre son beau corps d'argent, avec le jupon plein de falbalas de dentelle d'argent, semés d'émeraudes. Sitôt qu'elle entendit qu'on heurtait à la porte et qu'on l'appelait pour aller chez le prince, elle remit promptement sa peau d'âne, ouvrit sa porte; et ces gens, en se moquant d'elle, lui dirent que le roi la demandait pour lui faire épouser son fils; puis, avec de longs éclats de rire, ils la menèrent chez le prince, qui lui-même étonné de l'accoutrement de cette fille, n'osa croire que ce fût celle qu'il avait vue si pompeuse et si belle.

Triste et confus de s'être si lourdement trompé:

«Est-ce vous, lui dit-il, qui logez au fond de cette allée obscure, dans la troisième basse-cour de la métairie?

—Oui, seigneur, répondit-elle.

—Montrez-moi votre main», dit-il en tremblant et poussant un profond soupir.

Dame! qui fut bien surpris? Ce furent le roi et la reine, ainsi que tous les chambellans et les grands de la cour, lorsque de dessous cette peau noire et crasseuse sortit une petite main délicate, blanche et couleur de rose où la bague s'ajusta sans peine au plus joli petit doigt du monde; et par un petit mouvement que l'infante se donna, la peau tomba, et elle parut d'une beauté si ravissante, que le prince tout faible qu'il était, se mit à ses genoux, et les serra avec une ardeur qui la fit rougir; mais on ne s'en aperçut presque pas, parce que le roi et la reine vinrent l'embrasser de toute leur force, et lui demander si elle voulait bien épouser leur fils. La princesse, confuse de tant de caresses et de l'amour que lui marquait ce beau jeune prince, allait cependant les en remercier, lorsque le plafond du salon s'ouvrit et que la fée des Lilas, descendant dans un char fait de branches et de fleurs de son nom, conta, avec une grâce infinie, l'histoire de l'infante.

Le roi et la reine, charmés de voir que Peau d'Ane était une grande princesse, redoublèrent leurs caresses; mais le prince fut encore plus sensible à la vertu de la princesse, et son amour s'accrut par cette connaissance.

L'impatience du prince, pour épouser la princesse, fut telle qu'à peine donna-t-il le temps de faire les préparatifs convenables pour cet auguste hyménée. Le roi et la reine, qui étaient affolés de leur belle-fille, lui faisaient mille caresses, et la tenaient incessamment dans leurs bras; elle avait déclaré qu'elle ne pouvait épouser le prince sans

came to fetch her and knocked at her door. From the moment she had realized they were looking for a finger that her ring would fit, some ray of hope had induced her to do up her hair with greater care and to put on her beautiful silver bodice, along with the skirt that was full of silver-lace flounces and spangled with emeralds. As soon as she heard a knock at her door and people summoning her to the prince's presence, she swiftly put her donkey-skin back on and opened the door; the people there, making fun of her, told her that the king was sending for her to marry her to his son; then, with lengthy roars of laughter, they led her to the prince; astonished himself at the girl's odd garb, he didn't dare believe she was the same person he had seen in such pomp and beauty.

Sad and embarrassed at having made such a gross mistake, he said:

"Are you the one who lives at the end of that dark lane, in the third farmyard?"

"Yes, my lord," she replied.

"Show me your hand," he said, trembling and giving a deep sigh.

Heavens! Who was surprised? The king, queen, all the chamberlains and grandees of the court were, when from beneath that black, grimy skin there emerged a small, delicate, white-and-pink hand, whose pretty little finger the ring went on without difficulty. When the princess made a slight motion, the skin dropped off her, and she appeared there in such ravishing beauty that she prince, even in his weakened condition, fell at her feet and clasped her knees with a passion that made her blush; but this was hardly noticed, because the king and queen came over to hug her with all their might and to ask her whether she was willing to marry their son. The princess, embarrassed by so much attention and by the love that the handsome young prince displayed for her, was nevertheless on the point of thanking them, when the ceiling of the salon opened and the Lilac Fairy, descending in a chariot made of sprigs of the flowers that bear her name, narrated the princess's story with matchless grace.

The king and queen, charmed to learn that Donkey-Skin was a great princess, were twice as attentive to her as before; but the prince was even more appreciative of the princess's virtue, and his love was increased by his better acquaintance with her and her past.

The prince's impatience to marry the princess was so great that he hardly allowed time for suitable preparations to be made for that royal ceremony. The king and queen, both mad about their daughter-in-law, showered attentions on her and constantly held her in their arms; she had declared that she couldn't marry the prince without the consent of

le consentement du roi son père: aussi fut-il le premier auquel on envoya une invitation, sans lui dire quelle était l'épousée; la fée des Lilas, qui présidait à tout, comme de raison, l'avait exigé à cause des conséquences. Il vint des rois de tous les pays: les uns en chaise à porteurs, d'autres en cabriolet; les plus éloignés montés sur des éléphants, sur des tigres, sur des aigles; mais le plus magnifique et le plus puissant fut le père de l'infante, qui heureusement avait oublié son amour déréglé et avait épousé une reine, veuve, fort belle, dont il n'avait point eu d'enfant. L'infante courut au-devant de lui; il la reconnut aussitôt et l'embrassa avec une grande tendresse, avant qu'elle eût le temps de se jeter à ses genoux. Le roi et la reine lui présentèrent leur fils, qu'il combla d'amitié. Les noces se firent avec toute la pompe imaginable. Les jeunes époux, peu sensibles à ces magnificences, ne virent et ne regardèrent qu'eux.

Le roi, père du prince, fit couronner son fils ce même jour, et, lui baisant les mains, le plaça sur son trône, malgré la résistance de ce fils bien né; il lui fallut obéir. Les fêtes de cet illustre mariage durèrent près de trois mois; mais l'amour de ces deux époux durerait encore, tant ils s'aimaient, s'ils n'étaient pas morts cent ans après.

Moralité

Le conte de Peau d'Ane est difficile à croire:
Mais tant que dans le monde on aura des enfants,
    Des mères et des mères-grands,
    On en gardera la mémoire.

her royal father; and so he was the first to be sent an invitation, out informing him who the bride was; the Lilac Fairy, who took ch. of everything, which was only right, had insisted on that for fear of t consequences. Kings arrived from all lands, some by sedan chair, oti ers in a gig; those who came from furthest away were riding elephants, tigers, and eagles; but the most splendid and powerful monarch was the princess's father, who had fortunately forgotten his improper love and had married a very beautiful widowed queen, who hadn't given him any children. The princess ran out to greet him; he recognized her at once and embraced her very tenderly, before she had time to throw herself at his feet. The king and queen introduced him to their son, whom he honored with his great friendship. The wedding was celebrated with all imaginable pomp. The young couple, hardly aware of the magnificence around them, had eyes only for each other.

The king, father of the prince, had his son crowned that very day; kissing his hands, he seated him on his throne, despite the resistance of that well-born young man, who had to obey. The festivities connected with that royal marriage lasted nearly three months, but the love of that couple for each other would still endure today, they loved each other so, if they hadn't died a hundred years later.

Moral

The tale of Donkey-Skin is hard to believe literally,
but as long as the world contains children,
mothers, and grandmothers,
the memory of it will be preserved.

with-
rge
ne